Learning Sex Roles

American and Scandinavian Contrasts

Learning Sex Roles
American and Scandinavian Contrasts

Joseph E. Ribal
El Camino College

CANFIELD PRESS ⚥ San Francisco
A Department of Harper & Row, Publishers, Inc.
New York   Evanston   London

102156

International Standard Book Number: 0-06-387164-5

Library of Congress Catalog Card Number: 73-12195

74 75 10 9 8 7 6 5 4 3 2

Cover by William B. Nagel

Photographs are illustrative only; they do not depict the people represented in the case studies.
Photo Credits: Page 1, Roger LeRoy Miller, Inc.; pages 7, 27, 47, Karen Petersen; page 66, Carol Simowitz.

Library of Congress Cataloging in Publication Data

Ribal, Joseph E   1931–
  Learning sex roles.

  Bibliography: p.
  1. Youth—Sexual behavior—Case studies.
I. Title. [DNLM: 1. Sex behavior—Case studies. 2. Sex education—Case studies. HQ21 R482L 1973]
HQ27.R5   301.41'75   73-12195
ISBN 0-06-387164-5

preface

This is a casebook about sexual learning and behavior in different social and cultural settings—about how young people acquire sexual ideas, feelings, and behavior in the framework of sex roles, and about the problems and experiences they have. The book contains the accounts of American, Swedish, and Danish students, and the focus is mainly on what they think and feel about sex in their lives. As a casebook, it offers an opportunity to understand the realities of sex education for many young people in the United States and Scandinavia. Each case is a narrative of the student's sexual development from childhood through adolescence into adulthood.

The book contains thirty-six case histories, of students who were attending a community college in California, a Swedish university, or a university in Denmark. The material was originally part of data for a comparative study of American and Scandinavian school sex education programs. In this study twenty-five American case histories were experimentally used with Swedish and Danish university students to draw out comparable data about Scandinavian patterns of sexual socialization and learning. The American students had been enrolled in a marriage and family living course, whereas the Scandinavian volunteers were studying in the various social sciences, education, and the humanities. The cases reflect to some extent the guidelines that were set up to structure the personal commentaries along chronological and developmental lines, but each student was free to express any ideas and feelings he wanted to about his life and the role of sexual learning in it. As you will see, many of the Scandinavian students used the American case they read as a model and point of reference for discussing their own experiences and for making observations about what is important about sex in society. Scandinavian opinions of American sexual behavior are seldom very flattering, but their criticism should stimulate critical thinking of your own about the social and sexual contrasts between the United States and Scandinavia. You the American reader have the final *say on all the comparisons the Scandinavian students have made between themselves and the Americans.*

The case histories have been organized in groups of three to reflect the methodology of the study. The first student in each triad is American, the second Swedish, and the third Danish. The other aspect of organization concerns the division of cases into three developmental periods: childhood, adolescence, and adulthood. The cases have been selected with a view toward their appropriateness for each part and have been edited to eliminate commentary that was not essential either to our understanding of the developmental period or to important attitudes or behavior that follow. Further changes have been made in identifying data to preserve the anonymity and privacy of these individuals. Specifically, when necessary and appropriate, analogous biographical data selected from unpublished cases of the study were used editorially to prevent individual identification. Because of the personal and intimate nature of much of our data, this responsibility received very careful attention. Swedish and Danish translations have sometimes been amended to avoid confusion and improve readability, and certain distracting language errors in the American cases have been corrected.

An outstanding group of reviewers from the fields of psychology, psychiatry, sociology, and the health sciences reviewed the cases selected for publication, and most of them felt that the cases are a "gold mine for interpretation and analysis." But they also felt there should be some effort to suggest some of the implications and inferences to be drawn from the accounts. To this purpose I have inserted questions and annotations, to assist you in making your personal interpretations on the basis of biological, psychological, and sociological concepts as they apply to sexual development. Each part of the book also contains a short introduction and conceptual overview of the developmental period in question, and each case is preceded by a brief headnote. This organization should provide sufficient flexibility for a variety of academic situations and make possible a variety of creative uses of the book by imaginative professors and students.

If you are not now a student in a college course on human relationships and sexuality, but are simply reading this book out of general interest, I hope that the result will be greater understanding of the sexual feelings and behavior of others—and perhaps even yourself. Parents, teachers, and other adults do not often have access to the innermost feelings of young people struggling with the problems of social and sexual development. The various kinds of normal feelings, attitudes, and patterns of behavior that occur in childhood and adolescence are not always well understood, and of course problems may be even more subject to distortion and misconception. I hope that these cases and the editorial material accompanying them will contribute to understanding in ways that can be meaningful to all readers.

Joseph E. Ribal
Huntington Beach, California
July 1, 1973

acknowledgments

This book would not be complete without an expression of my gratitude to the many individuals who made it possible and who worked on it with me. Foremost in any statement of appreciation must be recognition of the students who contributed so generously of their thought, time, and energy.

Swedish and Danish students who assisted in translation tasks or other project responsibilities include Jacob Sjöberg, Hans Schiønneman, Lene Hansen, and Bo Møllor. Stefan Ekroth deserves special mention for his translation work and valued consultations on the Swedish data. Stig Troels Lund was similarly helpful with some of the Danish cases. Members of the faculties at Stockholm University and the University of Copenhagen were often encouraging and supportive. I am grateful to Professor Hans Hessellund of the Psychology Laboratory of the University of Copenhagen for his general helpfulness.

The research project brought me in contact with many different institutions and organizations in Scandinavia, and I am very grateful to all the people who answered my many questions. A number of individuals stand out because they made especially significant contributions to my analysis of our data. Mrs. Birgitta Linnér, a noted authority on Swedish sex education, and her colleague Mrs. Barbro Marnell, a counselor in the Stockholm Family Counseling Center, were generous in their time and interest in the study and provided many insights into some of the problems of sexual learning experienced by Swedish young people. Mrs. Elisabeth Wettergren, then an executive secretary for the Swedish Sex Education Association (RFSU), was very cooperative in arranging professional contacts and offering suggestions. Mrs. Kaisa Turpeinen, M.D., the director of a Finnish sex education organization, and Mrs. Kerttu Larjanko, Chief Inspector of the Finland National Board of Education, were very kind to give their time that I might be aware of some of the differences in Scandinavian sexual attitudes and behavior within the Nordic community. Gratitude is also due the Swedish Institute for Cultural Relations for its help at various points in the research.

In the United States I am grateful to El Camino College for the sabbatical leave and financial support that enabled me to conduct the necessary field work in Scandinavia. I should also express my gratitude to the School Board of the Huntington Beach Union High School District, of which I was a member, for the leave of absence that gave me the opportunity to study sex education programs in Scandinavian schools.

This book has profited greatly from the critical comments and suggestions of reviewers of the manuscript at various points in its development. I am indebted to the following individuals in this regard: Bernard Goldstein, Anita Fisher, Elton McNeil, Richard Maslow, and Abraham Levine.

The people at Canfield Press gave this project their careful attention and were most generous with their help and encouragement throughout. I particularly appreciate my editor Howard Boyer for his guidance and editorial skills. And I would like to thank Pat Brewer and Sam Haynes for their editorial help.

Finally, every book undoubtedly has its toll in time taken from people and other things. Therefore I think it proper to express my appreciation to Louise and the children, who were often moved aside for the sake of the writing. Their understanding and support have meant a great deal to me.

J.E.R.

contents

Learning Sex Roles

American and Scandinavian Contrasts

part one

childhood
and preadolescence

introduction

The years of childhood are filled with many significant social experiences, and they all have a bearing on adult sexual attitudes and patterns of masculine and feminine behavior. For many individuals, childhood ideas and feelings about the human body, body functions, and sex differences persist into adulthood. Although much of this early learning is subject to modification in the course of physical maturation and continuing social development, the effort to understand a person's sexuality inevitably requires an accounting of initial experiences and learning.

The impact of early learning upon adult sexuality involves some complex relationships among biological, psychological, and sociological factors. Our understanding of these relationships is far from complete, but there is agreement that childhood experiences have great impact on human personality and behavior. Let us briefly touch on some of the important social and sexual learnings that you may identify in the case histories.

Experiences of Infancy and Early Childhood

The basic needs of American and Scandinavian infants are not different, but the ways that infant needs are perceived and understood by parents and adults in different social and cultural settings can vary considerably. The responses of parents and adults to needs for security, intimacy, and physical contact usually play an important part in influencing certain patterns of personality development. The feelings expressed toward the child during his earliest years can be significant in the formation of his feelings toward others. The capacity to experience social intimacy, to feel secure with others, and to relate to others with physical warmth is associated with opportunities to experience these emotional elements in infancy and childhood.

Sex roles are learned in early childhood. In practically all cultures boys and girls are treated differently as soon as their sex is revealed at birth. Some cultures emphasize sex differences more than others, but there do not

3

*seem to be major differences between American and Scandinavian parenta.
responses to a child's sexual identity in early childhood. As the child
matures, however, the contemporary Scandinavian values of sexual
egalitarianism tend to mute sex role differentiation, whereas American values
tend to preserve distinctive sex roles (though there are notable exceptions in
current countercultural movements and trends).*

*In the first years of childhood the individual develops some
impressions about himself, which we may call the* self concept. *Included in
this imaginative construct are ideas and feelings about the human body.
Inevitably he forms positive and negative feelings about body functions, sex
differences, sensuality associated with genital or other erogenous areas, and
the system of social control that is woven around these experiences. This
social experience continues to form the self concept as the child develops,
and he begins to develop an image of his adequacy, particularly his moral
adequacy. This early learning becomes a foundation for the growth of sexual
attitudes and patterns of behavior, and may determine the course of sexual
learning and experience throughout childhood, adolescence, and adulthood.
The role of parents in managing toilet training, the learning of modesty
controls, the development of body attitudes, masturbation, and sex play
with other children are influential factors related and sometimes interpreted
by the American and Scandinavian students.*

Experiences of Middle Childhood

*This period usually begins with the first years of schooling, when
the child makes his way out of the home and learns to adjust to an outside
social world in which peers and other adults often become more important
than parents. The learning of sex role behavior is no longer just a matter of
fulfilling parental expectations. Outside the home, often in association with
older children, the child may confront different ideas and feelings about sex
roles and sexual matters. He may even become interested and involved in
sexual experimentation. These activities present opportunities for new
learning, but sometimes they also result in conflict with previously learned
sexual ideas and feelings. Fortunately the stresses of sexual learning and
unlearning at this age are rarely so intense as those of the adolescent or
adult, but occasionally such childhood experiences can have residual effects
not conducive to growth and healthy development.*

In Scandinavia the educational system assumes a great deal of responsibility for basic sexual education, but in the United States the schools have not been so active. In many of the cases you will see differences noted, but the comparisons do not always account for current educational programs. In many of the cases the role of parents as sexual conditioners is also often a matter of crosscultural comparison. The school-age child not only responds to parents and teachers, but also to peers. As the cases indicate, the main interests of children at this age level are not with the forms of sexuality that may delight or alarm adolescents and adults, but with needs for companionship (usually in same-sex friendships and peer groups), with the social requirements of just being a boy or a girl, and with satisfying parents and teachers in the process. There is normally no sustained pressure for sexual experience at this age.

Experiences of Late Childhood and Preadolescence

At about the age of nine or ten biological and social developments begin to signal the approach of puberty and adolescence. (Puberty is the period of physical maturation, whereas adolescence is the set of social and psychological responses to this maturation.) Prior to the major endocrinological changes and to the learning of adolescent behavior patterns, there is a time of preparation, often identified as preadolescence. From the standpoint of social development there is normally an acceleration of new experience: the child touches many parts of the adult world and consequently begins to develop interests, identities, and ways of behaving that are closer to what is expected of adults. Among these experiences may be an increased awareness of sexual realities, heterosexual or homosexual experiments with others, and overt and covert modeling of the sexual feelings and behavior of older peers. Of course there is much individual variation in this realm, as is evident from both American and Scandinavian case histories.

By the time a child has arrived inside the time brackets of prepubertal change and preadolescence, he has already learned a great deal about human sexuality, even if it is wrong by most standards. Almost all children at this age have developed a sexual consciousness that has important emotional implications for future sexual functioning and social interaction. In preadolescent children the role of fear and guilt associated with sexual behavior can sometimes cause a variety of social and psychological *difficulties. Most of the cases here deal with experiences within the realm of what is typical and normal. The lives of these young people have not always been free of problems in sexual learning, and some of these problems occurred during late childhood.*

Sexual frustration and anxiety can be a reality before the advent of puberty and adolescence, though the manifestations may not be identical with later experiences. Children are not always particularly skillful in dealing with their sexual tensions and the social implications of their sexual activities, as many of the cases show. Responses to frustration and anxiety often take the form of defense or adjustive mechanisms, most of which are learned in childhood. Among the mechanisms identifiable in the cases are: projection, repression, suppression, displacement, compensation, sublimation, identification, fantasy, rationalization, intellectualization, regression, denial, insulation, undoing, and reaction formation. Annotations have been provided in the cases to assist you in identifying, defining, and understanding these mechanisms.

Prologue to the First Twelve Cases

As we noted in the preface, the autobiographical cases are organized in triads to reflect the method of data collection. The first student in each triad is an American, the second Swedish, and the third Danish. The case histories in Part One have been selected because they are most useful for developing understandings about the period of childhood as it relates to sexual learning. Because of space limitations, some of these cases have been edited to eliminate commentary that was not essential to our understanding of this developmental period or of its effects on attitudes or behavior.

Finally, note that we are dealing with subjectively reported data about people, events, groups, whole societies, and, in a number of philosophical observations, the world. Sometimes there may be a big difference between subjective and objective perceptual processes. But the benefits of reading about how young people feel and think about themselves need not be diminished by this problem. Understanding can almost inevitably come to every reader who approaches these students with sensitivity, empathy, and a spirit of caring about the wondrous process of sexual maturation and social learning that causes the development of human sexuality.

chapter I

Lois, Ulrika, and Sussanne

LOIS

Lois describes and interprets the childhood relationships and experiences that have influenced her sexual attitudes and behavior. Her story shows how certain parts of the traditional female role are often learned in the context of family experiences. Her parents seem anxious to "protect" her from sex, yet Lois was neither protected from nor necessarily prepared to deal with many sexual realities. She emerged from childhood frightened, inhibited, and anxious about sexual matters. She seems to have had some difficulties in developing social relationships with her peers during adolescence.

     I am twenty years old. I have two younger sisters, fourteen and seventeen. As far as my relationships at home are concerned, I think everything works smoothly; we often participate in activities together. My mother and I are fairly close, but we don't confide frequently. My father likes to hold the disciplinary stick in the family, but it's all on the surface; I know he's soft inside. As for restrictions on our activities, they placed few, as long as they knew where we were and what we were doing. Though they may have kept too many tabs on what we were doing all the time, they

developed a sense of trust in us. I respect my parents more than
any other persons in the world, even though I don't agree with them
in all things—including the kind of sex education I got at home.

My recollection of significant events in my early childhood
is not too clear. I have always heard that I had a lot of problems
with my oral stage. Until I was five years old, I apparently sucked
my fingers. My mother couldn't get me to stop this unsanitary
habit, which they thought would deform my mouth and ruin my fingers for life. As I got older, she resorted to more extreme
measures. She covered my hands, but I sucked through the cloth.
She tied my arms in cardboard so that I couldn't bend them to suck
them. Finally she got me to stop with bad-tasting lotion on my
fingers. Now I can't stand to see people biting their nails or putting
their fingers in their mouths. One of the things I look for in a boy
is whether his nails are clean and well manicured. I think nice
hands on a boy are very sexy, if you know what I mean.

I believe that as an infant I was nurtured sufficiently by both
my mother and my father. I was the first child and the center of
attention until my sister was born. I must have been somewhat insecure, though, because they say I would never fall asleep by myself but would always have to be carried and rocked to sleep or I
would cry until someone came to pick me up. I don't know whether
I got my fear of the dark from this, but I hate the dark very much.
I don't like to sleep in a room by myself, and I'm very glad my
sisters have shared a room with me, even though it has been
crowded. Even at parties in high school I used to want to have
some light on when all the other kids wanted it pitch dark.

We have lived in an apartment since I was enrolled in kindergarten. I remember being dragged there kicking and screaming. I
was terribly frightened because I had never played with other kids
very much. Gradually I was able to find some playmates—always
girls. Most of my friends for the next few years were older girls
in the neighborhood. I liked dolls very much, especially the baby
dolls that wet their diapers and drank from a bottle.

I didn't like to play with boys. I always thought they were
too rough. I must have had no awareness of the differences
between a boy and a girl until kindergarten. Then I must have
learned that there was a difference because of the different bath-
rooms. I was playing one day with two boys, brothers who were
younger than me, and they got very dirty playing in the mud. Their
mother put them in the bathtub while I watched. This was the first

time I saw a penis. I was confused because the older brother had a smaller one than his brother. This comparison was amazing and thought provoking. But I suppose it is just like I recently read— some boys have big lips and others have small ones, and it doesn't matter very much for satisfaction. I never told my mother about seeing the boys in the bathroom, which seems a little funny to me now. I must have felt that she wouldn't have liked the idea.

DISCUSSION   *How typical do you think Lois's reaction to the discovery of sex differences is? Could this learning have been improved? How do you think these first impressions can have social and psychological consequences?*

My mother and I can talk about boys now, but she never said anything to me about sex or how babies came into the world. The few times I can remember asking about babies, she told me that I'd understand those things better when I was older. Everything I know about sex I learned on my own.

I think I was made to feel a terrible shame about nudity from watching my father dress one day when I was about seven years old. He was examining his penis in the bedroom mirror, and I was peeking around the corner. He saw me, and for the only time in my whole life he gave me a spanking and sent me to my room. I am sure he was only just looking at himself for some reason, because my father could not have been doing anything else. He is a perfectly normal man. It was wrong to sneak.

DISCUSSION   *Lois reveals here her response to seeing her father and his punishment. Concerning the father's behavior, is this an example of the defense mechanisms of projection and displacement?* (Sexual projection *is attributing sexual feelings, motives, and behavior to others in order to alleviate personal guilt feelings.* Displacement *is selecting others, who are usually weaker, to receive punishment for one's own disapproved behavior.) How common do you think it is for children to develop personal sexual attitudes around parental sexual defenses?*

When I was about eight, I found some girlie magazines in my father's dresser. I must have felt pretty guilty about looking at them, for I'd only do it when my parents and sisters weren't home.

I was really scared they'd find out, so I'd leave everything in the exact order I found it. These magazines were not pornographic by today's standards; they were mostly the kind men could buy on the magazine stands. I didn't think there was anything wrong with his having them, but I could see how he didn't want them where my sisters and I could get the wrong idea. I remember being fascinated by the naked breasts, and by how much kissing there was in them. Our family wasn't very affectionate in a physical way with each other. I have seldom seen my mother and father kissing with any passion. This is not to say that we lacked love for each other, because we express it in ways that are more disguised. Our love is one of true understanding and respect.

DISCUSSION   *Might her family's pattern of limited outward affection have caused her to feel some anxiety as a child? How important are parental models in the development of attitudes toward social and sexual intimacy? Does their absence from the home always foretell a problem in the life of the individual, or can models be found elsewhere?*

When I was much younger I had seen a mother nursing her child. My mother never nursed any of us. I could not believe how huge her breasts were. Later, when I was playing with my sister, I tried nursing her on my bare chest. When my mother found out what we were doing, she yelled at me and wanted to know where I had gotten such an idea. I told her about the lady, and she told me not to go there anymore. I was fascinated by the fact that a baby could be fed in such a way.

I had two traumatic experiences in the fifth grade. The first happened on the way home from school just outside an underpass. A man was smiling and manipulating his penis outside of his pants. I can never forget the sight of this man fingering the end of it with his thumb while he smiled. I ran for my life and was so scared I did not even know until I stopped that I was crying. I wanted to tell someone about this man but couldn't even tell my friends at school until several years later. I think I felt terrified by my own curiosity about what he was doing. I had no idea that he was doing something called masturbation. I should never have stopped for those few seconds to watch him.

DISCUSSION   *Lois's description of this experience gives us some idea how serious fears about sexual behavior can develop in child- hood. How may her parents have prepared her to cope with such experiences? How can such encounters affect social contact with the opposite sex?*

Shortly after this happened, an older boy—I think he was about fourteen or fifteen—pulled me into some bushes on the way home and tried to kiss me. I remember how desperately I strug- gled with him. Nothing happened as far as sex is concerned, but I ran all the way home as soon as I could free myself. I must have been aware of what would have happened to me if I wasn't able to get away; I was really scared. I never told my mother about this either. Since then I have tried to be careful in places where things like that can happen.

In the seventh grade we saw a film about menstruation. Until then I had never heard of this matter. I had wondered about the Kotex boxes at home but had not felt secure enough to ask my mother about them because she kept them with her hidden personal stuff. It would have been much better to see this film in the earlier grades when we were just having our questions about it, because one girl in our class started menstruating many months before we saw the film. The school really made a big thing of it: only the girls could see the film and only with a parent-approval slip. Furthermore, our mothers were also invited to attend. The fact that everyone made such a huge production out of it seemed very strange to me. I was embarrassed and scared. I wasn't looking forward to the time when I would start menstruation at all. The nurse in charge spoke in a hushed and nervous tone, and her voice cracked whenever she came to something that had to do with becoming pregnant from "doing it with a boy." The girls in the class tried to laugh at the nurse afterwards, but I think they were frightened by her.

I do not think I was very popular. I cannot remember hav- ing a real close girlfriend until maybe the eighth grade. I spent most of my time with my sisters at home. I was frightened to death of boys, and I think they knew it, so they often teased me. The girls in my class were very cliquish. I was a little lonely until I found a very nice friendship with a new girl, Nancy, in the eighth grade. She knew much more about boys and sex than I. Naturally I was very interested in everything she could tell me. We started to talk a lot about boys, but we were both too frightened to want to do anything with them.

Finally there was the graduation party from eighth grade and a day at the beach with the class. I had never been out on a date until that time. Anyway, my mother would never have let me go with a boy at that age. I was thrilled when a boy named Carlos asked me to be his date. My father was less thrilled, because he has a prejudice against Mexicans. I remember practicing a sexy image the whole week before, probably because I felt so unattractive. While I was quite normal in my development, I had felt much embarrassment until then about my physiological changes. I had become very conscious of my developing breasts and would hide them from my sisters and my mother if I could. When I started menstruating at the beginning of the school year, I felt much secretness and privateness about it. With the start of my menstrual cycle, I always locked the bathroom door whenever I took a bath, even though my father was the only male around the house. I had become aware of my sex in a way that may have been a little strange, but who am I to say for sure? Suddenly, with my first date with a boy this changed. I tried to get myself ready by exercising my bustline in hopes of developing a cleavage. I tried on my mother's dresses with low-slung necklines and wanted very badly to buy one for the party, but my mother wouldn't let me. I was even jealous of the girls who had more developed busts than mine. I wanted Carlos to feel that I was as well developed as the other girls.

The party was at a very nice house with a pool. We wore bathing suits most of the night. It was a very nice, clean party until some of the kids started sneaking off into the garage to "warm up" after swimming. As you might guess, Carlos wanted me to go in the garage with him. Till then I had been kissed only by my father and two uncles. I was scared beyond belief, but I went. Two other couples were there necking when we got there. Unfortunately it was dark except for a boy who was smoking. Carlos and I climbed on the hood of an automobile, and he put his arm around me. We kissed. I felt a wonderful feeling from being held by Carlos. I forgot my fear of the dark, at least for those minutes we were necking. I think I was as pleased by the fact that other kids knew we were making out in the garage. My friend Nancy was the only one at the party who knew for certain that this was my first time with a boy.

We were only there for a short while, and then it was time to eat. Carlos lost no time deciding that food was more important than sex. The next day at the beach we took up where we had left off. My excitement was as much social as sexual. I was glad to "belong" for the first time in my life. All the teen magazines, books, TV, and movies had only given me envy until then.

DISCUSSION   *Lois speaks here of a sense of liberation from some of her childhood social and sexual fears. She claims that contact with the opposite sex has become a desirable objective. How would you evaluate her perspective, and the significance of some of these new influences?*

The beach party was also very nice. Our teacher was the only adult. He didn't mind at all when kids started making out around the fire rings. I learned how to French kiss. It seemed dirty and unsanitary to have a tongue put in my mouth. I let Carlos do it because I didn't want to lose him to another girl. That was a very dangerous date for me, now that I think of it. I think he could have done almost anything to me. Fortunately he didn't. I was quite happy to just have him hold me romantically and kiss me without opening our mouths. Maybe I was a little stiff and scared from the newness of it. Also, I was very distressed to feel his penis through his bathing suit when he held me. I could tell that he was excited several times, but I think he was embarrassed from it, because he always moved it away from me when it became hard. For that I was very grateful. I was not interested in learning more about male anatomy for several years. I think the dirty old man in the tunnel had destroyed my curiosity for such a thing. I even recall thinking how much better it would be if Carlos did not have a penis, and all we would ever do was hold each other and kiss. Remember, I was only fourteen.

My first romance ended the next week when my father told him to leave me alone. I know that my father knows that it was wrong for him to say such a thing. I think my mother agreed with me, even though she did not want me to begin dating until I was sixteen. All summer I was miserable, even though the family took a lot of trips. I would spend most of my time reading and dreaming about boys. I also knew that it was important to respect the wishes of parents. My love for Carlos went away when I heard he was spreading a story that I had let him feel my breasts and the "other place" but that I was <u>frigid</u>. I had no idea what this meant, but I thought it was a pretty mean thing for him to say. After all, I had apologized to him about my father.

During my freshman and sophomore years I had only one date. I think a lot of the kids heard about what my father had told Carlos, and they took it out on me. The problem was complicated. My parents wouldn't let me date. The braces on my teeth made me look ugly. My complexion when I was a sophomore was a mess. I was too shy to let anyone near enough even for innocent talk. And the thought of sex made me <u>sick</u>!

When I became a junior my braces came off, and my life improved a little. A boy in my English class—let's just call him Shakespeare—asked me to go to a school play. He was really my only boyfriend all through high school. Shakespeare should have had braces, but I guess his parents couldn't afford them. He also should have had a dermatologist. My parents—especially my father—liked him very much, probably because they knew I was safe with him. We became attached to each other because nothing better happened for us. All through high school I dreamed I would become very popular, but it never came true. Except for Shakespeare I could never really talk with a boy. I think Shakespeare was worse off than I was. He had no friends at all because he was so conservative in his thinking. His only interest was the debate squad and becoming a lawyer like his father.

Shakespeare was not all bad, but as far as romance goes he was very awkward. We would sit for hours in his father's car before he would kiss me. I think he was too preoccupied with world problems to ever be an interesting person with a girl. It almost seemed as though he used me as his audience for his debates.

I think we just used each other to go to parties and be with other kids. Everyone thought we were going steady, but he would never give me his ring. During the whole time we were together, I never had to fear about myself sexually.

The party on the beach after the junior prom was a very wild affair. Some kids were so high they were running around in the nude. Naturally I would never have done such a thing, but Shakespeare became very disturbed by it, and he wanted to go home soon after we arrived. I think he was a little jealous of what he saw. I thought some of the boys were terrible to exhibit themselves like that, and I felt embarrassed for their dates. We went home. After a big fight about his attitude, we decided to end our relationship. My senior year ended with a kind of strange loneliness, but at least I was not pregnant and still 100 percent virgin.

ULRIKA   *Ulrika apparently comes from a typical Swedish family,*
              one of rather conservative persuasion; but grown up she is
              independent, self-sufficient, and egalitarian in her sexual
              outlook. Thus she articulates much of what many Swedish
              girls today think, feel, and do about sex and social
              relationships. Ulrika views Lois's story with biting frank-
              ness, and rejects what she believes to be the sexual values
              and norms of American society. But behind her strong
              statements we can see much of what Ulrika thinks and feels
              about herself, and we can begin to understand differences
              between American and Swedish sex roles and patterns and
              the ways that sexuality is expressed within these patterns. As
              Ulrika's commentary indicates, childhood is an important
              time of sexual learning.

This case history about Lois is very confusing to me in many ways. On the one hand, I find it very difficult to believe some of her statements about herself. And on the other, what she is saying is very simple and filled with childish thoughts about herself. Anyway I cannot believe that someone with such irrational ideas about herself can be counted on to tell a story of her life successfully. Furthermore, it does not seem correct for a person to talk only of the sexual matters in her life, as if nothing else is important about the individual. Your society's habit of enlarging sex into something enormous is ridiculous.

The sexual insecurity found in almost everyone's life is a normal thing. Sex is just one of the things a person must face. It is stupid for girls like Lois to worry themselves to death over it. Girls should do what they want to do and not feel and act so immature about sexual behavior.

Sweden is through asking people what they feel and do with each other sexually. That is old knowledge for us and deserves no serious attention. Now we have only the problem of teaching these views to children. Sex education is compulsory in Sweden, just in case some parents should be as stupid as American parents like Lois's. Our schools teach children all the things that must be learned about sex. Children do not have to rely upon parents, each other, or older playmates for knowledge or attitudes. Everyone learns the facts and then makes his own decisions about using or not using this knowledge. It is an individual right to decide what to do without demands from home.

Lois is much too limited by her parents. She could not stand on her own legs. Sexual behavior is not much different from other things people do with each other. Fucking is one of the many pleasures you can have with others, if you like. If you do not wish to do this with someone, it is your choice. It is like eating food and breathing air.

What will happen to Lois when she finds that fucking is just fucking and nothing more than a pleasure and a way of being with a person you love? How can so much of her life be looked upon as healthy, when she speaks of all her fears and frights about sex as she struggles to run from the few boys who want to make love with her? Foolish religious ideas and dead traditions have no place in a society, when they cause troubles in the mental health of the individual or the society.

This girl does not believe that she is equal to men. She thinks of herself as a poor, helpless creature who must find a man to care for her. She cannot stand on her own legs because her parents made her so helpless. They gave her insecurity and anxiety by keeping her a child, only because she was a daughter instead of a son. Sexually healthy women are not possible in America until men stop striking down their daughters and until the mothers stop feeling jealous of daughters who try to fight their way to freedom. The sons should be taught from the first moments that they are equal but not superior because they have a penis instead of a vagina.

DISCUSSION   *Scandinavians often speak with a frankness that others interpret as hostility. How do you interpret Ulrika's style of communication? What kinds of defense mechanisms may be expressed as hostile communication?*

My boyfriend, with whom I have lived for a year now, is a student at the Psychology Institute. He read this case and says that Lois has her thinking about Freud all wrong. She is not free of her oral fixation. I agree with him. She still wants to suck just like a little baby who wants to be taken care of by someone. Instead of doing such cruel things to make her stop putting her hands in her mouth, her mother should have let her alone until she grew away from this habit naturally. But I think that even that would not have been enough to make her normal and intelligent about herself. Her experience of seeing her father naked was terrible. Such a man should not have children. Is it not clear that he gave his guilt about playing with his penis in the mirror to his daughter? To beat a child because of her wanting to see her father naked is a barbarism. I can remember wanting to see my father naked when I was quite young, just to see if he was like my younger brothers. He did not hide himself from me when he was dressing or in the bath. I thought he was a very strong father and made nothing sexual out of it. Perhaps if Lois's father had let her see him, the thing in the tunnel with the man's penis would not have been important to her. Of course, it is easy to see why she stopped to watch him for some time and then could tell no one but her friends later.

DISCUSSION   *Ulrika's reaction to Lois's episodes with her naked father and the sexual exhibitionist centers on her point that Lois should have been taught a more natural awareness about the male body and sex differences. To what extent do you believe American attitudes about nudity have changed since the years of Lois's childhood? What might the implications of such changes be for future generations? How do you feel about nudity and sexual exposure by others? Why?*

My own family consists of my mother, my father, and my two brothers, who are one and three years younger than I. I am twenty-one. During my growing period I felt a strong connection with my family. I lived at home until I was nineteen.

My parents did not bring me up in an authoritarian way. My mother was a very good educator. In some ways I think my father did not wish to educate his children and preferred to have my mother do most of these things. My mother would help us make our decisions until we could make them ourselves. My father was very quiet with us. Maybe it was because his own education was extremely authoritarian, and he wished to avoid such experience for us.

I think how a girl feels about her father is very important in how she will feel with men and her husband, if she should get married. I think my father should have taken more interest in us. I never talked with him about my personal problems, and the same was true for my brothers. Of course, we have always talked about ordinary things. During my adolescence I accused myself of not liking my father, and this caused a deep hurt in me for him. I know that my father spent a lot of his time with us children. On Sundays and weekends he spent all the time he could with us; we went on

Sunday picnics together. And he is still very glad when I come home and dine with the family on weekends.

As I grew older, I became a little embarrassed at this connection with my family. I did not want to feel so bound. It went so far that I did not want to follow them in the summer to our country house. It was terrible to be caught in the middle. My parents made me feel like a great pig, who only thought about herself and being with her friends. When I decided to go to the university in Stockholm instead of Uppsala, they thought I was being very unkind to them. In spite of all this, I like both of them very much. I visit them often now, and I think it is fun to see my brothers and find out what they are doing.

I feel my relationship with my mother has been very positive all my life, in spite of some problems when I was a teenager. I think this contact with my mother was unusually good in helping me understand about sexual matters. She encouraged us to ask questions as we became older. My brothers and I often bathed together until I was about nine. I do not remember thinking it was unnatural to look at them or to be seen naked by them. Until I was coming into puberty, I did not hide myself from them while dressing. I often washed the penis of my youngest brother without giving it thought. I never played any sex games with other children, and only once did my brother who is two years younger and I have any physical contact. When I was about ten, he came to my bed at night, and we put our hands inside of each other's nightclothes. We quietly giggled over this experience, and I remember being a little surprised that his penis became so hard with its end coming out of the skin. I do not think it was very important, but it did not happen again, although my brother wanted to do it another time. My curiosity was satisfied by this fondling. I knew then how the penis could become straight to go into the vagina, a thing my mother had told me about but that I did not clearly understand until then. I have not thought of this incident for many years. Now that I think about it, I am glad that we had such sex play with each other.

DISCUSSION   *Sexual play between siblings close to each other in age is not unusual. Few parents encourage it, and many punish children when they discover it. Some parents ignore such activities, so as not to develop feelings of sexual guilt in the children. How do you evaluate Ulrika's impressions of her experiences with her brother? How do you compare them to the sexual learning reported by Lois?*

One of the things I found upsetting in my sex education was that children at school used sex words different from those my mother used. Generally I reacted violently against those bad words. I think it was mostly boys at school who used those words, and they were boys I did not like. I wish I could remember why I felt so strongly about those words, because now I feel very free and open in using them if it is the correct place. Still, I do not use them at home with my parents or brothers, although I would sometimes like to shock them. I think my mother would not mind, but my father and brothers have a conservative attitude in some ways.

I always played with many children. In the beginning I played as much with boys as girls. At about eight years old I started to play mostly with girls, except during the summer holidays, when I always wanted to be with boys. I loved climbing mountains and trees and playing your cowboys and Indians game with them. My brothers were very good comrades. I often made my youngest brother play with my dolls at home. These creatures seem to take most of my time for several years. I loved them; I hated them; and I adored them. As I became older, I played less with my dolls and more with my classmates.

I began menstruation when I was just thirteen. I did not mind this and had even looked forward to it. I was mature for my age and looked older than I was. Many of the older boys at school would look at me with interest, but I knew pretty well that these boys were often only hunting sex. I would laugh and make jokes with them but did not wish to go to bed with any of them. At that time I could not even think of such a thing, although there was a lot of talk around school about girls and boys who had done it.

When I was fourteen I had a boyfriend. He was a very nice boy from the older class. We went to many parties together. During this time we would kiss, but there was no petting because neither of us wanted to become too excited sexually. We often talked about how bad it would be to get pregnant, and he had the idea that a condom could break. Both of us were very intolerant of those students who were fucking with no care for pregnancy. It is very strange that Lois was so unhappy about her time with the boy from her English class. She seems to feel that he was a waste because they only kissed, but what more did she want to do? What would be the use of petting if she did not like him? To become all excited and not have sexual intercourse is not healthy or fair to either the boy or the girl.

Between fifteen and nineteen I had many boyfriends. Some of them were only for a short time, but two of them were very good friends for over a year. Until I was seventeen, I did not want to fuck with a boy, and then it happened with the first of my two good friends during the time before I left home to live in Stockholm. I would have had my first time with a boy earlier, but I did not consider any of the boys from school as lovers for such seriousness and passion. Perhaps it was a mistake not to have acted differently with several of those boys, but I did not mind acting like an "ice mountain" when fucking was all they wanted.

My first fucking came after I had known the boy for several months. It happened very simply after we both decided that we liked each other very much and it was time to fuck. We did it at his house one day after school. Both his mother and father worked, and he had no brothers or sisters to concern us. There is not much to say about the first time. It was easy for me, although I did not have an orgasm. The second day we did this, it was much better for both of us. He said he had done it with another girl during his holiday earlier in the summer, but I think he was without any experience. But we learned what had to be learned very quickly. Both of us had full theoretical knowledge of what to do. Of course, we used condoms very carefully during the dozens and dozens of times we fucked with each other, all the time at his house, where we could be alone and undisturbed. We had a very fine sex relationship after a while. Near the end of our year together, we became bored with each other and started to have sex less often. I wanted to be with another boy I liked in the older class. At the same time my girlfriend fortunately began to fall in love with him, so my boyfriend was not hurt too much by my interest in another.

My second serious boyfriend was not so quiet and shy. He was also very popular at school. Right from the beginning we had very exciting sex times together. He was much more experienced. We did everything, if both of us liked it. There were many parties with older students from his class and also some from the university. I stayed with him all night at several parties, and we always had a very good time with each other. It was during this time with him that my mother and I had some difficulties. While she is very free and open in her sexual thinking, she did not like me to be away so much with this boy. The times away from home all night were very disturbing to her and my father. But I had to make my freedom for myself. I thought I had the right to do as I pleased, so I did. I was in love with this boy, and it was my business how we would behave with each other.

It would be wrong to say we were having free love. Everyone talks so much about free love and does not understand what it
means. To be able to say that you have free love, you must be
free yourself. It is not just fucking together that makes it free.
You must be able to love and not regret it afterwards or not feel
shameful. How to talk with a boy about fucking is important in
knowing how free you have become. I can now talk that way freely.
But with this second boy, I was not yet free, so it was not a free-
love matter, although we fucked too many times to remember. It
is only with my present boyfriend that I feel what free love must be.

SUSSANNE   *Sussanne's view of her childhood illustrates some of the
differences between Danish and American parental approaches to sex education. Lois has internalized many of
her parents' sexual values, whereas Sussanne has exhibited
resourcefulness and ingenuity in working around those of
her parents. Sussanne compares her sex education at home
and with peers. Her parents' attitudes are traditional and
conservative, yet by the time she was nine they had
imparted to her a basic understanding of sexual behavior.
Sussane's parents, unlike Lois's, sought to ensure her social
and moral well-being by giving her understanding along
with advice.*

I shall start like Lois with my connections to my family. I
am twenty and have a younger brother who will soon be fifteen. My
home has been very good. Both my mother and my father have been
very good to us. Although I love my mother very much, I believe
my father has been the most understanding. But earlier it was sometimes impossible for him to understand that he had an almost grown-
up daughter. I do not know why he was so concerned about me
several years ago, but perhaps it is because he is a schoolteacher
and knows so much about the problems and troubles of being a
teenager.

Like Lois, I do not remember very much about the time
before I went to school. My parents have told me that I was very
sick for the first years of my life, and I even spent much time in

the hospital. It made me speak and walk later than other children. It also made my parents extra careful with me. Although my father did not have money for all the things we would have liked, they were very thrifty, so we had good food and clothes.

We moved from Korsör to Copenhagen when I was eight. I had to learn to live in the big city. And there were many changes living in an apartment instead of our little house. I had played with many children, both boys and girls, at my old house. It took me a long time to find new friends, and I do not know why. I became quite shy when we moved.

About sexual matters as a child it is difficult to say very much. In my family we always could walk around naked in the house or the apartment. I have been in the bath with my parents when I was young, and I have often seen them dressing and undressing. Nakedness has never been unnatural. But my parents have been very puritan in all other sex ways.

DISCUSSION   *What factors cause many American parents to treat nudity as an important moral issue?*

Although my parents love each other very much, they did not kiss each other except on special occasions. Once I asked my father why he did not kiss my mother as much as my brother and I were kissed. He said that kissing was mostly for showing love to children by mothers and fathers. He also told me never to kiss a stranger. It is probably because of this that I felt that I did not like boys when I moved to Copenhagen. I did not want to play "kiss each other." When I was about nine, my girlfriend, who was more interested in boys than I was then, told me how much fun it was to kiss boys and that I should not be afraid of doing it. I remember trying to kiss with my dolls after she had told me how exciting kissing could be. But still I did not play the game until I was ten.

My education about sex began with the story about the stork. When I was a little girl, I wanted a brother very much. My mother and grandmother told me that he might come with a stork and that it would help to put a little piece of sugar in the window. I put the sugar there every day, and it was not long before my brother came. I liked having him very much. I tried to help my mother feed and wash him. Although he is five years younger, we have a very fine, loving relationship.

DISCUSSION   *Such folktale evasions as the stork story may be as common in Scandinavia as they are in America. What kinds of problems can occur during childhood as a result of invalid knowledge about sexual anatomy and behavior?*

I was about nine years old when my parents told me about menstruation, babies, and sexual love between people. It was over several days while we were on a summer holiday when I asked why my mother needed her cloth pads. I certainly knew some things before they talked with me, but I had not known about menstruation. Soon we girls talked a lot about it, and we read books. I never found any sex books or magazines in my home. I had to read what the others gave me.

When I was ten years old, I began to feel different toward boys. About this time I heard some dirty stories at school. I laughed with the other children about these jokes, but they never held any great interest for me. My mother and father had never used those bad words, and to hear them from friends at school in the jokes made me feel shy. I would never say them myself.

This was also the age when we were educated about sex in school. But I must say that this education was not very good. All the things that really mattered, such as preventing, were not discussed. Such a thing may not have been of much interest to me so young, but it should have been mentioned in school instead of only by the older children in dirty jokes. One boy in my class chased the girls around the playground with a contraceptive on a stick. All the girls wanted to know what it was but were scared of it, for it looked terrible with the sperm inside. We did not want such a thing to touch us. I believe the boys in the class knew what it was because they made a big joke of it. It was not so important because the teacher could only laugh when she saw him doing it at first. This experience may have been a little like what happened to Lois in the tunnel on her way home from school. But I have never met a man showing his penis.

DISCUSSION   *How would you compare Sussanne and Lois in terms of their capacity at this point to deal with sexual realities among peers or with adults seeking sexual contact?*

When I was twelve, my mother gave me a book from our church about sexual relationships and love between men and women. It was a simple book which told me nothing I did not know. It was mostly to tell children not to become sexually excited because God would not love them anymore. My mother and I did talk for a bit about sex then, but she preferred that I read books from the library and then ask her questions. I read two books I thought were interesting, but they were not interesting enough to ask questions about. There was nothing more I cared to know then.

I was thirteen or fourteen when I started going out to parties with both boys and girls. These parties were held without drinking and when the parents were home. We danced a lot and played games together. I very quickly saw the fun that could come from being with boys. It was new and exciting to be liked by them. I forgot my old thinking about kissing and found pleasure in the games we would play. It was also very nice to be held in the arms of the boys while they kissed. But for some of the boys I was too shy. I did not kiss them with passion, like some of my classmates. One day my girlfriend asked me whether I would let the boy go into my mouth with his tongue. Of course I had not. But at the next party I did this with a boy and was very excited by it. It was only a few minutes before I also put my tongue in my boyfriend's mouth. Such passionate kissing was the start of having dates with boys.

My mother and father were very concerned about my dating. My mother was very kind in her way of telling me not to have sexual intercourse with boys. She talked a lot of morals and religion. But such beliefs were of little concern to me. I began to think with my girlfriends that the only important questions were whether you loved the boy and whether pregnancy could be prevented.

When I was sixteen I met the boy who gave me my first sexual intercourse. He was the same age as I, but quite experienced in making love. When I first danced with him at a party, I knew he would be my first love in bed. I dated him again and again. Each time he tried to tell me how much he was in love with me and how nice it would be to go to bed. Finally we decided that we would do it after the next party if we could find a nice place. Such a place was at the party of one of his older friends. It was only a very small party, and all of the students were strangers to me. I was glad because I did not want my friends to know what we were going to do with each other.

It was not long before all of us were drinking too much. At first there was only kissing and petting in the dark, but soon other

things began to happen for all of us. The spirits were very strong.
I let my boy feel my breasts and put his hand between my legs. I
could see that the other couples were doing much more and was
very excited by what I could see. One boy had taken off his pants,
and his girlfriend was stroking and massaging his penis. When the
others saw this, they too went further, and several of the girls
took off their blouses and bras so the boys could feel their breasts.
At first I was very scared, but still it was very exciting. My date
was very experienced with his gentle but firm touches to my sex
parts. He kissed my ears and neck with his tongue and teeth in a
way I cannot even today describe for another boy to do.

It was very nice to feel his penis in my hand. Its hardness
felt funny at first. I had before wondered what made it become
hard. I could not find the answer even in my books. As the party
went on with more and more lovemaking in the furniture and on the
floor, I could see that everyone there was to have sexual intercourse. It was not such a surprise, because my boyfriend had
told me that these friends often did it at such a party. At first I
had not believed him. I also thought that it would not be right to go
to bed with others watching. But it was exciting to see.

My friend and I found our way into the bedroom when I
thought the time had come for me. It was a narrow bed with a very
poor mattress. We took off the rest of our clothes, and soon this
boy was inside of me. I felt no pain. It was a strange feeling to
have the penis moving gently inside of me after he went through my
hymen. I suddenly felt the same pleasure I got from my own masturbation, which I had been doing for two years. It was only
different in the feeling of fullness, as the penis moved inside me.
I was surprised as he was suddenly giving way in quick movements
as he had his orgasm in me. The way he jerked and trembled for
his orgasm was thrilling. I felt very close to this boy and trusted
him in every way, but we had been very foolish. We had not used
the contraceptive he had brought. I think it was because of the
spirits and because we were so excited and passion-filled so quickly
once we had started to hold each other in the bed with our naked
skins. I worried about pregnancy the moment we had finished, and
so did he. All of the other couples at the party were having sex
again and again, but we only sat in the dark holding each other with
this terrible worry upon our minds.

After this first time we started to go to bed with each other
as often as we could manage for me to be away from home and find
a place. During the summer days this was no problem. We both
enjoyed the forest, which was not too many minutes from my home.

We hid a blanket in the forest which we used as often as the rain would let us. This was a very nice summer. My father liked this boy very much because he behaved so well with my family. Neither my mother nor my father knew what we were doing. This did not bother me very much because I knew they would be shocked and hurt by knowing of our times together. Yet I think my mother may have suspected because I did not want to hear her talk about sex any longer. She would tell of girls becoming pregnant, and such talk was not pleasant for me to think about.

At the end of the summer my love for this boy disappeared. I heard that he had gone to bed with a classmate of mine. He admitted it, and the love I had for him was completely gone in a few minutes. Naturally, I was very unhappy for a long time. Afterwards I talked with him again, but I could not bear to go back with him. My parents were very interested in what had happened between us, but what could I tell them? They knew I was hurt and were very nice to me, giving me much comfort and advising me to find another boy. This I did.

chapter 2

Stanley, Olov, and Henrik

STANLEY
    Stanley has compressed a great deal of life into his first twenty years, much of which he recalls with tempered resentment and sometimes with insight and understanding. Stanley's childhood seems to have been a time for learning many negative feelings toward himself. His parents' beliefs and practices about raising children and sexual learning could almost be expected to lead to the kinds of problems Stanley describes. Obviously his parents were not aware of the impact they were having on his development. This case makes particularly clear the link between childhood development and later years, when the quality of the parent-child relationship meets its test.

    I was born in Los Angeles twenty years ago. The only other child in our family was my brother, who came along three years later. Up to the time of my parents' divorce, when I was fourteen, we lived a reasonably normal life together. While our standard of living was not all that great, we at least owned whatever we had, which is more than can be said for most of our neighbors. Neither my dad nor my mom had much education, but considering their way

of life it wasn't necessary. I am the first one in the family to go
to college.

When I was just little I can remember being pulled or pushed
around by my parents. Even when I was in school, I had little independence. I gave the obedience of a prisoner who didn't know
whether to conform or escape. Because of this confusion, I grew
up as a selfish kid. I couldn't master problems very well either,
because my folks were always criticizing me. Sometimes I felt I
wasn't much of a person.

I don't believe my sex training could have been done correctly. There was always a sense of shame whenever I had to go
to the bathroom. I would try to urinate on the side of the bowl, to
make sure that it wouldn't make noise. I was told when to have
my bowel movements and then that I should "hurry up and get out
of there." I was always worried about becoming constipated, because after four or five days I was sure to become a candidate for
the enema routine. I would do almost anything to escape that. God,
how my brother and I hated those things, but our parents never
believed in laxatives. I don't know whether my feelings about body
wastes has very much to do with my sex life or not, but I feel that
it may be connected in some way.

All their yelling and screaming at us must have been a big
drain on them. My brother wet his bed until he was almost thirteen,
and became a real mental case over it.

My brother and I were taught to be very modest about our
bodies. We were even careful about exposure to each other. A
feeling of shame about our sex organs was probably learned from
our mother. I never saw my folks naked and had no desire to do
so. Maybe this is where I got the idea that it was dirty to be seen
naked or to watch a naked person. Later on this made girlie
magazines especially exciting to me, but I always had a guilty feeling about such things as well. They were dirty but nice in an exciting way.

DISCUSSION   *Some of Stanley's experiences to this point show how
sexual learning is related to the internalization of negative
feelings about the body and its eliminative functions. To
what extent is his behavior the result of his parents' beliefs,
attitudes, and patterns of behavior? What has caused*

Stanley to feel that sex-oriented magazines "were dirty but nice in an exciting way"? Can this paradox become the basis of sexual behavior for an individual? For a society?

Related to this was the fact that in the first few grades I really liked to be alone in the house so I could take off my clothes and look at myself naked in the big mirror in my parents' bedroom. I would kneel in front of the mirror and kiss the image in the mirror. When I was a little older I would enjoy feeling my penis and balls, and several times I remember backing up into the mirror and looking at and fingering my anus. This activity was completely self-invented. I would always feel a great deal of shame in having done it, and for years it bothered me that it may have meant that I wasn't quite right in the head. Fortunately I know now it is just one of the many sexual zones in the human body. The last time I did this playing around in front of the mirror, I was about eleven years old. I was either stimulated or curious about some dogs who were having sex. I really thought they were doing it in each other's anuses. I still believed what a friend in the third grade had told me about fucking between men and women. He told me that men fucked with women from the rear like dogs. I remember liking and believing the story so much that I passed it around to other kids, in-cluding my brother. I enjoyed using words like <u>fuck</u> and <u>shit</u> with my friends, but it wasn't too long before I began to have a lot of trouble with teachers. I got a bad reputation for talking back using some of the forbidden language. I enjoyed this because it brought me attention. The only thing I was afraid of was getting a beating from my mother. Once, when I was eleven, I was getting the belt from her, she hit my face with the buckle, and my dad had to stop her. I feel communication was impossible with her after that. I did whatever I got away with, and I wouldn't stop until I was forced.

I had only two genuine sex experiences with other kids before the teens. The first one happened when I was in the second grade. I had heard about a girl who pulled her pants down in front of the boys. One day I was playing with this girl alone, and I asked her to do it for me. She didn't want to at first because her mother had told her not to do it any more. But it didn't matter to me that she'd promised her mother. I nagged and nagged until she said she would pull her pants down if I would pull mine down too. We went to a house being built about a block from her house. When we got there it was almost dark, and the workers had gone home. I remember removing the temporary door and crawling inside with her. She pulled up her dress and took her panties off, and I got out of my pants and hung them with my underwear on a rusty nail. We didn't do anything but crawl around inside the house and look at each other. The only thing that came from this except the satisfaction of my curiosity was the beating I got at home for being so late.

I was not very interested in sex through most of my child-hood. It was enough to me to know that babies grew inside the mother and crawled out of the "mother's hole" when they were ready to be born. I was only baffled about how a large baby could get out through the hole. The opening I had seen in the girl had seemed very small. I thought the reason the mother had to go to the hospital was so the doctors could cut the "crack" to let the baby out.

When I was eleven or twelve I had a homosexual experience with a boy in my class. Just north of Manhattan Beach there are some beautiful sand dunes where Neil and I would hike. You had to climb over some fences, and if the guards saw you, you had to run like hell to get away. We were never caught. I know now that what Neil and I did with each other was just silly kid stuff, but for years it bothered me.

Whenever we had a chance in the dunes, we would strip down and walk around naked. At first we would just throw sand at each other and then chase each other until it got to be wrestling. The first few times we horsed around nothing much happened except to grab each other in the crotch. However, the more times we were together, the more homosexual the play became. I hate to use that word, but I guess I have to admit that this was my homo-sexual period. I really hated women, and even girls, then. One time when we were both tired and just lying there letting the old sun beat on our bods, Neil and I just sort of started to tickle each other. He got an erection almost right away. It was the first time I had noticed such a thing in another boy. I had had them occasion-ally, but they were unrelated to anything sexual except one time in front of the mirror. After he got hard, he stroked me, and soon I was just as big as him. It was quite an experience. Neither of us knew the significance of what we were doing. We did this about a dozen times. The activity was confined to feeling each other's penises and spreading the cheeks of our posteriors so we could see each other's anuses. He played around a little with mine, but nothing erotic happened beyond this. Both of us forgot those two summers and never talked about them with anyone else, as far as I can tell. We were very good friends through all the rest of grade school, and in eighth grade both of us started to take some interest in girls.

DISCUSSION   *Coping with forbidden or disapproved homosexual experiences in childhood is sometimes a problem. Defense mechanisms (rationalization, suppression, repression) are often employed to help diminish guilt and anxiety. Rationalization is the unconscious effort to justify behavior and thus protect the self-image and gain self-approval. Suppression is the conscious control a person has of his behavior, feelings, attitudes, and thoughts. Repression is the act of forgetting matters that threaten the self-concept. To what extent does Stanley use any of these mechanisms to deal with his homosexual behavior? How common are these experiences? How should they be evaluated by young people, parents, and adults?*

I started kissing and petting with girls after I was thirteen. No sooner had I started kissing a girl than I would try to feel her breasts. It was a great game to see how far the girls would let me go. I didn't care much about what they thought of me, anyway. My reputation at school was so lousy it didn't matter. The only thing that kept me in line was my fear about girls and the guilt I learned at home.

When I was fourteen my parents separated and divorced. My father had become a complete alcoholic, and my mother was as mean as possible. It was a terrible time for my brother and me. I think my sexual behavior was affected greatly by all of this, and I was deeply depressed. At first I decided it was my mother's fault, so I thought all women were morbid and cheap. Then my father would do things that caused me to think he was the bad guy. I never had much respect for him, but he really took a lot from my mother. My friends asked me about the divorce, and I didn't know what to say. My life was on a real downhill course for the next three years. I lived with my mother, but did just about what I wanted to do. Both of my parents continually played for my affection, which they never got.

DISCUSSION   *Stanley's manipulation of affection to accomplish social ends, including hostility toward parents who fail to meet his needs, seems important in his personality makeup. How does a child learn to withhold love as a weapon in social interaction? What is the role of parents in such learning? Once an individual learns to deal with frustrations and anxieties in parent-child relationships in this way, how might it affect intimate relationships in adulthood?*

I can honestly say that my friends in high school were not of the best character. I was always out late. My grades didn't matter. My respect for people in general had diminished. But in many ways I was having all the privileges and pleasures of being a grown-up. By the time I left high school, in the middle of my junior year, I had built up quite a record for goofing off and telling off the teachers and coaches. I had also picked up a police record for being investigated for some small thefts. I had no respect for girls. I was sixteen before I had what you could call a real date! I was ashamed of my family and the company I was keeping. I also started having some fun with beer, wine, and pot with the guys. Then Joan happened to me.

Joan was the first girl I ever dated. We met at a beach party, where there was a lot of beer and dope being smoked. She was only turning fifteen, but she had already been to bed with another boy, a surfer. We started dating every weekend. Both Joan and I could be out as late as we wanted. Her mother was also divorced. Actually, except for dates we had at the drive-in with another couple, I didn't mind spending time around her house, because her mother was seldom home. We would spend hours during the beginning of our relationship just kissing and petting in her living room. To be honest, I was unsure of myself, afraid of having sex with her. I was used to having wet dreams since fourteen.

When I was sixteen I quit school and went to work in a gas station. I had become very interested in cars, and it was a big thing for me to save money for the day I could buy my own. As soon as I quit school, I started to spend more time with Joan. Her mother was happy to have me around the house—more so than my own mother, I think. I used to fix things for her. I didn't think at first that she liked me at all, but we gradually began to get along real well. She was very open about sex. I remember her saying, "If you two kids start to get serious about sex, I don't want no babies around here." She must have known that we had not done anything with each other yet.

When I was seventeen, my mother threw me out of the house. She said she did not like me corrupting my younger brother and a lot of other complaints. I moved into Joan's house. Her mother almost seemed pleased about it. At first I had my own room, and there was the understanding that I could get tossed out if I became a pain. When

I moved in, I knew it would be only a very short time before Joan and I would have sex.

It happened the first week, when her mother was reading in her bedroom. We screwed standing up in the kitchen, almost fully clothed. It was easy, and I enjoyed the new thrill. I think I expected more, but it was still good.

The opportunity to go all the way sexually came almost as often as we wanted it. Joan would stay home from school, and we'd stay in bed all day. Her mother worked. Everything I know about intercourse I learned from Joan, and she was only fifteen. Everything was focused on our love, which was purely sexual. In many ways we both used her mother to get what we wanted. I am now a little ashamed about how we both treated her, because her intentions were good.

Soon Joan was pregnant. We both wanted the child, despite our ages. We probably thought we would automatically become mature people. We talked about birth control, but Joan said it wasn't the same for her with rubbers, that she liked the feel of loads rushing into her during my orgasm, but I am now convinced that she wanted to get pregnant so we could be married. We told our mothers, then went to Mexico to be married (without my mother's consent). Joan's mother, after a few screams and tears, accepted it in no time.

Marriage to Joan was very beautiful until the responsibilities started coming. Our first problem was that we had to live with her mother, and she was finally putting her foot down. We had no money to live on. My job at the station was cut to part-time, and I couldn't find another.

In the third month of pregnancy, Joan lost the child. It was really a blessing for all of us, as things have turned out. After that our sex life was never the same. It was actually very odd from that time on, but of course I had little to compare it to. Joan taught me everything I knew about sexual intercourse, but the lessons were very simple and ordinary. We would remove our clothes at the bed or under the covers. Both of us avoided looking at each other if we could. It was crazy. I think we both felt a lot of shame about having sex, even after we were married, when everything should have been all right. Maybe it was our age. I can't say for sure what caused the coldness that came over us. Joan did not want to have sex anywhere near as much as I did.

Near the end of our first six months together, it became apparent to everyone that trying to live together was a big mistake. The crush of responsibilities and the sexual fiascos changed both of us. I know now that I was a lonely person when I met Joan. For almost a year she gave me some tenderness and satisfied my needs for mental and physical intimacy, but the dreams of pure sex had become like a picture of my parents trying to do it. The fun and excitement of sex was over for Joan, and I only had my need for satisfaction. Near the end, whether she wanted it or not, I forced her to have sex. I thought it was the very least she could do for me. She had quit school but hadn't gone to work. I would sometimes think at the station that the whole setup was wrong. It was certainly not what I had in mind for the rest of my life.

DISCUSSION   *From childhood Stanley remembers his feeling of helplessness, loneliness and denial of affection. Joan did not cure all that. What connections do you see between his childhood and the events and outcome of his relationship with Joan?*

OLOV   *Like Stanley, Olov came from a broken home. Through Olov we can see how this problem is confronted in a Swedish family. The way everyone works out the loss of the father is a critical factor in Olov's life. Olov's commentary provides impressions of values and norms that guide the development of sexual learning and relationships in Sweden. His ability to discuss sexual matters is typical of Scandinavian candor. Olov appears to be a relatively secure and self-confident young man who has had some success, beginning in childhood, in fulfilling his basic needs.*

My first reaction to this American student is "poor Stanley." How much you have lost. Throughout his story there is fear and guilt about sex, which has almost ruined his life. Not once does he say he learned anything from his school about sexual matters. And, of course, he was all alone with his sexual experiments, with such fright about almost normal, and even expected, experiences. His parents must have given him a bewildering way of thinking for him

to become a failure in so many ways. I am glad tha[t]
some idea of his predicament and is going to try to o[v]
stupidity of his family and society. It must have been
for him to talk so freely. "Poor Stanley" has my good

I am the youngest of three children. My sister is four and
a half years older, and my brother is six years older. From my
earliest childhood I just recall certain moments of joy and a few
times when my mother and father quarreled with each other. But
I also remember when they kissed each other and held hands like
real lovers. My relationship with my father was very short because
he became very ill when I was almost eight years old. During his
illness he gave up his life in suicide. This was a terrible shock
when it happened, but within a year the loss was mostly over for
me. My mother never did remarry while I was growing up, and I
did not mind this at all. Perhaps it made my connection with my
mother stronger, but mostly it meant something to my sexual development because of the greater freedom I got by not having a
father restrict my activities with other children. I was always
free to be myself, and I feel I used that freedom very wisely most
of the time. I was a much better student than Stanley.

It was probably very fortunate that my mother worked several
years before my father's death, for she was able to become a very
important and successful manager of a business in Stockholm. I was
sent to the kindergarten near her job while my sister and brother
were in the lower schools. At kindergarten I received my first remembered lessons about sexual matters. I had often seen my sister
naked at home and was curious to see if other girls were the same
way in their sex organs. It was in the toilet at school that I attempted
to look at a girl when the teacher and other children were out for play.
This experience went very well for me. She freely let me see her. I
have no idea now what I said to her to get her to permit this, but she
must have thought my interest was not so very strange. I do not remember touching her, but she felt my penis. As it happened, she was
more interested in me than I was in her. My curiosity about her was
gone very quickly. It was nothing I wanted to do again. Now I do not
even remember her name.

The next sexual event in my life was when I was about seven
or eight. We grew up in an apartment house in which five families
lived off every gate. Across from our door lived a family with
three children, including a girl of my age. Since we lived so close
together, there were many possibilities for us to play with each
other. I do not remember when or how we were first led into sex
play, but our games often did turn out to have a sexual experience

for us. When no one was home with her, in her darkened bedroom we would pretend that we were a mother and father. She explained to me what she had seen her mother and father doing with each other. Our own attempt to do this was very simple and even innocent. We would take off our clothes and get into her bed and rub our bodies together as if we were fucking. I do not remember getting an erection from it, but I nevertheless was excited enough to want to do it with her whenever she would want to.

I remember losing interest in this game as soon as my father died. It could be that I felt deeply that it was very wrong behavior and not just something you should not do because of fear of punishment if you were caught. I must have felt that my father would not have done such a thing, even though I believed that her father would. For me it was not so satisfying. I was too young for sexual climax.

DISCUSSION   *People often have a difficult time imagining their parents engaged in sexual intercourse. Does Olov reveal here an attitude that sexual intercourse for adults is somehow wrong? Are Scandinavians who perceive themselves as sexually liberal and free necessarily without learned anxieties and fears about sex?*

When my father died, there was much loneliness in our family. I was very unhappy and became somewhat distant with other children for the next couple of years. This was not helped by my being forced to wear glasses when I was nine. I was often teased at school because I was so thin and had to wear these glasses. I had only one friend who could truly be called my companion. I believe he was also a lonely person, because his parents had come to a divorce. Gunnar and I gradually came to be with each other more and more.

In the fourth year of school we heard about sex and the birth of babies from our teacher. She was very clear in her talks with all of us. I think I felt some embarrassment at becoming aware of the bigger meaning of my earlier sex experience with my neighbor girl at home. Other than this, the sex instruction was without event. I only avoided the girl who lived across from us at home. She also avoided me. Now it is quite different when I visit my mother and occasionally see her, and we laugh for reasons we will not express but only think to ourselves. She is a beautiful girl who no longer needs to curl up in bed with impotent little boys! At this time my mother gave me a very good book about sex and the changes that were to come to my body. But it would have been better if I had had a father. I must say that I worried about whether I would ever mature in the way the book said I surely would as a grown man. I did worry some about my appearance, and this grew worse when some of the boys my age were ahead of me in their sex growth. Perhaps it is good that Gunnar was also at my stage of physical development.

Gunnar and I did not talk very much about sex because each of us was unsure what the other would think, but finally it was Gunnar who asked me one day whether I was starting to grow hair around my penis. I was probably in my twelfth year when this talk came out. Fortunately, I was able to report such a beginning, and it was from this that our conversation turned to masturbation and what some of the other boys were talking about concerning sexual matters between boys and girls. One night when he was invited to sleep at my house so we could go out early for skating and hockey, we talked of how it would feel to fuck with a girl. Such talk gave us both erections, which resulted in our trying to jerk off.

My first summer away from home in camp was not very important in giving me experience in sexual matters. At this age masturbation was something you did not want to talk about with other boys. It was still a very mysterious and private matter. The second summer I went to camp, it was more open. I remember all the boys in my cabin competing to see who could make his cock the largest. But it was not completely open among us. Such sex play often was followed by teasing the winner. The boy who was usually the victim of such teasing was more than a little dull. He not only would end up showing us his large cock but he would shoot out his sperm in his hand while we all watched. I now feel very sorry about how we encouraged him. From these summers at camp I learned some freedom about masturbation and did it often, but from that time not with other boys watching. By the time I was fifteen, I had masturbated hundreds and hundreds of times, and I am sure that I was without bad feelings concerning it. When full maturity had come to my sex organs, I had no feelings of worry.

DISCUSSION   *Compare the preadolescent homosexual experiences of Olov and Stanley. Was it more significant socially and psychologically for one than the other? What defenses did Olov and his friends use to cope with this experience? What should parents or teachers do to help children deal with these experiences?*

When I was fourteen or fifteen, I had my first real interest in a girl. It was also a matter of sexual interest, but I kept that all in my mind and did not let it out in anything we did together. It was very good to just walk home with her from school and hold her hand. I would only dream about how exciting it would be to touch her large breasts and feel between her legs. Eva was a very good first girl for me. We went to all the school parties with each other. We never did any of the touching I wanted to do with her, only a little kissing and close dancing. I feel now that she was ready for much more, but it was too frightening for me to try. Eventually, she started to go with other boys more experienced than I. But from her I learned how to be with a girl and was better able to go on to the other girls in my life.

The years between twelve and sixteen were very important because of the many changes in my life. Perhaps it was the summer when I first went to camp that I learned to be with others. I did not feel all of the loneliness of my childhood any longer. While my mother was even busier with her work, my older brother became a very good friend. We enjoyed each other more than was possible when I was very young. We could talk freely about girls and sex. I think he has been a good influence in my life. As for my sister, she has gone her own way in a fashion best for her. She now lives with a medical student while she is completing her last year in the school for nursing.

All things considered, it is to my mother's credit that she was able to give the three of us a good home while making a life that seems satisfying for her. Her direct contribution to my sexual patterns are not too clear to me. While she always answered my questions (of which I had very few), I am sure that her attitude of letting me discover sex without giving me feelings of guilt was best. I thank her in my heart for her simple words of understanding when she accidently came upon me while I was masturbating. I feel she had very healthy attitudes about sex. She has now married a very fine man, whom we all like very much. The only time my mother and I had a serious difficulty was in my second year in high school when I neglected my studies and almost fell into a pattern like Stanley with his girl Joan. Fortunately, it never led to the serious business of marriage, which I owe to some good advice from both my mother and brother.

After Eva my time with girls went very easily. I had good friends of both sexes and could enjoy myself much better. Although I no longer have anything to do with the church, I probably should report that being confirmed when I was fifteen was important--not for any religious reasons, but because it made it possible to spend four beautiful summers at a church camp. That camp made my first fucking, with a girl named Christina, possible.

It happened the second summer I was working at the camp as a counselor. Christina had been only fourteen and a half years old when we had met during the very first summer. I thought she was very cute then, but when she came back the second summer to work in the kitchen, she had turned into a very mature girl. I was ready for her, and I am sure that we felt the same desires as soon as we saw each other outside the kitchen door the first day of that summer. This was the summer I almost completely forgot about my family, my friends, and, indeed, about everything else. There were many romantic nights together—long walks along the sea, the fun of naked swimming under the lightly darkened night sky, and the excitement of our bodies coming together for kissing and petting. It was a love dream come true, I thought. Her beauty was without a single flaw. It was the summer for my sexual feelings, and it is true that at no time before, and even since, have such instincts so ruled my every judgment and action. It was like being insane.

My times with Christina at first were very frustrating for me. Until the last week of camp there was only kissing and petting. Both of us would have orgasms whenever we could do it for each other. Still, I would leave her and go to my cabin and masturbate again, just thinking of the time we would fuck with each other. I loved her so much I confessed this to her, to my own surprise. Perhaps it was this confession that brought us to end our virginity. During the last week at camp the desire to fuck could no longer be beaten back. I now realize that we took a great risk in doing it without a contraceptive, but we were lucky. It happened on a beach not far from camp on one of the most beautiful nights the Lord has ever given to the archipelago. The sea was warm, the air filled with a balmy, gentle breeze, and the touch of our bodies was electric with the desire to have each other in the final act of love-making. I shall always remember her pulling me down to the wet sand after we walked away from the water. After only short moments of kissing and caressing, I placed my cock at the entrance of her cunt. Her only word, "now." I pressed my hard cock against her virginity, and it was cracked with little more than a firm push. At last we both had a real fuck. For an hour we lay together upon the wet sand, only thinking and feeling the beautiful sensations of what we thought was a forever kind of love.

HENRIK   *Henrik also had only one parent during much of his childhood, but unlike Olov, Henrik shares with Stanley the need to escape a difficult mother. Henrik demonstrates how to use the resources of the peer group, and perhaps the permissive social conditions outside of the home, to deal with the parent-child conflict. One of the important things to note in Henrik's commentary is the role of the parental model in forming attitudes toward sexuality and social relationships with the opposite sex. Henrik's views of his parents provide interesting contrasts.*

Stanley and I have some experiences in common, although I must say that I look at them differently. Both of us come from totally spoiled marriages. My mother and father were always fighting. Their divorce came when I was nine years old. At that time my father fell hopelessly into drink and could not even work at his factory job. Although I always wanted brothers and sisters, it is fortunate that none came to share the little affection and love I was able to get from my parents.

I feel Stanley tried to be free in telling of the events in his life, but I wonder how good some of his interpretations of these experiences are. I also believe that he has exaggerated the significance of sexual matters in shaping his life. Perhaps he has read too much Freud. When he tells me that he always tried to pee on the side of the toilet so no one would hear him, I wonder how important this is. Out of curiosity, I asked several of my friends about this, and we all agreed that we pee on the side of the toilet so it will not splash so much. But of what importance is such a matter, whatever the reason? He has also talked a lot about how his childhood experiences influenced his later youth in some important way. I am inclined to feel that childhood experiences are of less importance than he has made them out to be.

Young people in Denmark find early in adolescence that the sex ideas of parents are not a good guide for finding sexual pleasure and satisfaction. Our friends turn out to be more important in forming our sexual style, and we quietly leave the views of our parents behind. We are also able to leave the childhood sex experiences behind, whatever they may have been. Our liberal and permissive point of view probably makes it easier for us to do this than for Stanley in his society.

There are two examples of what I am trying to point out. First, I have masturbated for as long as I can remember. Yet I have many memories of my mother's punishing me for doing it. I never really believed her when she would tell me how bad it was. I must have known in my own mind and body that it was a very good thing to do. I only learned not to do it when she could see me. I liked to be naked and look at my body, even though she told me such displays of the self were shameful. Yet I liked to do it, and especially with other children whose parents did not seem to care very much. There were many summers, even when I was as old as ten, that I would play with other children this way.

The second type of experience was my first homosexual event, when I was twelve. Another boy and I would often go to his house for the sole purpose of playing with each other in a sexual way. We knew of other boys who did it as much as we did. I never felt any guilt about it. We only wanted our parents not to find out. Even when we were as old as fifteen, I did not attach any bad meanings to it. It was a very satisfying activity, especially after we were able to come by some very good porno books and pictures. Both of us were quite normal. It was at the age when it was much less trouble to masturbate, looking and thinking about the sexy girls in the pictures, than to try to do those things with the ones we knew. But all of this was quietly left behind without guilt or remorse. Of course our parents would not have liked any of these things, but so what! Children have a right to be themselves in their sex interests if it does not hurt themselves or others.

DISCUSSION　　*Henrik's view of what parents ought to do about sex play between children is not to be taken as the Danish norm. While Danish parents tend to be permissive rather than punitive about such matters, they usually do not encourage such experiences among children. Would Henrik impose no limits on his own children?*

What is much more important is the total love relationship between parents. I am now almost twenty-two years old, but I swear that until only a few years ago I totally hated the idea of anything resembling marriage or family life. I am now living with a wonderful woman who has two young children, aged two and four. We have been together for over a year. I like being called Father. But I would never have had this if I had not been able to get away from the terrible experiences of my own childhood. My mother punished me very severely for wrongdoing, just as Stanley's did. Such memories must be thrown into the sea, as I finally managed to do. I had to face the fact that I did not like my mother and girls who were like her. I was fortunately able to discover, after many false beginnings, that there are very good persons of both sexes who are unlike my parents.

As I have said, this discovery came not too long ago. I had a time much like Stanley's, except my sex experiences seem to me to have been much fuller. Many of these experiences ended with discouragement about finding the good type of person, and others ended even in sexual failure. But now this bothers me not even a little bit, and I can talk about it without feeling very much.

When I was thirteen, I was almost completely controlled by my mother in all matters, but I gradually was able to break away from her. I spent more and more time with boys from the school. We seemed to begin together to take an interest in girls. At first it was just our conversation. Then we started to watch the older boys we knew. I feel this is important in growing up. You do not learn to be with girls by studying them at home.

DISCUSSION   *Like Stanley, Henrik is determined to break away from his mother, but the results are not the same. Could this contrast point to the importance of the peer group as a social and psychological influence? Does Henrik seem more secure with his peers than Stanley? How does rebellion against parents succeed and fail?*

By the time I was fourteen, after going to parties with various girls from school, I had a steady girlfriend. My time with Margit did more for my social growing up than for my sexual satisfaction, except that I certainly had feelings strong enough to do some masturbating about her. The two of us would only risk kissing, and near the end I petted her naked breasts. She never minded letting me play with them but would not let me touch her below. Our time together was ended when I wanted to match the experience of some of my friends, who were feeling their girls in the vagina. Margit did not take kindly to my forcefully pushing my hand under her dress. I was very angry at this refusal, but after all she was only fourteen, and I probably would not have been able to do anything that would have been satisfying for her anyway.

With the end of Margit, I continued to go places with my friends. By the time I was sixteen, there was much walking around on the streets, just looking for girls and talking with them, if they

would. I know I did not care much about being with them. I only
liked the idea of trying to look big with my friends. It was like a
game for me. There was much more talk about having sex with
them than doing it. At this time my mother again became a lot of
trouble to me. She did not like me to be out so late at night. Also,
she did not like it one little bit when I was found to have been drinking with my friends. She would tear me down, just as she had done
with my father. But the more she would tell me not to do something, the more I would go ahead and do it, including the drinking.

A friend and I had bought a great many condoms of various
kinds. It is amusing to think that when my mother discovered them
in my bedroom she thought she still had a responsibility to teach
me about sex. I am sure that she thought I was using them because
I had so many. Actually I only had been collecting them, except
for the times I would use one for masturbation. My mother's only
contribution to my sex education up to this point had only been a
concern about my masturbation. Two years earlier she had found
me in the morning doing it in my bed. Her reaction was as if I was
still the eight-year-old child. She talked almost without end about
the shame and unhealthiness of what I was doing. The embarrassment of this incident was soon of little consequence to me. At
least, this was what I told myself.

The condoms I had been collecting for close to a year finally
were put to use when I was just seventeen. My first sexual relationship uncovered in a very direct way a matter I had worried about for
some time. It was the question of what you do if a girl agrees to
fuck with you and you become so shocked that your penis cannot
become firm. This was very bad to have on my mind for my first
experience, and I am now honest enough to say that the influence of
my mother may even have been present in what happened.

I met the girl I was to go to bed with at a party with my
friends. She was at least three years older and lived in a rented
room alone in the centrum. I would have not thought that she
would take such an interest in me, but I was more than pleased
when in front of my friends she accepted my offer to take her home
"for a night of loving."

After walking many kilometers and much "big man" talk
from me along the way, we found our way into the privacy of her
little room. It was a fiasco from the beginning. I was no nervous,
I was shaking all over as soon as we got there! When she said we
should take off our clothes, I was really scared. Now I can see
the normality of what I was going through, but then it was different.

I thought at the time that it was absolutely necessary for the man to have a firm penis before getting into bed with the woman. Mine was completely small from my fright. While she got into the bed, I went into her toilet and with great strain tried to masturbate it into fullness. I must have been at this for at least ten minutes. I was a crazy picture of odd behavior, to be sure. I was standing there in the dark for so long with no reason to give her as she called to me. It finally ended when she came through the door and put on the light. Unfortunately, she immediately saw me doing self-stimulation, and without success. Worse than when my mother discovered me, she said nothing. This was nothing like what I thought it would be the first time.

Now I can laugh at my embarrassment and shame, but then it was quite different. I soon came from her toilet with no solution to my trouble and wordlessly started to put on my clothes. I was crushed by my shame. While I was still dressing, she came naked to my side and kissed me. There is no doubt in my mind that this was the most important kiss of my life. Saying that she understood, she did the next beautiful thing. She took off my clothes and led me to the bed. Naked upon the bed, we again kissed and held each other. Most of my nervousness was gone after a while, and it was a great relief that when she reached down to my penis it was as hard as a rock. She was very experienced, and after I stopped to put on a condom (at least this was done with experience) her hand guided my penis into her vagina. It was in the end as Stanley said—"I enjoyed the new thrill of fucking."

When we had finished fucking, we talked for several hours about ourselves. She had not known that it was the first time for me. We talked of what had bothered me at first and what she saw me doing in her toilet. It was a wonderful conversation, and I was relieved to be rid of my misunderstanding. There is no telling what would have happened to me if I had left her when I felt so much failure of my manhood. It was a simple misunderstanding of what to expect, having no experience.

The two girls who became my strongest friends before I became a student at the university were very important in teaching me about other matters concerning being with a woman. The details of our relationships would be very ordinary to tell, but for me they were very important. As I have said before, I had very bad feelings about marriage and being with a girl in a steady way. I had no sisters and had not been given much knowledge about matters by my female classmates. Certainly, my mother's attitudes and behavior were a poor example of how a normal woman behaves.

DISCUSSION   *Does Henrik's reference to his mother suggest the impor-*
tance of a parental model in forming sexual attitudes and
patterns of behavior? How did Henrik's negative impres-
sions about his mother influence his behavior toward girls
up to this point? What changes the course of this pattern
for many young people?

These two girls did much to give me knowledge about the
pleasure and satisfaction of intimate ways of living. They were different from girls who were only for sexual connections and fun at
parties. Both of these relationships ended for the same reason—my
eye for other girls at parties. I can confess my foolishness now,
but then I was afraid I was missing something in not taking advantage
of opportunities to have excitement and fun with someone new.

I was twenty years old when I became a student at the university. At the same time I completely cut myself off from my mother.
Both of these events made changes in my life. For the first year I
lived with three other male students in an apartment close to the
university.

I went to the many parties my new friends had on the weekends, but other than that the first year was filled with hard work and
a job, as my mother had stopped all financial help. Only twice during the whole year did I find myself in bed with a girl, and both times
it was without much satisfaction for me. The girls were very stupid
and had nothing of interest to say. Masturbation seemed like a lot
less trouble.

In my second year at the university I became very good
friends with the woman who is now my only love. Litta was two
years older than I and had been divorced from an older man, who
had given her two children before the marriage was finished. She
was a secretary at the university, and this was how I came to know
her. All the students liked her very much. For several months
we met only for a little talk and something to eat, but gradually our
times together became longer and more serious. I became acquainted with her children and loved them immediately. I tell you,
these children have made a much better person out of me.

Litta and I decided after a number of months to live together
on a trial basis. Good fortune came our way immediately, for it
was possible to move to a good apartment, which was less expensive
than anyone could hope for. Our sex life became freer when we
could finally have some privacy away from the children. Having the

experience of sex with many women, I can truthfully say that Litta is the best of them all. There is no substitute for deeply loving the person you fuck. I am sure that we shall be married to each other as soon as the true father of the children can be brought to his senses to give them up completely. This is my hope, but, even if this part of our relationship does not go as smoothly as I hope, it will be a problem we can solve.

chapter 3

Shirley, Birgitta, and Inga

SHIRLEY   *Shirley recalls certain childhood and preadolescent experiences that can be interpreted as the sources of her style of femininity and sex behavior. Her sexual attitudes and behavior are often the surface indicators of more basic responses to the opposite sex. Shirley appears less socially isolated and better integrated in the activities of peers than Lois was. She has enjoyed popularity as a dating partner. Her technical virginity, which she highly values, can be examined from the viewpoint of her attitudes and experience. Shirley's history reveals many connections between early sexual learning and young adulthood that instruct about a number of psychological processes and cultural variables that relate to common American heterosexual relationships.*

I am going on nineteen this month, and this is going to be my second year at college. I still live at home with my parents and younger brother, who is only ten, but a terror. We lived most of my first years in Kansas, where my father worked in gas stations as a mechanic. We moved around a lot, and, to hear my parents talk about those days, things were pretty rough. I can't remember much about my early sex life, only the hauling of all our stuff from one house to another in an old truck my father had then. My father is selling cars now for a Los Angeles dealer, and I think the money situation is better now. Neither my dad nor my mom had much education, but they always demanded that my brother and I get one.

My first childhood sex experience was limited to playing doctor with my girlfriends before any of us started school. We usually did this in one of our bedrooms, but never at my house. There was something exciting to me about having another's hands on my body. I would almost always urge the doctor to proceed further. While I never thought of doing it with boys, I don't think the game had much to do with sex. It was just fun to play it and satisfy our curiosity about each other's bodies.

My mother never found out about the doctor game, but she did find out about something else I did, when I was in kindergarten. I used to walk home with a couple of boys, and they used to give me pennies if I would pull down my pants and show them my genitals. My mother wanted to know one day after school how I got the money. Foolishly, I told her. My mother was furious and beat me with a little whip she kept with her ironing board in the wall closet. Since then, I have always been afraid to open that door. I still remember how much she hurt. She then went to the school and talked to the teacher, who punished the boys and sent notes home to their mothers. Those boys were always pushing me on the playground after this. I guess it was good that we moved away from there, so I could go to a new school.

DISCUSSION   *To what extent do you regard Shirley's earliest recollections about her sexual play with other children as normal? How would you evaluate her mother's behavior? To what extent do you suppose a parental punishment of sex play at this age forms life-long impressions and feelings? Does this episode also suggest that parental efforts to punish such sex play can result in social adjustment problems for children? What factors motivate parents to relate to their children in this way?*

I was still in kindergarten when I asked my mother where babies came from. Her answer was that God placed the baby in the woman's stomach after she got married, and then it came out the bellybutton. I told some of my girlfriends about what my mother had said and heard other stories to conflict with mine. But I didn't doubt my mother's word.

When I was in the first grade, I had two girlfriends and a boy who lived next door to us. Bill was the only boy playmate I ever had. We would play with him in his fort. One afternoon Bill and I were alone. I saw him take his penis out of his pants to urinate. I was very curious and asked him if he would show me his penis again. He agreed but wanted me to show myself. I told him it would be all right with me, but he'd have to do it first. After he took it from his pants, I thought it was a strange-looking thing, like a little baby mouse. I wondered what his testicles were for. He told me they were his eggs for making babies, which didn't make any sense at all.

I remember squeezing them, and, sure enough, they were like eggs. This more or less destroyed my mother's theory. When it was my turn to let Bill examine me, I told him I had changed my mind and was only fooling. Because of this trick Bill never wanted to play with me again, and I suppose he was in the right. I think I was still scared from what my mother had done to me earlier.

DISCUSSION   *Many American parents would take this last statement as evidence of the effectiveness of fear in preventing sex play among young children. How do you feel about it?*

In the third grade a woman was baby-sitting with my brother and me. Her twelve-year-old son was with her. He and I played hide-and-seek until I caught him in our garage. Instead of continuing to play, he insisted I sit down with him there in the dark and talk. I complied, as I figured him to be older and smarter. He then proceeded to describe the sex act to me, as only a twelve-year-old would know how—very crudely, with all the basic four-letter goodies I already knew were dirty. I was a little repulsed, but I was also very curious. I didn't realize the connection between what he was talking about and having babies. As he went into all the details about how the penis goes into the vagina, I became entirely fascinated. He then prodded me into the shed adjoining the garage, where he went on to the next part of his lesson. He pulled down his pants. I can remember being horror-struck at the sight of his organ. It was huge! He convinced me to pull down my own pants, but when he said he was going to do that which he had described to me in the garage, I pulled up my pants and ran into the house. I never told my parents or the baby sitter what had happened. I was afraid I'd get in trouble. I never liked to see this boy in school or in the neighborhood. I don't even remember his name, and I only hope he doesn't remember mine.

After hearing his story about what might go on between old people, I became more aware of the differences between boys and girls. I also knew that my mother had lied to me in the bellybutton story. For the rest of grade school I just relied on what I could find out from my girlfriends and what things I learned from the boys and some of their dirty jokes.

DISCUSSION   *Shirley makes clear that she could not discuss sexual matters with her mother for fear of being punished. Furthermore, the mother has demonstrated her unreliability in answering questions. To what extent is this a fairly typical experience for American girls? How effective is the peer group in providing information about sexual matters, especially at this age? How do the opponents of school sex education programs argue this matter?*

After a lot of kissing parties I fell in love with a boy in the eighth grade. I liked Allen because he took me to movies and was just fun to be with most of the time, when he wasn't horsing around with his friends. The first time he got fresh with me was at a party, and I blame it all on his friends. I suppose it was not too terrible a thing he tried to pull off, from what kids do now with each other. But I remember being shocked when Allen tried to put his hand under my dress when all of us were necking in the dark. He kept trying to do it all night, just because some of the girls at the party had let their boyfriends do it with them. I was really shocked to find out that the girls were willing to go so far. I think I was the only girl at the party who did not let her date have a feel. Allen got mad at me and told me that we were finished. I remember crying about it for a couple of days, and then I decided that I would let Allen feel me if that would bring him back.

DISCUSSION   *What psychological, social, and cultural factors went into this decision? Was this decision shaped more by her peers or by her elders?*

We were sitting in the darkest part of the movie theater. I felt as though I were on trial. We weren't very far into the picture when the test was on. Allen started kissing me and rubbing me through my sweater, and then his hand came under my dress. I think I was a bit scared from it and also wondered if anyone else could see him doing it. But it wasn't too long that I began to feel real excited from the way he was rubbing his hand on my panties.

I was very hot from it, even though it was my first time with a boy. The next thing I knew his fingers were under the elastic, and he was feeling me bare. Strangely, I really was very excited by this. Suddenly the back door of the theater opened, and the manager shined his light on us. I know he saw the whole thing—Allen's hand, I mean. I absolutely froze with embarrassment. After a few moments Allen and I left, without seeing the rest of the movie. I think Allen was even more embarrassed.

I went with Allen for the rest of eighth grade and the beginning of my freshman year. During this time we did a lot of petting. The summer before high school began, Allen and I went to the beach a lot. There, under an ugly green blanket, much of the rest of my sex education with Allen took place. We never had sexual intercourse but did a lot of other stuff that was very educational. Both of us would be under the blanket and slip down our bathing suits so we could feel each other. I remember one time putting suntan lotion on Allen's penis and moving it until he had an orgasm. That was quite a surprise to me. I had no idea what was happening when suddenly all that white stuff came shooting out all over us. The couple of other times we did this at the beach, I was more careful to have something ready to catch his discharge. I was really feeling grown-up in having come so far with a boy, in spite of my very slow beginning.

DISCUSSION   *What are the psychological and social implications of Shirley's sexual behavior with Allen? Does her behavior at this point reflect any of her childhood learning about sex? Have her peers completely eclipsed her parents as a source of guidance for sexual attitudes and behavior?*

During this summer my menses began, and I think this also changed my attitude about boys and sex. My mother had given me a booklet to read about a year earlier and at the same time put some Kotex in my closet with a belt. She never said anything about what to do or anything, but the physical education teacher at school had told us about it, so when I started to have the period I knew a little about it. After the first time I used to get terrible cramps for a while, so my mother knew the menstruation had started. Her only advice was for me to stay in bed. We did not have any sex education at the school, but I learned enough from my friends to know that I could become pregnant with a boy now. It was this idea that kept me from going all the way with Allen. I am sure he didn't have the first notion how to prevent babies.

From the kinds of things that Allen had done to me, I was learning little by little about masturbation. I found that I could do this while having some far-out fantasies and could even have an orgasm from it. Most of my dreams like this had to do with body rubbing, caressing, squeezing, and hurting. If I did this during the day, I would become very wet in my pants and would have to go to the bathroom. These fantasies greatly excited me, and I did not have to touch myself very much to have an orgasm. I thought I might be going crazy for a while, but I think that the more I actually touched myself the more physical the thing became and then the thing about going crazy was less important. Unfortunately I didn't know a single person I could talk to about this, and it would have really helped because I was mixed up.

My second year in high school went fairly smoothly. I had a lot of dates with different boys. A lot of them were clods, but a few of them will always be worth remembering. I never went all the way with any of them, but got pretty heavy with one boy when we parked at the airport for some necking after a movie. Bert used his hand to give me an orgasm, while I played with his penis. I was surprised by my fervor. I guess it had been bottled up since my experience with Allen on the beach. I only dated Bert one other time, when we did much the same thing overlooking the bay. He tried to have sexual intercourse with me, and I got real scared about the way he was forcing me to give in. First he gave me a lot of talk and then started to pin me down in the back seat. I may have had some of it coming to me, because I had been a little more aggressive than I ever am with a boy now. I remember unzipping his pants as soon as we started kissing. I took out his penis and started stroking it before we had even been petting. I think he got the wrong idea. I don't know how I managed to keep from getting raped that night. I was just certain that I did not want to have sexual intercourse yet. I thought, and think, that once a girl gives in the boy takes less interest in her. The most popular girls are those who hold back and make them earn it with true love and affection.

When I became a junior I knew quite a lot about boys. During high school I never dated a boy who was younger than myself. I felt much more attracted to older boys, who always seemed to have much more to offer in the way of interesting things to do. During my last two years I had very little to do with kids at school. I went to parties with the beach crowd and college kids. There was a lot of wine drinking and pot smoking at most of these parties, and by the time I graduated I was pretty well aware of all this in a personal way.

In the spring of my senior year I went to one very wild party that had a lot of older kids. My date, Paul, turned out to be twenty-four years old. It started off with dancing and drinking. I'd forgotten that I wasn't good at holding my liquor, so it was not long before I was really bombed. Paul took advantage of the situation and wove me into the bedroom. I was feeling very happy, and once on the bed Paul had no trouble taking my blouse and bra off. He stayed fully clothed. I became extremely excited when he toyed with my breasts. He was quite the operator, the way he caressed and fingered me. I don't remember how long it took him, but I remember his hand in my pants and how his fingers felt around me while he was kissing my breasts. I had done this with Allen and Bert, but never had I felt the kind of beautiful sensation that was coming from Paul.

Suddenly pain was everywhere. He had stuck three of his fingers up me, and I struggled to get him out, but he held them there despite my twisting and cries. He told me to relax. I don't know what got into me, but I let him keep his fingers in me and tried to relax. He continued to kiss me all over my breasts and neck. Finally he withdrew his fingers but did not stop that lovely caressing. He begged and pleaded with me to go all the way, and I almost thought I'd relent because of the excitement I felt. Surprisingly, though, I had more control than thought. I summoned all my strength to push him away and say "NO!" He continued pleading, but within minutes I'd got my bra and blouse back on.

When I started my first year at the college, my social life took a new jump forward. I met quite a few new guys and dated almost everyone who asked me out. I enjoyed some of the college dances last year, but it was mostly the private parties with friends that were exciting. The strand crowd is still a bit fast for me, but I think I can meet and handle all types now.

The guy I liked best to date was Robby. He was always a lot of fun and had a new Pontiac Firebird. The trouble with Robby was that he was too popular. I never knew when to expect him to call, because he was so busy with other girls. I still have a lot of respect for him because, when I told him I was a virgin, he didn't try to push me into anything. We have a lot of fun just talking when we see each other on the campus. He always asks me if I still am a virgin. About that, I don't think he can understand.

I'm not going with anyone right now, but this doesn't bother me much. I haven't yet decided when I should give up my virgin status. I am starting to feel a little strange about it, seeing that all my girlfriends have been having intercourse regularly with their boyfriends, but I am worried that once I start doing it with boys there will be nothing left. Also, as I mentioned, I think boys will begin to take you for granted and the challenge of their getting to know you and doing things for you will be lost. Love is something that should go with sexual intercourse. Until I feel that with a boy, I will be content to do the other things with him.

BIRGITTA   *Birgitta vigorously tugs at several of the main strands of Shirley's social and sexual experience. Part of what she unravels includes what she alleges to be sexually wrong with American society. Despite the overtones of personal superiority, her commentary discloses some of the important differences between American and Swedish sexual learning and development. Birgitta's childhood sex education reflects the contemporary norms for much of modern Sweden, and she is candid in describing her heterosexual interests and activities.*

To speak of Shirley's life is not the easiest thing for me to do because there is much about her that I do not know. But of course I have many feelings about this girl and her society, which gave her some of her ways with boys. I am one year older than she, but that cannot be the reason for all the differences between us. Her experiences in her society must be why we are so different. Frankly, I am very glad that I am me and not her.

Shirley has a way of talking with two tongues and has herself all mixed up over it. Inside herself she likes to be a sex creature with boys, but on the outside she has to seem pure and innocent of sexual happenings. She likes to think that boys are the only ones who can rightly encourage sex to happen. She acts like a virgin, saving herself from bad boys, when inside she really wants to be fucking.

I am not a virgin. When I first had sex with a boy, I did not think I gave the boy what Shirley feels about her virginity. I feel that I took the boy's penis into me for the pleasure it gave me and him. We had a wonderful time in my first fucking, and the very

first time was bad only because there was some blood on his penis
when he took it out of me. How crazy it seems to me that she thinks
that there will be nothing left if she has the experience of fucking with
a boy. My life is much better now.

My sex education was very good in most ways. My knowledge
came from my shy but honest mother, and later I learned some things
in school. I do not remember playing any sex games with my friends.
Our bodies were never hidden from each other at home, so there was
no special desire to do things like play doctor with other children. I
know this is a common game for many children, but I cannot remember ever being interested in it. Both my older and younger brothers
did not hide themselves from me. I do not think I thought very much
about wanting to look at the penises of my brothers, and I did not
even have much interest in looking at myself. I am sure that I must
have placed my finger in my vagina when my mother told me about
how the baby came from the womb through this tube. I remember
now doing this a number of times in my bath and think this was very
natural.

DISCUSSION   *Does Birgitta's current thinking that this behavior is "very
natural" help her to remember these experiences? If she
felt such experiences were bad or abnormal, is it possible
that she would not have been able to remember them as
well?*

I suppose Shirley's mother feared her doing this, so the babies
had to come from the navel, so she would not be curious. Such foolishness. I do not think my mother was always comfortable about my
questions in her talks with me, but she never told falsehoods. In
talking about this matter with children I believe it is normal to have
some embarrassment, but that should not discourage mothers from
such talks. Even in Sweden, most mothers have some upsetting feelings when they imagine their children growing up sexually. Mothers
do not easily see their little children as persons who will be fucking
someday. But there is no need to lie like Shirley's mother. And to
beat a child because of sex games is barbaric.

Before school everything at home was quite normal and just
like that of most of my friends. My mother and father never yelled
at each other, as Shirley says her parents did. They were very
democratic in their relationship, and this is how I shall expect my
own life with a man to be, if I become interested in having a child
and desire to be married. But I do not wish to marry for a long time.

I do not know whether I liked to play with boys or girls more. I think when I was playing outside I liked to be with boys, but when I was inside I liked mostly to play with girl classmates. I never had the kind of sexual experience Shirley told about with the twelve-year-old boy. Perhaps such a thing would not have happened if her mother had told her about sexual matters. I think she could have had a very dangerous time with that boy in the garage because of her ignorance. To have sex at such an age would have been tragic for her. My mother had told me quite young how fucking was done and that the reasons were both to have babies and because the mother and father tell their love for one another in this beautiful way. Yes, my mother said it was a beautiful way. She also told me that it was best to wait until I found a boy to love as much as she loved my father, and by then my vagina would have grown enough to do it. It was not all told to me at once and then forgotten, but I remember hearing these things many times. I think my mother was very shy until she read some good books about this, which she gave me to read when I was older.

I was about eleven when I went to my first party with a boy. All of us walked together that first day, and I think we just naturally paired off without much reason. After this my wanting to be with boys had more cause. When I was twelve and thirteen, the boys in my class acted quite different with us than they had earlier. I doubt that any sex thoughts changed the way most of these boys behaved. They only wanted to act like the older boys in school. I think the boys were very shy with us because we were more developed than most of them at this time.

Menstruation began for me when I was halfway through my thirteenth year.   This was a very new thing for me to feel and understand, although I knew all about the theoretical part of it. I believe it made me feel much more grown up. Soon after I started menstruation, I made another discovery. I found that I could have some very pleasant feelings from gently rubbing my clitoris, although I could be quite satisfied from gently caressing all of my genitals with the palm of my hand. Later it was pleasant to find that I could get a very nice feeling by touching my nipples with the ends of my moist fingers. I did this kind of masturbation without knowing very much about why it felt so good. I do not think that there was any regularity or pattern to my activity.

It was not until I was fifteen that my masturbation was such that I had an orgasm. I shall always remember that beautiful feeling. I was experimenting with some of my mother's contraceptive lotion to see how it would feel in my vagina. As I was thinking about how it would be to take a boy's penis inside of me, I moved my hands very forcefully across my genitals, and it was not long before I had this sudden awakening inside my body and mind. What my mother had told me about the pleasure of fucking was in a big moment finally clear to me from the work of my own hand. From this time I have masturbated quite a lot, with good results. Unlike Shirley, I knew enough about this so I did not think it would cause me to go mad. It is very hard for me to believe that such a thing could be true after her boyfriend had been able to excite her so much in the theater and on the beach. This must be another point of ignorance in her sex education.

DISCUSSION   *Birgitta implies here that masturbation was a matter of self-discovery and experimentation. It seems that she organized some thoughts about it after she began the practice, probably much in the same manner as Shirley. What do you think should be taught about masturbation, and at what age? Is masturbation a subject psychologically and socially approachable for most parents?*

When I was fifteen I also began to have some more serious thoughts about boys. My girlfriends and I would spend much of our time talking about the boys we liked (mostly the ones who liked sports). These sports always seemed to keep romance away from us. I grew tired of watching and waiting at games of hockey, football, and basketball. Finally, I took some interest in a boy who was a year older. We went to a school party and had a very fine time dancing. We stopped on our way home from the party in a park near our home to kiss. I found this to be a very nice feeling with this boy. It was not just kissing that made me feel good, because I had done that a lot when I was thirteen and fourteen. I knew at once that I would like him for other things. I went with this boy to many school parties and several at the homes of classmates of mine and his.

The summer brought me a new boy. He was a lifeguard at the swimming pool in the centrum. I swam often that summer. I think he noticed my interest in him from the start, because he would always smile at me when he knew that I was looking at him. One time after a night swim, he walked me home. After becoming more familiar to each other, at the pool, we went to a party at the home of a friend of his. It was a very nice party, with many people I did not know, so I could be myself in all ways. At this party we kissed for the first time, although we had known each other for almost a month. I found this kissing especially exciting, and it had a new influence on me. I would lie awake in bed at night and dream of his having sex with me. I would think his hand was the one that was touching and caressing me, and it was his fingers which were playing with my breasts and touching the ends of my nipples. I would have orgasms from such thoughts but afterward would feel it was silly to expect that he would ever do this with me. He was so very shy and slow in such matters.

However, I was not disappointed for long. This boy and I spent a very exciting time with each other in the pool after we closed ourselves in alone one night. We kissed and petted upon a cot in the lifeguard office after swimming alone with each other for a short time. I cannot easily forget the awkwardness of lying together on this cot in our wet bathing suits. Both of us laughed at how our teeth chattered from the cold, but we were really both more than a little frightened by what we were doing. Soon we were very warm from holding each other. I suggested that we should change into our dry clothes, but I think I was also thinking of becoming naked. When we took off our bathing suits, I could see that he had become very excited sexually. His beautiful penis was standing very hard before my eyes. We did not put on our clothes, but instead fell to the cot again to embrace with our naked skin touching each other at all parts.

This whole thing had not been planned at all. I knew very deeply in my passion that I wanted to fuck with this boy, but we weren't prepared to prevent a baby from coming, so he would not do it. I am grateful for his care, for to become pregnant would have been very bad for both of us. Instead we kissed and petted on the cot. It was almost enough that he put his finger into my vagina and kissed my breasts with great passion with his lips and tongue. For the first time I was shown how to move his penis back and forth to give him his satisfaction without fucking. He had an orgasm, with his sperm falling upon the towel under my hand. We stayed together holding each other for almost an hour before we dressed and went home.

I was very much in love with this boy for several weeks until I discovered that he already had a true girlfriend who was away for the summer. I did feel very bad for myself when I made this discovery. I had known that they were good friends but not that they were steady lovers. When school came, I was changed a little and may have gained some new wisdom about love. My old boyfriend didn't interest me. Perhaps it was because I wanted a boy for fucking and did not feel my old friend was going to be very good at this—

with me, anyway.

When I was seventeen, I had my first experience with fucking. After knowing this boy for several months, I went to his house after school to work on some mathematics homework. At least this was what we told our friends. But I think they all really knew that we were going to use the time his parents were away for other things. I liked this boy very much but could not say that I loved him. He was very athletic and handsome. It was mostly a physical thing that made him so attractive to me. Some of the girls I knew had made love with him and said he was very good. I think it was mostly a matter of its being my turn to be with him. He was somewhat cold and matter-of-fact in inviting me to his house that first day. I did not know that he was entirely serious when he told me that when we tired of mathematics we could make love.

We did not do any mathematics. As soon as we were inside his apartment, we began to kiss and hold each other. It all happened very fast without much romantic holding or touching. I became so hot all over from the thought of what we were doing, and I think he immediately knew that I wanted to fuck with him, although I was very nervous inside. He took me into his bedroom, and after some kissing we took off all our clothes after I had unbuttoned his shirt to feel the hair on his chest. He was even more handsome without his clothes, and his penis had a very nice look to it. In his bed we kissed and caressed each other. My vagina became very wet from his fingers. I thought it was right to tell him that this was my first time, and he was very surprised but not upset, as I thought he might not like to do it as much. I think my fingers in my masturbation had made it possible for me to be entered so well by his penis. Unlike some of my friends, who had felt some pain the first time they had fucked, it was very easy for me. I only found some little smears of blood and felt no pain from this first fucking. He did it very well with me.

We were in bed together for the rest of the afternoon, just kissing and holding each other. I loved him despite his cold way except in bed. But it turned out that his interest in me was limited, and it did not take too long for me to feel this way about him as well. I also worried about this time because I thought the condom had become too loose after we had stayed together too long with his penis still in my vagina after his orgasm. It had slipped off inside me when he pulled his penis from me. I thought he was very careless toward me in this. It was not enough for me to hear that I should not worry about it when I talked with him about this the next day at school. He almost seemed angry that I should bother him about this.

After all, I did not know everything about such matters.

In the past year I have been going with only one boy. He is a student at the university and has a very promising career ahead of him. We are very good lovers. At least, there is not very much that we do not find exciting and pleasant with each other. Sex is very important to both of us. We can talk about what we like to do best, and I think this is very good. Talking about fucking should be like talking about eating good food. It is like having a menu from a very expensive restaurant from which you can pick out anything you wish and order as much of it as two people can eat. I still do not know that I shall marry this man when we are finished with school, but I think we could be very happy for the rest of our lives. I think to have children is the proper reason to get married.

When I came to the university this fall, I moved from my parents' home to live with my boyfriend. This arrangement does not make my mother very happy, although my father says it is fine for me if I like him very much. It is the modern way, he says. I see my mother and father many times each week. Both of my brothers like my boyfriend very much, and they have both even come to dinner with us several times. My family is still very close, and I know that we will always help each other in any way needed. To leave home was not easy to do, but I am very happy now, living with a very good boy who understands and loves me very much.

INGA   *Inga represents a more gentle Scandinavian response to the American case history. She ignores many of the issues that caught Birgitta's attention. Inga implies in talking of her parents that many of her attitudes were obtained at home, and that there was little room for scorn in personal attitudes. Their family life appears to be happy and fulfilling for all the members. In imparting information about sexual matters, the mother's role appears to be the most important. Inga gives no ideas about how her mother could have done things better. It is interesting that by the time of Inga's adolescence the family recognized that there were some differences in sexual values between herself and her parents. Seemingly the factor of permissiveness functions to prevent conflict within the parent-child relationship.*

I am the oldest of three sisters in what I believe has been a very happy family. My father and mother have been very good to each other, and especially to my sisters and me. We lived most of our time together as a family in Hilleröd, but for the past seven years we have lived in Copenhagen. Since I was seven years old, I have always been in school. I am now twenty and in my first year at the university.

It would be nice to know Shirley. She talks in an open way that makes me think she is honest about what she tells about herself. I do not think it would take us much time to know each other. I certainly do not have much to hide from anyone. In many ways Shirley is like me, but many things are different about how we feel and behave with our classmates.

As the oldest one in my family, I was often the leader for my sisters. They would ask me things, and I felt that I should know, to help them understand. We always knew that boys were different and had penises instead of vaginas, because several boy cousins would come to our house for visits. We were just naturally shown their bodies when they were little babies. I do not remember asking my mother about the difference, but my sisters and I took care of them as little mothers in play, so nothing was hidden from us about it.

My mother told me about having babies in the natural way they came when I was quite young. I am sure that I passed on my knowledge to my sisters. At first I was a little confused about what my mother had told me, because she said that children were a gift of God that came from a seed from a mother and father coming together inside of the woman. I was only concerned at first about those couples who did not have children. I thought that God did not like them. When I was in school, my mother told me about how the seed comes from the penis and is placed from it inside the mother when they are in love with each other. She explained that the testicles make these seeds for the father to put in the mother. I learned all of this without much interest.

I also learned some of the practical things of such knowledge by watching our dogs mate. Without my mother's knowing about this, I tried to get our dogs to have sex with one another because I wanted puppies to give to my friends at school. It did not turn out that way for some reason not clear to me then. I had explained to all my friends at school that I had done this for them. I was something very special in my first grade as an animal breeder, even without success.

DISCUSSION   *How did it probably happen that Inga was not interested in discussing with her mother the effort to breed puppies? Does this possibly suggest that even in relatively permissive settings children learn to feel some anxiety about sexual matters? How do you think adults unintentionally condition apprehension about sex in children?*

Shirley tells of playing doctor with her girlfriends. I do not think I ever played that game, although my younger sister once told of playing it with some of her friends. I recall only one game that we played about sex. My youngest sister and I slept in the same bedroom. We had to go to bed very early, even if we were not tired. My sister and I would often play very quiet games which would not let anyone know that we were still awake. One of the games we called "we are a boy." We would put one of our toys between our legs and pretend that we were boys. All we would do is take turns touching and feeling the other's toy, asking how it felt and things like that. We also would rub these toys between our legs, so we could feel what it must be like to have a penis. It was a very funny game which was very simple. Perhaps it was just an excuse to get pleasure for our tiny clitorises.

I believe it was from this game with my sister that I learned the joy of masturbation quite early. It was a joy like many other joys. I did not connect this stimulation with the other sex. I did not connect it with sexual living in any way. That came later. I cannot remember how often I did it. As I became older, maybe around the age of nine, I do remember that I was afraid my sister would hear me doing it and that my parents would find out, even though I do not remember that they tried to forbid us to do such a thing or even that they had mentioned it. Somehow much is missing in my memory of how I got my attitudes about sexual matters.

DISCUSSION   *Much sexual learning is unconscious, but feminine patterns and sex roles reflect social norms that may be quite explicit. Do you think that knowledge about how individuals learn these patterns unconsciously in the course of experience with others can be helpful in guiding the social and sexual learning of children? Does recall of this unconscious learning by the adult usually result in a positive or negative experience?*

Even though my parents were rather old fashioned, they were very free people about sex in that they never talked ill of any people who lived in another way. I know my mother would not gossip like some of the women we knew. I think they always wanted me to make decisions that would be good for me, but they did not force anything on me. I was free to play with whomever I wanted to. We almost always would play in big groups with both boys and girls together. I do not think any of us took an interest in sex matters until we were about twelve years old.

Then the school gave us some instruction on technical things about conception and birth and menstruation. I liked the movie we saw about all of this, but it did not tell anything I had not heard from my mother. Some of the girls in my class learned quite a bit from it. Some of them laughed afterwards about the pictures of the penis and how it was shown standing up, as if they had never heard of such a thing. We made a joke to one of the boys in our class about this and asked him if he could do that with his penis. It was somewhat cruel to do this to him, but until that day he had been making fun of some of my girl classmates who were developing.

The talk of the girls and sex education in school made me start to think about sexual living between boys and girls. I remembered my mother's saying several times that sexual living was a joy to both husband and wife, but I did not know exactly what she meant. I could not understand that it would feel nice when anyone went into you with a penis. She did not tell that it was because of the clitoral satisfaction that it was so nice. I do not remember exactly when I began to feel that sexual living between a man and woman was related to the things I had done by masturbation. The connection seemed to come to me gradually. When I was about thirteen, I had an orgasm one night from masturbation. Then I knew for sure that what I was sensing could be true.

DISCUSSION   *Inga at age thirteen has had ample opportunity to put together a fairly complete understanding of human reproduction and to discover through personal experience the meaning of her mother's statements about the pleasure of sexual behavior. Would you say Inga's masturbation is positive or negative learning? How does this experience compare with Shirley's experience of masturbation?*

Soon after I had had this experience with my hand, we moved to Copenhagen. My new school had more sex instruction. The school doctor came to talk with us and answer some of our questions. I was too afraid to ask anything, but some of the girls asked very good questions. None of the boys would ask questions, but only make jokes, which disturbed the teacher and the doctor.

The only question I asked was whether it hurt to have sex with a boy for the first time. He said it usually did not hurt, but for some girls it could hurt very much, especially if the boy was not very careful. I cannot blame this doctor for my fears about this, because even with my mother's talks I had wondered about it. And one time when I was masturbating I put my finger into my vagina and felt some hurt, which was a little frightening then and perhaps stayed in my mind. I worried a lot about the penis's hurting me some day. It is too bad that the doctor did not say what to do about it. I wonder if Shirley avoids sexual intercourse for the same reason, although she does not mention that idea. But it was such a problem for me that I did not wish to do anything with boys except kiss until I was seventeen years old. I did not even like to have my boyfriends feel my genitals, although I would let them do it if they would not go further than the outside of my vagina. I would always wiggle away from their fingers when they tried to put them inside me. It was very strange, and I was very unhappy about it. I wished that I could have talked with my mother or someone about this. Finally, when I was seventeen, I talked to our family doctor about my fears, and he examined me. He was very kind and gentle with his hands, but he only told me that, should I have a problem with a boy, I should go to a specialist who cared for such things in girls. I did not worry about this until I tried to have sexual intercourse for the first time. Then it was clear why he thought I might need to see the specialist.

My first experience with a boy was very bad. He was from my class at school, and we had always liked each other very much. For several months we went together to many parties and school activities. I had dated three other boys before Jens, but these romances had only lasted a few weeks and had only involved kissing and petting. Jens was a much more serious affair. He was really my first lover. But for Jens I was a complete sexual failure. After several months of loving each other in romantic ways only, we tried three times to have sexual intercourse in his brother's apartment. Each time it was very painful, and he could not get through my hymen. It hurt me very much even to have him put his finger up into me. I cried so much in his arms that I think his love for me was mostly sympathy after those three times together. He did everything he could to help, but boys at seventeen know very little of such things. He tried putting cream on his penis. Then he would put cream on his finger, but nothing would work so I could relax and not feel the pain from my hymen. He pressed a lot the last time we tried to have sex together. I felt awful, as if I would faint. We had to give up. It was very bad for Jens, as it made him feel very guilty. The next time we tried it, I did some masturbation for him with the cream on his penis, but I know it was not satisfying for him. I think he was too embarrassed to have an orgasm that way with me. We left each other feeling very bad about what had happened. Jens and I stopped seeing each other, and I knew it was my fault.

I knew that I should do something to correct my problem. I decided to see the specialist my family doctor had told me about. It was not easy to go behind my mother's back, but I did not think I could tell her about what had happened. She had asked me if I was sleeping with Jens, and I had lied and said we only kissed.

I told the specialist's nurse that I was to be married and wanted to consult with the doctor about a problem, which I explained to him. He was very nice, although I don't think he believed that I was to be married. He said that my hymen was very thick, and it needed to be given a simple cut. I remember his putting something up me to produce anesthesia. After a few moments, he made the cut.

This doctor also gave me birth-control pills. He was very open with me. I asked him about having pain with a boy the first time even though my hymen was cut. He told me that it could still happen, but that I would then be a case for the psychiatrist and not him. He suggested that I try masturbating by putting my fingers inside with a lubricant for a few weeks.

Near the end of the school term a boy at one of our school parties became very interested in me. Hans was quite different from Jens. He was very sure of himself with me. We went dancing several times and to a party before there was more than kissing. I never told him that I was still a virgin. I did not think it would make him feel interested in me. For some reason I tried to give him the impression that I had been to bed with several other boys. After knowing him for only about three weeks, we went to a room of a friend of his who was gone for a weekend. For a whole month on weekends we would be together in this room having sexual intercourse and making other kinds of love. Hans was truly my teacher in all the ways of sexual living. Although he was only eighteen, he had been going to bed with girls since he was only fourteen.

chapter 4

Chris, Stefan, and Poul

CHRIS

Chris's case illuminates a number of the social and sexual themes of childhood that some adults find difficult to remember and communicate. Chris makes clear the importance of sexual secrecy—how sex is learned as something separate from love and intimacy, how sex is something simultaneously good and bad, and how the male should supposedly relate to the opposite sex socially and sexually.

Before I get into sexual behavior, I should let you know a few things. I am a male, twenty, have a high IQ, and am taking my last course before transferring to one of the state colleges. I'm a history major and hope to be a high school teacher. I have lived most of my life in the Los Angeles area, but we moved here from a small town in Nebraska when I was eight. My family is working class with a lot of middle-class ornamentation. I have a brother four years my senior and no sisters.

In early childhood I was already masturbating. I don't remember how I learned this. I probably regarded it as a natural thing to do because I enjoyed it. During this period I can't recall being "caught" at it or reprimanded for it, but I was aware that my

66

parents wouldn't be too pleased if they found out, so I was careful. Neither do I recall using any female sexual stimuli for it until I was older.

Evidently I wasn't content to keep this good thing to myself entirely, for I can remember instructing a neighbor, who was four or perhaps five, in the technique. He was not overly enthusiastic about learning, but I had certain toys he wanted to play with, which I used as a bribe. I remember us in my bedroom with the door closed. We were under the bed so that if my mother had come in we could have told her that we were playing a game with my toys. At first I had to demonstrate what to do, because he knew nothing about the practice. After I experienced an orgasm I allowed him to stop trying and just play with my toys. I do not remember much else except maybe a fear that his mother might find out. From that time on I had no interest in sharing masturbation.

DISCUSSION   *Infants and very young children invariably discover that stimulation of their genitals can produce pleasurable sensations. In America a masturbating child can cause parents intense anxiety and embarrassment. Chris has probably locked away in his unconscious memory the specific circumstances of his negative conditioning. What are the implications of learning that something that is very good is very bad? Did Chris acquire an important component of the sexual ethic of his society as a toddler?*

During this period I was exposed to many members of the opposite sex who were approximately my age. The one who held the strongest attraction for me was my cousin. Our parents thought it was cute for us to kiss and encouraged it in public. I detested the audience, but enjoyed the kissing. Even at the ripe old age of six I would have preferred to do more of the kissing in private.

I vividly recall one day when our two families had returned from a picnic. We were given a shower together. Of course we couldn't keep our eyes off of each other's genitals. This was my first experience in seeing how girls were built.

Sometime later that same summer my cousin was visiting again. We were playing in our car with my brother. It was my brother's idea to play doctor. The three of us covered as much of ourselves as we could with a blanket. When my cousin's panties were off, he examined her while I watched. After a short time of feeling her between the legs, my brother and I opened up our pants so she could feel us as well. Finally I had my turn with her. We only tickled her, more or less, but then my brother got the idea of taking her temperature. He used an old lollipop stick as a rectal thermometer, but when he tried to force it into her bottom she started to cry. My brother and I were afraid our folks would hear her, but my brother got her to stop crying by convincing her that it wouldn't hurt if she would just stop crying. As a clincher, he told her she could stick it up my tail if she wanted to. She took him up on the promise. I can still remember the awful pinching sensation of that stick being shoved into me by the "nurse." I didn't cry, but I sure as hell wanted to.

We must have felt that we had been doing something wrong because the three of us sat very sheepishly all through dinner, and our folks wanted to know what was wrong with us. The three of us never discussed this, but I thought through the years that I could hold it over my brother's head in case he might discover me masturbating.

DISCUSSION   *The fact that Chris recalls how he could use this incident against his brother suggests another way individuals attempt to cope with their own sexual anxieties (in this instance possible discovery of masturbation). If Chris had reacted as described, would this be a good example of sexual displacement?*

The next sexual incident also occurred with my cousin and my brother. Her folks were on a trip, so she stayed at our house for a night, on a cot in our bedroom. After we were in bed and the door shut, I climbed into her cot. We were both wearing pajamas. After a lot of tickling and giggling, I remember getting on top of her and placing my genitals in proper proximity to hers and beginning a rhythmic up-and-down motion on her. While I was thoroughly enjoying myself, my brother became very uptight about all the noise and threatened to tell our parents if we didn't stop. We stopped, but I was mad at him for some time. I think this also made me aware of the need for privacy in anything sexual.

Later, when I heard the word fuck, I more or less figured out that rubbing a girl in this way was what it was all about. Even at this age it was something I wanted to get into. But for years my activities with girls were purely social.

I often saw my father naked, but I never quite accepted his nudity. Perhaps I was jealous of his sexual endowment. He is really hung, as we say.

At the age of nine I saw my mother nude from the waist up for the first time. I was lying on their bed talking to her, and I noticed her slip falsies into her bra. I asked her what they were for. I don't know why my mother felt she had to make her breasts any larger. They looked plenty big to me. She told me she wore them to keep the material of the bra from cutting her skin. Naturally I didn't question the answer, but I suddenly got a big interest in breasts. For laughs in school I would draw figures of women with big breasts.

My mother kept a small doll on her bed. One day about this time I decided to examine it when I was alone in the house. I removed its dress and looked at it. It had what seemed to be breasts, although there were no nipples. The area between the legs wasn't right either, only a smooth curve. Even so, I became excited over this doll. I remember holding it next to my erect penis and rubbing against it, but just rubbing the doll against my penis wasn't bringing the desired result, so I masturbated.

DISCUSSION   *What might have happened if Chris had been discovered in this activity? What are some appropriate adult responses to such behavior by a child? What factors should a parent keep in mind in dealing with such situations?*

During this period I became aware that the male impregnates the female through copulation. Perhaps I learned it by watching our dogs or listening to my father talk about breeding them. I knew that our bitch was going to have pups and that our other dog was the father, so I watched her stomach swell up and knew the pups were growing inside her. I heard my father comment on her swelling tits being filled with milk. She had the pups in the deep grass behind the house. I watched from a distance and was fascinated to see them emerge from her. I was also fascinated to think that it started from the other dog's giving her a good fuck.

In junior high school there was more freedom, and the other students were a lot older. It was a mild shock for the first few months. I noticed my sexual interest in girls growing stronger. For one thing there was physical education. The good side of it was being able to see a lot of girls running around in their shorts, but the bad part was the traumatic experience of taking a shower publicly. Not that I had an aversion to water or cleanliness, but now I was compelled to compare myself physically to my peers, especially the older classes. Needless to say I was envious of those with muscular bodies and embarrassed at my own scrawny frame. But that was a minor problem. I had seen my father, and was aware that my genitals would in time be similar to his in size, but as I looked around at some of the guys—even in my own grade—I wondered what might be wrong with me. For a couple of years, until my growth caught up, I felt somewhat inadequate.

DISCUSSION   *Chris has experienced a common preadolescent problem (for some it may last well into adolescence). Rates and patterns of maturation vary within a wide range of normality, but those who feel they are lagging behind often feel intense anxiety. They may deal with it by using the mechanism of* sexual compensation, *or overcompensation.* (Compensation *is the unconscious covering up of feelings of inadequacy by diverting attention to expressions of strength and adequacy.) How common is this mechanism at this age, in your opinion? In what ways can it become the basis of problems? Is this mechanism ever so common that it becomes a cultural norm?*

Near the end of the eighth grade I noticed that my penis was growing a lot larger when I would have erections, that hair was starting to grow around my organs, and that I got erections just by thinking about girls in a certain way. I imagined myself fucking girls I couldn't even talk to. From this I could masturbate. It was during this period that I first ejaculated. At first I thought I had urinated, but after a visual check I realized it wasn't urine but semen. I don't recall how I knew what the substance was, since I had had no formal sex education or any little talks with my father. I was elated because I felt I had the power to impregnate girls, but fearful because I would have to be careful not to become a father. Even as a virgin I was fearful of becoming a father.

I started reading anything I could get my hands on concerning sex. My first material was the "literature" that accompanied pictures in magazines that I stole. Then I graduated to porno paperbacks. Along with the thrills of reading about some guy who had every girl he came in contact with came a bonus I hadn't expected. The techniques of these heroes who were more stud than

human became the basis of my knowledge not only of how to seduce
girls but also how to copulate with them.

DISCUSSION   *How do you evaluate Chris's sources of sex information?*
What impact does such material have in forming sexual
attitudes and patterns? Would Chris have benefitted from
a formal course in sex education? Is contact with such
sexual material a typical experience in growing up? Does
such material provide models for traditional sex roles in
American society, or does it serve the interests of those
who promote the sexual values and norms knows as the
"sexual revolution"?

Books were not my only way of learning about the art of
copulation. I recall one other incident that happened quite by accident, but turned out to be sexually exciting. My father had come
home for lunch. I watched him go in from the back yard. Later I
burst into the house and called for my mother. I could see a mirror
in their bedroom through the slightly open door. The reflection was
of my parents copulating. Without breaking stride, I walked straight
through and out the front door, then around to the garage and thought
about what I had seen. I was embarrassed at having walked in on
them, but I was also excited and I masturbated.

As my early adolescence came to a close, we got some new
neighbors who had a daughter in my class. I became her constant
companion. I learned procedures for all the little things I was expected to do on a date, and being seen with her sent my ego soaring.
This happy situation came to an abrupt end when her family moved
to Iowa, and for a while I was lost, because now I had time but nothing to do with it. There had been nothing physical, but we had
developed a kind of love for each other, and I had developed a definite love for her body. I had never missed a chance to look down
her dress or up her skirt. She had become my main fantasy, and
suddenly she was gone.

During the summer following my sophomore year, I
promised myself that by the end of my junior year I would ball some
girl. In my junior year I began dating in earnest. After I'd dated
my best friend's girl, he convinced me that I should ask her to go
steady, which I did. After a few weeks our relationship had progressed to the point where I felt brave enough to try something. The
first night I tried, it must have taken me a half hour of rubbing
everything under her blouse <u>but</u> her breast before I finally put my

hand on it. I gave her every chance to say "stop," but when she
didn't I was shocked. I was very surprised when she finally did
stop me, when I put my hand under her bra. I later learned she
stopped me because she was embarrassed about their smallness.
I finally got her to the point where I could unhook her bra and put
my hand under it. Then the problem arose of her not wanting me
to see them. After I assured her of my undying love and that they
couldn't look as funny as she said they did, we progressed to a
prone position with me on top sucking on her breasts. After a few
times of this, I finally got my hand down her pants and my finger
up her vagina, but we still hadn't balled. That was the next problem.

Surprisingly, this was the simplest one to overcome. She,
of course, wanted to remain a virgin until we were married. After
convincing her that she wouldn't get pregnant because I would be
wearing a rubber, I used one of the oldest lines in the book. I told
her that she would still be a virgin because I wouldn't put it in all
the way. We had plenty of opportunity to be alone at her house, so
one evening we took advantage of it in her bed. We didn't remove
all of our clothes, and I promised her I wouldn't insert more than
the head of my penis. There had been enough foreplay that we were
both aroused enough not to have any physical problems, but as I got
started the promise I made to myself came through stronger than
the one I'd just made to her, and I went in as far as I could. We both
experienced orgasm. She wasn't a virgin any longer. I was sorry,
but I just couldn't help myself. After all, we would get married
some day.

At the time we all believed that any couple that went steady
for more than six months was balling. Some of my friends tried to
get me to admit that we were and to talk about it, but I never did
give them a straight answer.

During this period my parents never questioned me directly
about my sexual activities, although when I was going steady they
did hint around about the possibility of my having sexual activities.
I ignored such comments. I think they were worried that I would
become a father and have to get married and quit school.

We broke up the first summer after high school. We still
saw each other now and then, but it was usually for sexual satisfaction. When she became engaged that fall, I was deeply hurt. I
wanted to strike back at her.

I now know that I was too young to get married. I have enjoyed these past two years living in my own apartment. The freedom

is great. While attending college, I have managed a full-time job,
which has given me enough money to do almost all the things a young
bachelor has a right to do before settling down. I have had a ball at
the college with a lot of girls I know on both social and sexual levels.
While there have been many times of sexual frustration, I feel my
early-established patterns of masturbation provide me with enough
sexual release to not make for problems. My apartment has become
a Grand Central Station on weekends. Despite my slow start in life,
I now feel completely at ease with a lot of good friends from work
and college. I also find myself extremely occupied with the job of
being a student, something I neglected in high school. When I look
back on all my troubles of growing up, I feel pretty good about how
things have turned out. Now that I understand myself better, I think
my chances for a happy marriage someday are much improved. And,
for sure, I know that if I ever have some kids, they will have a
father who will understand the problems of becoming sexually mature.

STEFAN   *Stefan makes an emphathic effort to understand and*
                  relate to Chris's story. At the same time he provides a
                  clear view of many of the typical experiences in the life
                  of a Swedish boy. The contrasts between Stefan and
                  Chris can be instructive in understanding certain differ-
                  ences in the sexual cultures of America and Sweden.
                  Stefan's feelings about his body and sexual play with
                  other children have a Scandinavian orientation, in that
                  modesty controls do not produce patterns of introverted
                  sexual secrecy and insecurity. His early experiences with
                  sex were not associated with pain, violence, and exploita-
                  tion, but seemed to combine sexual behavior with feelings
                  of affection, intimacy, and friendship.

       I must say that I like Chris very much. I think he must be
a very honest individual to have told so much about himself and his
problems of maturing. He has surely read his Freud very well,
for he is well acquainted with his kind of thinking. His memory about
his early life also seems very good, while my own experience comes
to my mind only in short glimpses. Perhaps some people would feel
that much of what happened to Chris was abnormal, but I think his life

is quite as normal as my own. In many ways Chris and I had the same difficulties as we were growing up. Nevertheless, there were some differences, which I shall comment on as I try to compare my life with his.

I grew up about ten kilometers from Stockholm in a smaller city. My mother and father lived with the three of us children on the edge of the city, where there was opportunity to run and play in the surrounding forests. Because my father's business was in another city, he did not spend much time at home, but my mother was always home, where she managed a large house with a large vegetable garden and many beautiful plants and flowers. My two brothers and I had a rather typical Swedish childhood, if there is any such thing. The family would spend every July in the mountains at my uncle's holiday cabin, where I had many enjoyable experiences with other children. It was the only time of the year when my father had time to spend with us without having his business interfere.

When I read about Chris, I think about how all the sex experiences of children would disturb the parents if they knew. While I did not share his interest in masturbation until much later in my childhood, I too had many experiences of discovering sexual things. However, I feel that his experience with sex in childhood was much more important to his way of thinking than mine was. He seems to have been more excited sexually about girls than I ever was as a young boy. My brothers and I spent much of our time playing games and sports with other boys. The sexual things were usually quickly forgotten, although they are now interesting enough to remember as I try to recall the past.

Chris's feelings about being too thin seem very funny to me because everyone in my family is thin. We did not try to cover ourselves from the sight of each other. My brothers and I often bathed together, and the family would even take sun together in the nude when we were away in the mountains. It was fun to run in the forest naked when we were small. Our mother seldom said anything about this, and she seemed to enjoy our fun. Even when my girl cousin came to visit, it was not forbidden. Perhaps Chris would have felt different about his body if he had not lived only in the city and could have had the same experiences. I, too, came to puberty a little later than other boys my age, but this was not a problem, as no one ever laughed at me for it. I remember mentioning something about this to my father, who was very good in what he told me. Growing hair around my penis was not all that important, although I do remember being in the forest alone one time and drawing hair around my sex parts with a piece of charcoal when I was about nine years.

DISCUSSION   *The body attitudes that Stefan has described here are fairly ordinary by Swedish standards. Compare these with typical American attitudes. What interpretation do you give to Stefan's mild anxiety about his sexual immaturity at the age of nine?*

I cannot remember asking my parents about human sexual matters. Because we always had many animals around the house, I think I learned about reproduction from them. I recall at the age of about six playing dog with a neighbor girl who was a year or so younger. We had both watched our dogs having sex in the morning with interest. Later that afternoon, when the two of us were playing in the forest building a little house from sticks and tree branches, we took off our clothes and "played dog." I remember how I smelled her from behind and tried to rub my penis near her vagina. I think we had more fun from our barking at each other than sexual satisfaction. I do not remember having an erection.

The first time I can recall having an erection happened in the second year of my schooling. The girl I mentioned and I had a very long way to walk home from school. We always used to do things on the way if we could find some trouble or something especially interesting. One day we stopped to dig a hole in the forest to bury a dead little bird we had found by the roadside. Suddenly I got a very strong wish to touch and kiss her and see her again without her clothes on. We both agreed to take off our clothes, as it was warm and the place we had stopped was hidden. She played with my penis, and I remember feeling very strange in having it get hard from her play. She mentioned that it was coming out just like one of our male dogs and wanted me to rub it against her vagina, which we did. I think we were both very excited by this, although it never occurred to either of us that I should put it into her vagina. The rubbing was very pleasant for her, and when I became tired of it she did not wish me to stop. I did not feel that we did anything bad, although it made me feel very grown up. Later that summer we did it several more times with the further excitement of kissing and hugging. However, I remember a feeling that it was not a fully satisfying experience for me, although it seemed very thrilling to her. From this age of seven to nine there is a gap in which I cannot remember any sexual activity.

When I was nine, I started my homosexual period. My best friend and I often used to go out in the forest and take off our clothes and lie down and press our bodies together and touch each other's penises. Both of us would instantly become excited, even before we took off our clothes. I told him one day about the girl I had played dog with, and we tried it ourselves.

However, for the first time I felt that something I was doing sexually was not right for me because I worried about my friend's telling the other boys in our class about our activities. We knew nothing at this age about homosexuals, so that did not bother me then, although several years later when we found out about them it did concern me. Then I did worry about others finding out what we had done. My friend was not so lucky. When I was on holiday he did the same thing with another boy, who told his father about it. The result was some very cruel punishment for my friend. He was badly whipped and was forced to read the Bible every day for the rest of the summer. Also, he was not permitted to play with other children for a long time. I am sure that my father would only have ignored what I had done, although my mother would certainly have been shocked.

DISCUSSION   *Stefan is undoubtedly more "Freudian" than Chris. Has he rationalized away his anxiety about these events of his "homosexual period"? Evaluate the Swedish father who punished his son. Why would Stefan's mother be more shocked than his father if they had discovered his activities?*

Again, these sexual incidents did not seem to get me interested in masturbation. I believe I was twelve before I developed that habit. It first happened when I was taking a shower and had soap all over my body. When the hand-held shower touched my penis, a sensation that I had never felt before ran through my body. It was part pain and part enormous happiness. By and by it led to a climax. After this I began to masturbate. Fortunately, I had heard other boys joke and talk about it, so I knew it was natural. I was only concerned that my penis had not yet developed to its full size and I was without any body hair.

Perhaps my interest in masturbating became a substitute for my underdevelopment. There was a time when it was almost all I could think of, just as there was for Chris. I even remember doing it in school when it was dark in the classroom during a movie. At about the same time I started to look at those sex magazines that all of us boys collected and shared with one another. Just like Chris, I read magazines and tried to imagine it, and then I would mastur-bate. My brother discovered me once doing it in the toilet, and he forced me to show him the pictures. His only comment was that I was too young for such things, but later that week he showed me some even better pictures, which he had found in our father's cabinet. I was very upset that my father should have such things, but I soon overcame that and was even glad that he had sexual interests along with me. My next older brother and I became very open with each other about sex. He was very popular at school and was having sex with girls, which he told me about in great detail.

About this time the school had many lessons about sex, which gave all the facts I needed to know. We had a very good teacher, who answered all of our questions. I was not yet physically mature sexually and felt much more able to excel at sports. Unlike Chris, I felt no strangeness in taking showers with other boys who had larger penises and body hair, because there were others just like me, too.

When I began high school, I began to combine my interest in sports with an interest in girls. I became the favorite of several girls in my school. We began to have our own parties, and even some of the school parties were fun for me. Dancing with girls became very exciting. I quickly learned what there is to know about petting with girls. Several girls I dated during these first two years of high school made fucking almost unavoidable, but I was still too scared to do it. I would take condoms with me on dates but only use them later at night to masturbate into in the toilet after I came home. I was seventeen before I had my first fucking, with a girl I liked very much.

This experience turned out to be very bad. Her parents were on holiday, and she was staying alone, but still we were both worried about her grandmother's checking on her, as she had been doing regularly at night. One night her grandmother had chased me out of the house when we were just kissing and drinking her father's wine. We had petted with each other a lot and thought we were very much in love. We had even spent several hours naked with each other, and both of us had reached orgasms by fondling and kissing our sex organs. So, ignoring our fear of her grandmother, I rolled on a condom that night and tried to enter her vagina. It was very bad for both of us, as I could not go through her virginity. She cried a lot, and her pain soon became mine. I could not push through. When we put on a small light, both of us saw some blood, and we became very frightened and wondered what we should do. After taking a shower together and much kissing, we went to sleep in each other's arms. I left early in the morning with much sadness.

The next evening was better. We drank a lot of wine and

tried to forget our frustration of the night before. I used my fingers much more to feel in her vagina. She was very wet there and begged me to try again. This time my penis was able to go all the way into her, but I reached my climax after only a very short time. I was satisfied, but she was still wanting more. So after a few minutes I again had an erection, and we fucked once more. This time it was good for both of us. Our love became very intense and for the rest of our time in high school we had sex regularly without any difficulty. On two occasions we had sex without a condom, but this was only because I had foolishly been forgetful. Our worry about pregnancy was too high a price for that pleasure. Our most difficult problem during these two years was to find a place where we could be together. We had sex many times in a schoolroom, a garage, in the homes of friends, at parties, and during the summer in the forest.

Both of our families expected us to marry eventually. However, we began to have some difficulties. I resented her jealousy and the way in which she tried to order me about in various affairs. Even my brothers noticed that and sometimes made fun of me for it. She also began to think that I should buy her things and buy her tickets to films and such things.

Finally another girl came to my attention, which destroyed this relationship entirely. I soon fell in love with this girl, and within a few weeks we were fucking regularly in her home with the approval of her parents. My mother was very upset about this, and I was encouraged under the circumstances to leave home for a while. But then my mother changed her mind, and upon my return there were no further problems. She was very happy that I had decided not to marry this other girl and had chosen instead to finish my examinations to enter the university.

This is my second year at the university. I no longer live at home but share a small apartment with a friend from my home town. For the past year I have not had a girl to live with, but my friend and I often have girls spending the night with us. We respect each other's sexual privacy, although things often turn out to be funny and inconvenient. We only have a small curtain to separate our beds. We don't care about this, but sometimes the girls feel strange about it.

My earlier desire to marry every girl I went to bed with has changed. I can have a lot of fun with a girl when we both know that sex can be exciting without becoming more than that. Taking girls home from a party or a club is now an ordinary matter for both of us. Having fun now is important because later it will not be so easy. I think I shall be a very good husband and father when the time comes, but now it is not possible to think seriously of such things.

My roommate and I will leave at the end of this month to spend two weeks skiing in Norway. Both of us are also hoping to fuck with as many Norwegian girls as we can. They are very beautiful and very good in bed. My friend has told many stories of fun he has had in Norway with young girls who have liked him and gone to bed with him. My friend's father will let us have his car for the holiday. Of course, we shall both return to be with our families for Christmas holiday. It is a very happy time at my home, with the whole family coming together to drink and have fun. Playing with my brothers' children will also be fun. And, of course, my brothers will both be very interested in how many girls I found in Norway, so I better find at least one.

POUL

Poul, a very serious Danish sociology student, expresses rather vigorously his opinions about sexual values, norms, and institutions in modern society, in particular those in the United States. His hostile prelude may annoy some readers, but there is something to be learned from his commentary. Once Poul gets around to his own life, you may become more understanding and accepting. His home life does not seem to have measured up to certain norms expected for Danish families. It seems particularly fortunate Poul has found a love relationship that can meet the needs that were neglected during much of his childhood and adolescence. Poul's report of his youth makes clear the importance of peers when parents fail to fulfill their roles.

Unfortunately, this investigation seems like most of the other American research projects I have known. It looks like micro-sociology on the family level from which there will be generalizations to a broader level for the society as a whole. Furthermore, it seems to be harmless because it will not focus upon those arrangements and relationships in society that in fact carry power. I hope that the person making this study will face up to the kind of society in which he lives instead of making harmless microsociological investigations.

I am a twenty-year-old student of sociology who does not have a lot of time to waste on things that are not relevant, but I see in the case of Chris an opportunity to expose the bourgeois myths that most of us can easily identify.

In general, because of Chris's upbringing he has followed one of the sidetracks of the bourgeois myth, which splits love into purely biological and spiritual parts. Then in his story about himself he has fixed his eye entirely on the physical part, as he describes such things as masturbation, watching fucking, and himself fucking. He almost wholly forgets the more important aspects of the emotional connections between human beings, which are not based upon the sex organs alone. Thereby he steps into that part of the myth that is typically assigned to the men in the bourgeois society—the masculine power, which is supposed to suppress the feminine object in the physical race to achieve orgasm and pleasure for itself. It is good when a man has laid as many women as possible, according to this concept, but it is also good for a woman to be a virgin at marriage.

Chris is somewhat aware of this myth, but he never succeeds in all the pages of his statement in liberating himself from it. The myth is especially present in his thinking and feeling after he finally has his first sexual relationship with a girl. During the time that follows he has a latent coldness to almost everything that does not have to do with the physical race for orgasms. He probably felt that the female was only an object reacting to a stimulus, which was always a climaxing, erect penis driving into the sex organ of the woman to prove the claim of male power. This is the essence of the male belief in the bourgeois sexual myth.

On the other hand, the female part of the myth consists of the belief that happiness will come from romantic feelings and activities, even though the sex act is something bad, if not actual hell, for the woman. Such an idea results in women feeling that they are not supposed to get emotional and mental satisfaction from sex in the same way as men. A Big Romance is supposed to be happiness for women caught in this myth, while sexual fucking may in fact destroy the illusion. How Americans like Chris react after sexual orgasm is revealed in his statements.

During the past fifteen years or so, various sex prophets, oriented more or less toward medicine, have tried to change the female part of the myth by emphasizing that the female seeks the same intensity of physical satisfaction as the male. This is an oversimplification, but it probably covers most of what could be called really new. Unfortunately, most of these sex prophets have continued to put aside the emotional aspects of human relationship. The penetration of the penis is still the focus.

The alternative to the bourgeois conception of love is to emphasize the emotional relationships that can and should occur between men and women. Love should be something more than the penetration of a woman with a penis. The partition between what goes on in something called the Big Romance and what happens in the Fleshy-Fucking-Trip must come down and find dialectic resolution. The subordination of emotional activity to physical sensation and vice versa by both sexes must be smashed. The two things cannot be parted and understood as such. Such a change would cause women not to fear what will happen to their reputations as they engage in sexual behavior outside of marriage, and men would not feel that they had to prove their masculinity by using females one after another, like logs thrown on a fire.

I know that this all sounds like I myself am pretty saved, but for several years now I have realized that the bourgeois myth lacks proper awareness of what life is all about. I am now going steady with a girl, and we both feel that what I have just stated is true. Furthermore, we both feel that each of our lives together is rich in emotional being despite the meaninglessness and injustice of the bourgeois society in which we live. But do not be fooled about our letting things stay as they are! We are preparing to fight the power constellations in the Western world and the Soviet Union. One has to become a revolutionist in this mad world.

As for Chris, he must do something to stop his suffering under the masculine part of the bourgeois myth. To get out of this hopelessness, he must recognize the inseparableness of the two principles. This, I believe, is what I have been able to do and thus lead a somewhat more meaningful life in this specific area. However, this recognition of my advantage has sprung from my interest in developing critical interpretations of other arrangements and relationships in my society. Of course, this has led to a lot of other frustrations because of the injustices of bourgeois society, which have often imposed themselves most forcefully upon my life. These conditions have truly brought about a revolutionary consciousness in me.

DISCUSSION   *How do you evaluate Poul's sociological analysis of sex roles and sexuality? Do you feel individuals sometimes cope with their own frustrations and anxieties by intellectualizing about others? (*Intellectualization *is similar to rationalization, with a more elaborate use of reasoning, abstract generalization, and very logical kinds of argumentation to justify attitudes and behavior, often for repentant purposes.)*

Before I came to the university, I lived in a typically bourgeois home about fifteen kilometers outside of Copenhagen. My father was just another economic slave in the system, struggling to provide the simple rudiments of survival for my mother and myself. We were always poor, compared to the rest of the family and many of my friends in school. He worked very hard for our money, but was only used so that others could make their profits by his labor. And he would often use my mother and me for a release from his own repression. I never did like him, because of his stupidity and lack of courage in fighting those who caused his misery and failure. My mother did her best to provide human kindness and warmth in our home. Although it is difficult to talk with her about my present beliefs, I feel that she is a person who will some day be capable of understanding me and the social order that is coming. My best friends were the ones who were always getting into trouble with the school. My rebellion at school was never accepted by my father, who would beat me for matters which were not important. Only my mother understood how a child can be at the mercy of repressive authorities, who seek to make all children into robots which conform to meaningless values.

DISCUSSION   *When parent-child relationships have a meaning of such negative intensity as Poul's, does this affect the ability to remember the content of experience for that period? Does it also suggest that the frustrations and anxieties felt during this period are not yet emotionally resolved? In your opinion, could these be the childhood makings of a rebellious or even revolutionary adult personality?*

I do not remember anything relating to sex before the age of seven. All I can clearly remember is setting fire to our apartment. It was only a small fire with little damage, but I remember my father's beating me very badly with a large leather belt, which even made cuts on my naked ass. I think I still have these marks

on my skin, the cuts of a bourgeois father who could only think of
property without human compassion. I doubt that sexual matters
were of any interest to me at this period.

Until I was about eleven, I again do not remember very
much. However I remember being in love with a girl in my class
for several years. I remember walking with her hand-and-hand
and maybe kissing her on the street where others could see us. I
was so busy getting into trouble in other ways that I probably did
not have much time to think about sex. Most of my time was spent
with other boys, and while we occasionally talked about sex and
had fun learning and using sex words, there were no sex experiences
with other children which I can recall or which I feel are worth mentioning. Some time during this period I learned about reproduction
of both animals and people but did not feel much interest in it. When
I read what Chris had to say about himself, I wonder whether having
his experience at this time of my life would have changed my attitudes, but I think not.

From the ages of eleven to fourteen, I began to have something happen in my sexual ego. As a Boy Scout I remember playing
some sexual games when we went camping at various times. Perhaps they were only half-sexual games. When we went to our sleeping bags, we started to talk about girls and fucking. Erections had
become a fact of life, and we were all quite eager to make clear to
each other that we could have one from thinking about girls and
fucking. The game simply consisted of putting yourself over one
of your mates and then doing some fucking movement while you
grunted and giggled. I do not remember feeling that it was much
more than a game we were playing. We also told each other dirty
stories that had to do with fucking. It is interesting to me now that
none of these stories ever contained the idea that there were some
good emotional elements in sexual relations. Again, the masculine
myth principle is apparent in this early learned behavior. Big
cocks driving into cunts that surrendered with pain to the overwhelming masculine power was the typical theme. We told these
stories to each other as substitutes for our own powerless experience, and those who could tell the dirtiest ones felt the most
masculine.

Chris remembers that at about this time in his life he had
his first ejaculation. This was about the time I also had my first
experiences. I recall going out into the woods with some porno
pictures and masturbating with them, as I imagined myself with
those naked ladies in the pictures. I spent many hours with those
pictures, pretending that it was me who was fucking and kissing

their breasts and vaginas. Unlike Chris, I was very pleased about
the size of my penis, because it was bigger than those of other
boys my age. My first sexual climax did happen with the pictures.
I was not bothered by the sudden shooting of semen for the first
time, as my pictures had made quite clear that this was normal.

    I always felt that my parents should not find out about my
sex habits. My parents never told me anything about sex, so I
may have escaped from what was probably a very out-of-date view
about it. But only in my relationships with my parents was sexual
discussion taboo. At fourteen I could speak freely about sex among
my friends, and even my girlfriends.

DISCUSSION   *Poul's inability or unwillingness to communicate about*
                    sexual matters with his parents is understandable from his
                    commentary. To what extent do you believe programs of
                    sex education in schools would tend to solve this
                    problem? Are communication difficulties more a problem
                    for children or their parents?

    When I turned fourteen, I kissed a girl in a very real way
at a party. This first deep kiss was just an act of curiosity, for I
was then in love with another girl. The latter relationship lasted
several stormy months, but only involved deep kissing, in which
we would both use our tongues to stimulate ourselves and each other.
Much of our time was also spent sitting for hours feeling each other
with our hands. I could not be satisfied with this, as I knew what it
was all about and what it was to do something sexual that would
cause orgasm. I had really learned the male myth. I became quite
aggressive with her. She was on the Big-Romance trip only. At
the end we both knew that I was too often interested only in physical
excitement. But after this I became interested, much like Chris,
only in trying to find a girl who would fuck with me. I had a very
easy time getting girls, but I could not find anyone who wanted to go
to bed with me. It was still much easier to masturbate and forget
about fucking, considering the girls I knew then. I also had gotten
more pictures.

    Shortly before I turned fifteen, I met a waitress in a snack
bar near home. I began to spend much of my time and my little
money there, as I fell more and more in love with her. With her
I had my first fucking, which turned out badly for both of us. We
were both let down, although I know little about what she expected.
We fucked on the floor of the restaurant after she had finished

cleaning and closing it for the owner, who went home early drunk. It was not her first experience, and, despite my masculine myth of male power, she directed the whole operation. She took off her clothes, then took off my clothes, then kissed me once, then put my cock in her cunt. Almost immediately I had an orgasm, which partly spilled itself on the floor. We held each other on the floor, trying to kiss and act like it was still exciting, but it was over, with the main satisfaction being the idea in my head that I had finally really fucked a girl, that I had showed her the power of my male cock.

We did get to like each other very much, and several months later we had sex in her room at home when her parents were away. I learned with her to assert my aggressiveness in sexual matters, despite the fact that she was older and more experienced. Again, I must say that I was suffering from the myth, and this relationship deteriorated as I began to see her only when she was important purely as an object for fucking. For many months I pretended to be in love with her in a very indelicate way.

We went with each other with many interruptions in time until I turned 18. Finally she met another boy and found out how little I cared for her and how she had let herself be exploited by me. I had only begun to understand our relationship on an emotional plane. I knew at the end that she had finished with me for good reason. Because she has fallen very much in love with this older boy, it seems unlikely that we will ever be more than good friends.

At a party at this time I met a girl I knew in school. We had a good time with each other and went steady for several months. This is the start of the period when I changed my opinions about society little by little. This change was not of any interest to her, and we began to have some major conflicts about our ideologies. Both of us began to go our own ways. Our interest in fucking with each other also ended, as I wanted something more from girls than a hot, moist cunt. I wanted someone whose mind could join mine in the revolution.

After this last relationship I spent many months changing my social activities. I became very much interested in material that my previous schools had never seen fit to bring to our attention. At the institute I met the girl with whom I am now living. Something unique has developed between us. An almost inexplicable emotional connection animates our relationship. We have a most beautiful time together. And, of course, this includes sex (for those who are still suffering from the myth). By beautiful I do not mean that our lives are without problems. We are often, if not constantly, being driven down by the depression and repression of the society within which we are trying to live. But the feeling of mutual love and understanding that makes life worth living is there for us.

part two

adolescence

introduction

The experiences of childhood make indelible impressions on everyone's personality and sexual makeup, but adolescence is a more critical time for sexual maturation and development. Puberty and adolescence are popularly thought of as the time of sexual awakening. Such a conception ignores the importance of earlier development and the continuity of growth, but the years of adolescence clearly bring certain biological, psychological, and social changes that are unique to this point in the life cycle and have profound effects on adult social and sexual behavior.

Biological Factors

Many people think of puberty as a single event of maturation (the first menstruation for the girl, the first ejaculation of seminal fluid for the boy), but puberty is a period of physiological and anatomical growth that covers many years. Menstruation and the capacity for ejaculation are the obvious indicators of many complex biological changes in the human body. That these two signals of maturation should have significant social and psychological meanings should not be too surprising, however. Human sexuality includes much more than physiological functions and reproductive behavior. The perceived advent of sexual maturity, whatever the social and cultural definitions, is universally important in the lives of young people. How the adolescent views these changes in body form and function usually depends on certain psychological and social conditions. The biological course of maturation is not always well understood, and sometimes rather grave misconceptions about sexual maturation can leave lasting impressions. Failure to understand biological factors can usually be traced to the failure of parents to provide such knowledge, to limited or nonexistent information in schools, or to peers who may not possess or share sound knowledge. Experiencing the strains and stresses of this growth also requires biological understanding and in many instances the emotional support of others, and either may be absent from relationships with parents, teachers, and peers. There are numerous examples in the commentaries of both American and

Scandinavian students of how deficiencies in understanding of the sexual maturation process and in the ability to cope with insecurities and the negative responses of others can be the basis of problems during adolescence.

In the case histories the following kinds of concerns occupy the students: the rates and patterns of physiological growth; changes in sex characteristics; the onset of menstruation, seminal ejaculation, and nocturnal emissions; and the experiences of sexual stimulation, excitement, and orgasm. Much of this testimony suggests that young people need to understand better the nature of their bodies and the realities of human sexuality.

Psychological Factors

The psychology of adolescence is now an important realm of the behavioral sciences, because we now better appreciate that experiences during this period make lasting impressions on adult behavior, and that adolescence is a time of change in the individual's emotional life. Attitudes and feelings change, and so do adult and peer expectations of how the adolescent should feel and express emotions. Childish responses to frustration and anxiety are supposed to be replaced with more mature reactions. The adolescent is expected to behave more independently of parents, assume more responsibility for personal needs, and begin to manifest adult patterns of coping with problems.

Both American and Scandinavian adolescents typically face some new social expectancies about how to think, feel, and behave sexually. Often the young person must learn to deal directly with social and cultural conflicts about sex for the first time. Sexual values and norms may not be a matter of consensus among parents, adults, and peers. Sexual conflicts and contradictions that hang like clouds over childhood may often become hurricanes in adolescence; but perhaps even more significant psychologically are all the inner conflicts about sex that the adolescent may feel as silent storms of fear, guilt, and personal inadequacy. A number of our students have related many of these problems with sensitivity.

Among the common psychological problems are: frustration and anxiety about physical growth (particularly sexual maturation), insecurities about masculinity and femininity, worries about homosexuality, anxiety about personal acceptance among peers, problems of forming meaningful relationships with the opposite sex, moral anxieties about disapproved behavior, sexual fears, and feelings of guilt. Any of these problems can endanger the capacity to function in social situations and relationships and thus retard development. The individual may become caught in a vicious social and emotional circle: inappropriate attitudes and behavior result in social rejection and isolation, which result in more inappropriate responses (such as neurotic defense mechanisms). Fortunately many adolescents are caught in this circle for only a short time.

Adolescence is a period for much change in feelings and behavior, and the young person often has the capacity for flexibility and adaptability to change. Adolescent behavior often seems to adults to be unstable, undependable, and unpredictable, and understanding and accepting the psychological conditions of adolescent social development are not always an easy task. Our American and Scandinavian students, however, are not so old that they have forgotten this personal background. Many are able to relate with sensitivity and openness their social and sexual difficulties during this time.

Sociological Factors

The particular ways that sex roles and sexual behavior are organized within cultural systems play a large part in determining human sexuality. Much of an individual's sexual feeling and behavior is expressed in terms of his unique character, but a great deal of what he has learned is shared by others (though he may not always feel or realize that this is so). Perhaps you have already compared some of your own experiences with those of the case studies.

Sexual behavior is a social behavior we learn with others, so there is considerable similarity in our experience. We are always part of a social and cultural system that defines appropriate sex roles, provides sexual values and norms, maintains controls to produce conformity, and deals with deviation. Fitting into any contemporary society is not an easy process for all young people. Adolescent and young adult rejection of traditional sexual values and norms is not uncommon. However, it is sometimes so easy to get caught up in the rhetoric of "sexual revolution" that one loses sight of what persists from generation to generation in problems of learning to cope with sex in human relationships.

How young people view the experiences of sex role learning and handling their sexual needs reveals much about the ways the culture is sexually organized into separate social worlds for the male and female. We may think of these separate worlds as sexual subcultures. We do not always recognize the many lines that are culturally drawn between the sexes. Adolescence is often a critical time for internalizing one's sexual culture. Certain forms of behavior are either highly valued or less valued depending on whether they belong to one sex or to another. In childhood boys and girls learn the importance of sex typing and channeling of behavior, but during adolescence the pressures for conformity usually increase, and the social and psychological implications of failure to adjust become more serious. We briefly identify some significant common themes in the male and female subcultures.

The male subculture influences adolescent boys in many ways. Athletics and competitive sports that typically exclude active female participation are a central element. Pressures are brought to bear on the boy to acquire interests and skills in athletics if he has not developed them earlier, and participation teaches such approved male characteristics as aggression, competition, and physical prowess. The automobile and motorbike also have an association with masculinity in both American and Scandinavian cultures. Learning the mechanical skills, knowing about automotive products, learning to drive, and racing give the boy a sense of male identity and masculine accomplishment not encouraged for girls. For many adolescents the car is an imagined and real facilitator for social and sexual experience. Interest and participation in activities associated with the physical or natural sciences is often encouraged for boys because of the masculine identity of these fields. In early adolescence masculinity begins also to be measured by a boy's sexual interests and activities. At first the focus is simply on sex, but later it shifts to heterosexuality. The adolescent boy may take some time overcoming social inhibitions with girls, but peers and others will usually point him in the direction of heterosexual discovery. He is expected to learn certain manipulative skills to control girls' social and sexual behavior.

For many years peers may monitor each other's progress and compare notes. Early in adolescence, and sometimes much later, the desires for erotic pleasure and for social intimacy may be in conflict. This incompatibility is the result of male peer group support for the "double standard" as well as of the likelihood that boys of this age have not yet had much experience in combining sex with social intimacy in heterosexual relationships. The double standard is a subject of considerable interest to many Swedish and Danish students. The strength of this norm in each nation is left up to your judgment.

In the female subculture home relationships play a significant role in imparting feminine identity and skills. The male is usually set free of the home socially and sexually much earlier and more completely than the female. For the girl the mother and sometimes older female members of the family serve as models of femininity. The peer group usually reinforces this experience and learning. While the male subcultures emphasize physical performance and mastery over things and people, the female subculture stresses skills of sociability and popularity.

By early adolescence girls have moved beyond "mothering and house-playing" to the serious business of becoming physically and socially attractive. For a number of years this occupation is not actively directed at males of the same age, but later their physical and social attractiveness becomes valued in heterosexual relationships. Until then girls must be content only to imagine how boys will react to them. There are many exceptions to this waiting period, however. A girl has many years to develop romantic conceptions of boy-girl relationships, and most of her interest in sex appears to be channeled in this direction (boys seldom share her purely romantic conceptions). Traditional female values and norms encourage girls to use sexual behavior to manipulate boys in order to gain social rewards—affection, companionship, status, and security. Using romance as a means of meeting sexual and social needs requires learning some delicate strategies, for she may indeed be dealing with "double standard" males. The female case histories offer some perspectives of how female subcultures prepare the adolescent girl for adulthood.

chapter 5

Jane, Eva, and Dorthe

JANE

Jane, at eighteen, has left behind many of the strains and stresses she felt about sexual matters during adolescence. Some aspects of her relationships with her parents during childhood and adolescence are unusual, but many of her family experiences may seem rather ordinary. Her reliance on her peers for knowledge, understanding, and comfort in working through the problems of relating to the opposite sex has had its shaky moments. While there may be some frailty in her interpretation of important social and sexual experiences, Jane seems to do a good job in portraying her personal feelings and describing the common social and sexual patterns of her adolescence.

I was born eighteen years ago into a very modest household, an only child forever. No talk of sex went on, nor was there any way even to find out about it there. I don't know exactly when I figured out that my folks had a big hang-up about sex, but I think by the time I was in the sixth grade I knew enough never to ask my mom or dad about it. My dad would cuss all over the place, using all the four-letter words, but as soon as the TV would flash the word <u>sex</u> in some decent way, he would crumple into silence and look like a very sick sheep. My mother was a real strange one about sex. When I started to take an interest in boys in grade school, she made IT sound like such a horrible thing that I am surprised I ever was laid—and I mean ever.

When I was about seven, I tripped up to Mom and asked her where babies came from. She told me she had this operation in which they cut her stomach open and out I came. This really blew my mind! I felt almost like crying for her when she showed me her scar. God but was it an ugly thing. For weeks all I could think about was how a doctor cut her open with a set of knives, and the blood and all.

The way I got introduced to intercourse was by watching the dogs in the neighborhood. At first I thought the dogs were fighting with each other, but then one of my friends, an ugly boy who lived next door, pointed out that they were doing something called fucking. I became an expert on dog sex and could trace the various family lines in the neighborhood for my friends.

In about the fifth grade boys started to get interested in dirty stories. For a while we had a big dirty joke craze going. I remember telling a few the boys thought were great. I really loathed the boys in my class until the seventh grade or so. I was quite a bit bigger than most of them and was teased a lot. One thing that used to bug me was being chased on the playground by some of the older boys, who tried to see up our dresses. Finally I got smart and wore shorts under my dress. I probably would have had a lot more fun if I hadn't been so smart.

One day my best girlfriend and I went over to a friend's whose mother kept all kinds of sex books. They found all the good parts and let me read them. I remember now only a few things about what I read—the part that said the guy should be on top and the girl on the bottom with her legs spread wide so he could put in his penis. It said something about the guy moving up and down and the girl sideways. This was the only thing I read on human intercourse for years to come.

One day when I was twelve I was messing around with myself (I guess that's how you say it), and I had a climax through masturbation. I wasn't too sure what it was, but I thought it might interfere with my having babies normally, so I only did it occasionally. It wasn't until I was about sixteen that I got on with it in a way that was sort of heavy for me. Last year I got myself a little vibrator, which is really like finding yourself a secret little sex machine. When I have a shitty day going, I know that when I get home I'm going to tingle with beautiful vibes and let my bod and head trip out for a while.

DISCUSSION   *Is it appropriate to make a distinction between fear and guilt as factors that inhibited Jane's early practices with masturbation?*

At twelve I started to menstruate. The first time I thought that I was bleeding to death. Of course my first thought was that my masturbation had started it. I was frightened to tell my mom because I figured that then she would know that I might have been messing around with myself. I had had a close call once when she found me with my pants on the floor while I was "resting" on my bed. There was a big scene about why my pants were on the floor and how it was nasty for a young girl to take them off for any reason.

DISCUSSION   *What psychological, social, and cultural factors might explain the way Jane's mother confronted her sexual behavior? What kind of responses do you feel are in order for a mother who discovers a daughter Jane's age masturbating? What impact do you think this kind of situation has on communications between children and parents?*

Finally I had to tell her that I was having stomach cramps. All she said was that I should stay in bed. When some of my friends from school came over later that day, one of them told my mother that I was menstruating. Isn't that a mind-blower? After Mom pulled herself together, she told me a few things about it. The next month she was all primed with a booklet, but never again a spoken word from her on the subject, except to be careful with boys.

All this was in the seventh grade. I started to sneak around to read James Bond books then, and paperbacks. I also fell in love with the Beatles. I collected pictures of them, watched their TV appearances, went to their movies, copied their accents, tried to do whatever they did, learned all the words to every record they had out, and listened to any disc jockey who promoted them. My love was in its purest form. I once heard my father refer to them as "the fucking Beatles" and hated him for over a year because of it. I didn't think so much about having sex with Ringo, my favorite, as about just taking care of him and giving him anything his little heart desired. My thing with the Beatles kept me interested in older men and uninterested in my own age group.

By the time I was fourteen and graduated from eighth grade I hadn't been out on a date and had never been kissed. My other girlfriends were well ahead of me. I went to a few parties in the eighth grade, but the big game was spin-the-bottle, so I sat in the corner until it was over. My parents were glad I didn't date, and so was I. That summer a few boys tried to pick up on me at the beach, but I shut them down with no trouble at all. They all seemed so phony, the way they would strut their stuff like cocks looking for dumb hens.

When I started high school, I also started having my teeth straightened. Not only was I reminded by my father almost daily how much this was costing, but I had to look in the mirror a hundred times a day to see how ugly I had become. I think my folks, the Beatles, and my teeth kept me away from boys for another two years. Finally, near the end of my sophomore year, the phone rang with a boy on the other end of the line. The voice only asked before hanging up whether this was Jane's whorehouse, but I knew immediately that someone was interested in me. News of the obscene-phone-call nut spread through the ranks. I wouldn't have bothered mentioning this, except I think the story got a lot of guys interested in me. It was all the same at first—you know, they wanted to know if I was getting any calls lately. Then a little joke like, What's your number now? I really liked some of this attention.

Finally a boy named Roger asked me to go to a school dance with him. Roger was one of the last guys in the world I wanted to go with, but I was so excited about going with someone that I went. His father picked me up at home. As a first date it turned out to be dullsville. The school thing was not much fun for me, but there were some very groovy guys there. The juniors and seniors were especially cool-looking. The underclass pimple set was a lot less interesting to me.

DISCUSSION   *What do you think is the reason for the social incompati-bility between males and females at this point in adolescence?*

During the summer my girlfriend and I would go to the beach every day we could get someone to drive us—meaning the mothers, but no boys. My girlfriend and I did a lot of talking about boys, but neither of us was ready for much more and we knew it.

Near the end of the summer I met Hank, this tall, dumb surfer. It was infatuation at first sight. He was about two years older than me. Since I was so bashful, I couldn't talk with him, so I did normal things like steal the garden hose and some rocks from his house at night. I would phone his house and just hope he would answer so I could hear his voice. Then I would hang up. After four months of this, my girlfriend somehow got the word to him that I was madly in love with him, so he asked me to go to a football game. Mom had fits over my going with a boy who had a car, and the thought of Hank's being eighteen blew my father's mind. I really wanted to back out of the date at the end because the stuff hitting the fan was pretty heavy, but I didn't. Finally Hank rolled up in his wheels, blew his horn, and out I flew. The date was a 100 percent improvement over the farce with Roger. Hank was sort of neat. After the game we went to a drive-in for a coke.

I felt pretty big, sitting in that drive-in after the game. I imagined myself as a model in a TV advertisement from Chevrolet. Everyone there was watching me, I thought. After the cokes Hank drove down to one of the beach lots. When he tried to kiss me I jumped clean across the seat away from him. He was really sweet about it. I went into my life story about sweet sixteen and never been kissed. He suggested that it was a good time to get started, so after an hour of discussing it I laid one on him.

We dated each other for about six months, but it wasn't until our last few dates that I would let him get his hands on me. Finally one night I let him inside my blouse. I thought he was going to rip the straps off my bra if I didn't do something to help him, so I took it off, and we moved onto the next plateau. He was really kind of slow in picking up on things, for which I was grateful.

After a while he kissed and sucked my breasts. It was quite a turn-on for me. I had no idea that I was so sensitive to touch that way there. Hank was having a great time also.

The last date with Hank ended up again at the beach, parking in his car. After a short time he was back on my naked breasts, and I must say it was really a terrific feeling. I really had him turned on—too much, actually. His hand crept up under·my dress, and I remember his clever little fingers making their way around the elastic of my pants (I've changed to pantie hose since then). It wasn't too long before I felt his finger inside me. Suddenly something in me said "Stop," but Hank had a different set of buttons in his head—not many, but different. I got pretty scared, actually, and no joking now will make me forget.

Hank pulled off my pants and in a mad whirl of arms and legs had dropped his own pants to the car floor and suddenly showed me the thing I had only gingerly felt through the insulation of wash-and-wear slacks. Let's just say that I was something less than thrilled. It was a lot bigger than I thought one of those could be. After he worked a couple of fingers in my vagina, he just stopped the action and told me he was sorry for what he had done. It was really kind of sad, and I think Hank was even more embarrassed than I was, to stuff his hard penis back into his underwear and pull his pants up from the car floor. I didn't help him, chewing him out about maybe getting me pregnant and how I wasn't interested in dating someone who goes crazy in the head.

It was a good relationship in some ways. I think the first time a boy puts a finger into you it is almost like having sexual intercourse. I have even wondered whether I may have messed up by not letting him have intercourse with me. I ended giving my cherry to a real weirdo, a dude I didn't like at all.

After Hank I dated a bunch of other boys. I don't know what happened, but I started to hate anything that had to do with sex. I started hanging around more with my girlfriends. I soon learned to lighten up a little. I had no objections to doing some necking and petting at parties, but then they started to ask me how good I was in bed. When I would tell them that I was a virgin, they wouldn't believe me. I think it scared some of them off.

DISCUSSION   *Why do you think Jane makes this observation about her virginity? Were her feelings mostly focused on her own fears or on the possibilities of rejection, as she indicated?*

During my last year in high school my parents became impossible, and I began to ignore all of their rules about when to be home and all that. I didn't talk to my folks for weeks at a time. I had to start meeting my dates on the corner or in drive-ins. Still I made it all the way through high school as a virgin, but the summer suddenly brought a desire to be rid of my distinction.

DISCUSSION   *Jane interprets her reluctance to engage in sexual intercourse up to this point as unusual. What factors explain her attitudes and behavior? How accurate is her estimate of virginity for this age, in your opinion?*

Shortly after graduation I went out with Rudy, a guy about twenty-four years old. He was one of those hot-stuff, beer-bar dudes.

Rudy picked me up on the strand in the middle of the afternoon, because, he said, he was trying to get a party together. It was a party for two. It was a typical beach pad—no beds, kitchen sink filled with dishes and smelling pots, grime, a toilet seat splattered with puke, and all the other good things in life. We got on with it by drinking an awful lot of wine. He had a great record collection, though I never had the guts to ask for the Beatles, which is just as well. This was not the afternoon for the desecration of my four-year love affair. This was only the day to lose my virginity to a real jerk.

After we got into it on the mattress on the floor, I told him that I was a virgin. He started all that sweet stuff about how he was going to turn me on and make my first time into "the best fuck of my life." But it was just a lot of talk. I got out of my clothes after he stripped off his. After a few minutes of kissing and feeling each other, he eased his penis into my vagina. I thought it was going to hurt, but I didn't get that message at all. I just lay there riding out the storm above me for about ten minutes. He kept muttering things and asking me how good it felt, and I guess I played my part all right by telling him how wild he was. It couldn't have been all bad, because I had an orgasm that was just as good as my vibrator could do. As soon as he had his climax, he jumped off me like he had just finished being timed at a bucking bronc contest. I really couldn't think of anything else to say to the bum, so I got dressed. It was time to split to a drugstore and get foam. I have only seen Rudy once since, at a beach volleyball game. I had built up my hopes that one groovy guy was going to come and sweep me off my feet, but this thing turned out a little different. I'm not sorry I did it. I guess I learned what I didn't want in a sexual relationship with a guy. I also thought I was going to have some kind of sex hang-up, so I just had to get it over with. I don't know exactly what I ended up proving to myself.

Now I am living in a small apartment with a girlfriend. We

don't see much of each other because we have jobs that have us on duty at the hospital at different times.

About four weeks ago at the hospital I met Jerry, a pharmaceutical salesman and twenty-six years old. We ended up going to the beach on the first weekend. I was very infatuated at first, but I started to feel a little sorry for him. He's been married six years and is separated from his wife. When I found out, I wasn't mad at him, but I didn't think I wanted to start anything with him either. But we did. The second weekend I went to his apartment. He told me his problems, and I told him mine. He started telling me to take him away from his wife. That's almost a mind-blower. Anyway, it turned into sex in the bedroom. This experience seemed like it was a dream. Everything went perfect. Since that second weekend he picks me up at work every night, and I spend most of the night at his apartment.

The sex relation is very open and honest. He is a beautiful lover and knows how to make sex so satisfying. I have really fallen for him but can't quite believe that he will not want to go back to his wife. I wonder if I'm just taking him for what he can give me now. Jerry means something to me that no other man has ever been able to make me feel.

EVA

Eva has apparently been brought up in a Swedish family with a number of social and economic advantages that cause her to feel a good measure of pride. Her sex education at home would not by Swedish standards be considered unusual, but Eva seems not to be totally satisfied with her mother's approach. She reports rather briefly on childhood sexual learning, but goes into more detail concerning her experiences during adolescence. Through her commentary it is possible to see how the Swedish girl begins in early adolescence to experience characteristic independence and autonomy in heterosexual relationships.

Although I am two years older than Jane, this does not seem to be important in looking at our lives, because we have lived in completely different directions all along.

Jane says so little about her family that I think she must feel great shame about them. About her mother, it is a tragedy that she had such feelings about sex that she could not help her daughter through childhood and adolescence. To be shown the scar on her mother's stomach with such words shows how American parents like to frighten children away from sexual matters. I understand that it is fairly typical in the U.S.A. for parents not to be able to talk honestly and freely about sex. The attitude seems to be that sex is not for children and must not be discussed with them. I would not have wanted to live with Jane's parents, although her father seems to have a good sense of humor about things—I will say that for him.

I am glad that Jane has found a man finally who can satisfy her sexually. Of course, it would have been better if he were not married. I like the idea of being a girlfriend for older men, myself. So I can understand her point of view at the end of what she said about her love for this man.

I am a very ordinary young woman in most ways. I have had many boyfriends in school and during my summer holidays at the lakes. My first sexual intercourse took place when I was fifteen. But perhaps I should tell you some things about my family and my younger years first.

I have lived all of my life in Väterås, where my family has been for as long as we can remember. My family name and that of my mother are well thought of by everyone above and below us in the community. All of us have received very good educations, if that has been our choice. Both of my brothers have even gone to an American university in Wisconsin, and my sister has spent a summer with one of them traveling to various cities in the U.S.A. So you can see that I know a great deal about your country and the people in it.

My brothers and sister are older than myself, and I can see from their success in life that family matters have made things turn out well for them. We were taught from our earliest years to learn to take care of ourselves in every way. Although my mother did not ever have any interest in things outside of the home, she was very good with us children. I remember her reading a book to my brother and myself when we were very young about how babies came. I remember the pictures of the inside of the body and how the baby slides out through the vagina. It was very natural to hear this from my mother.

My knowledge about my own body was very complete in all ways. I saw my older brother naked many times. Only when his puberty began to come did he hide himself from me, and then I felt, for some reason, that his doing that should make me do the same. My father and mother often slept with each other naked, and I can remember going into their bedroom with my brother some holiday or Sunday mornings and trying to pull the sheets off them. My parents did not seem to mind such play.

Like Jane, in many ways I preferred the girls to the boys in my class until later in my school years. Perhaps the reason was different, because I was one of the smallest girls in my class, and I did not want to play some of the rough running games with the boys. Jane says that boys in her school would run and look up the girls' dresses. Such a thing seems very silly to me. I am sure that most of the boys at my school knew very well from their sisters and mothers what the sex organs looked like. But maybe it is again the American attitude about sex that makes it a very dirty thing for boys to see girls' sex organs. I wonder if the girls thought it was equal fun to try to look into the pants of the boys to see the penis?

It was the summer when I was ten that I had my only real childhood experiment with sex, and it was with a boy and girl in a little house on the lake where we kept the family sailboat. All summer we swam near this house. One day we played a little game of swimming without our bathing suits. After swimming for some time, Kjell would dive to play tag by touching the genitals of Sara or myself. Whoever was tagged then had to dive and swim for another. Sara and I never tried to tag each other, because we wanted to feel Kjell. I thought this was rather good fun, and I did enjoy feeling Kjell and even liked it when he caught me.

Finally, near the end of our holiday we had a time with each other in the boat house. It may not have been very important at all, except I remember becoming very excited for the first time in a sex way. The three of us played jungle natives, and Kjell was the chief and Sara and I were his naked slave girls. Kjell had the right to feel and fondle our genitals as he wished. I re-member thrusting my body toward his hand so he could feel me, and Sara did the same when it was her turn. I thought it was interesting to see excitement come to Kjell's penis while he was touching us.

The only thing I feel was strange and unnatural about this was that neither Sara nor I tried to touch Kjell. We may still have been thinking that it was not nice to touch him there if he did not wish us to.

These games with Sara and Kjell were very good for me. We liked each other very much, and these times together in this child sex way made us trust each other with our confidences. From that age until I was fourteen, I did not have any experiences with other children that had a sex-behavior part.

When I was twelve years old, my teacher showed us several films about sex. We also had some small books in school, which we studied. I was especially interested in what was told and shown us about menstruation. Unlike Jane, I was well prepared for the beginning of my menstruation just when I became thirteen.

I was about fourteen when I first had an orgasm from masturbation. I had often felt myself with pleasure since I was about ten or eleven. Perhaps Jane got her fears from her mother. My mother had told me only that my genitals were very special parts of my body, which had a lot of feeling in them. Perhaps my mother should have told me more when she discussed this with me. I know that I shall teach any daughter I have that masturbation is very pleasant and satisfying. I like to masturbate and do not see why children should be left out of such an experience. Fear of having sex with boys comes from not knowing about having sex with oneself beforehand. It is too bad that my school, unlike those of today, had nothing to say about masturbation.

My first boyfriend was from my brother's class. I was fourteen, and he was sixteen, although not very large for his age. Eskil was very good for me in overcoming some of my shyness about being with a boy. I do not think it was a very romantic relationship, because we had known each other too long for that kind of excitement. But for a whole year we went to school parties with one another. It was fun kissing with him, and three or four times I encouraged him to feel my breasts. But in many ways it was difficult for us to do very much more, because I think each of us worried about telling my brother, who was always very interested to know what we were doing. Eskil wanted to fuck with me, but he said my brother had told him once that any such thing would end their friendship. I did not really need to have physical sex with a boy then, as I feel I must now.

DISCUSSION   *How does this experience with Eskil compare to the same*
period of social development described by Jane? How
does it compare as a basis for learning later attitudes and
patterns of behavior with the opposite sex?

That summer I met Georg. He was older, sixteen or perhaps seventeen, and very handsome. I fell in love with him as
soon as I saw him. I think Georg knew I liked him from the very
start, because he followed me home to find out where I lived.

Two weeks after we met, Georg and I had a real chance to
be alone with one another. As soon as his parents were gone,
Georg came to my house to get me. Up to that time we had only
been kissing and petting, but I knew as soon as we walked into his
house together that day that we would soon be fucking. I felt very
grown up and sexual throughout my body. When we kissed each
other, I had an immediate longing for his hands on my body.

George was not very aggressive, although he had told me
before that he had fucked a girl at his school who did it with a lot
of boys all at once. I told him I thought that it was bad of him to
have sex in such a way. It was small comfort to have him tell me
he didn't really like the girl at all and did it only because of the
other boys. I had told him that I was also shocked that he had not
used a contraceptive to keep the girl from becoming pregnant.
While we kissed, I wondered if he had found a way to get some
contraceptives. I remember stopping our kissing in the living
room and asking him whether he had condoms to put on his penis.
Georg was rather surprised to hear me ask, but also grateful, I
think, that my mind was made up to do this with him. I was glad
to hear him say that he had them.

I think we were both more than a little scared by what we
were doing. After being in bed a few minutes we enjoyed the
wonderful and exciting feel of our bodies next to each other. I
think he was more scared than I though he had some experiences
with that other girl.

I have been to bed with many boys since Georg, but I
think I shall always remember the sensations I felt for the first
time in having sex with him. The first time must be important
for all women. When Georg entered me with his penis, I felt like
a full woman. His gentle movement of his beautiful penis inside
me caused a deep rush of passion.

Georg was a very nice boy, and I know that I loved him a lot for many months after our wonderful time together. We wrote to each other many times. However, Georg once wrote that his mother was very angry at what she had found in one of my letters. I never heard from him again, as they did not return to the lakes for holidays.

After my time with Georg, I soon returned to school and my friends. Two of my girlfriends shared with me their secret that they, too, had fucked with boys for the first time during the holidays. I think the three of us felt very grown up in a new way. Back at the school many boys from the older classes began to be interested in us. It was not long before we were going with them to places in the city for dancing and good times.

My mother began to worry some about how I was behaving with so many boyfriends she did not know. I remember her asking when I was about sixteen whether I was going to bed with any of my boyfriends. I was very honest and told her that I had been to bed with several, but that I was very careful with them and made sure that we always used a contraceptive. I do not think my mother was shocked. She only told me to be very careful, because sometimes men will not care enough to keep a girl from becoming pregnant. She also told me that I should not have sex with boys who were drunk, because they were the most careless.

DISCUSSION   *How do you compare the mother-daughter relationships for Jane and Eva in matters relating to sexual learning and activities? Are some factors more important than others?*

The fine fucking I had with Georg took hold of me in some way that I think often happens to a girl after she has a good time with her first boy. I had very strong needs to have sex. Masturbation was not enough any longer. I was very excited by handsome boys at school, and I think they knew this from the way I would look at them. I know I can look quite sexy when I look at boys I like very much.

My year back at school began in a sexual way with Filip. He was a fine hockey player with the school team. All the girls wanted him, but I was the one to have him for almost a full year.

Filip was very handsome in all physical ways. His only problem was that he was not very good in his studies. During the

year we were with each other, he was very kind. Filip had been to
bed with another girl at school before we were with each other. I
knew that he was a good lover from what she had secretly told me
about him. She laughed about how big his penis was, and I think
she tried to scare me about it. But later there was no problem at
all, although I found fucking with him difficult for the first moments
when he put it into me.

Filip lived with his family in a large apartment building
where his father was the manager. He had keys to all the rooms
below the lobby, and it was here that we would make love after
school, and even at night after parties. I think Filip and I just
learned to expect to fuck with each other after school if we could
find a place. My love for Filip changed to coldness when I found
that he had started to be with another girl in his class.

With Patrik, a new boy in my class, I learned something
new about sex. His father was a sea captain, and I think his family
was very rich. Patrik was not as handsome as my other boyfriends,
but everyone wanted him, just the same. His manner with girls was
quite filled with charm and friendliness as though he wanted to be
with you in a very close way.

Patrik and I had sex with each other many times, but there
was something missing in our way of doing it compared to the times
with Filip. I do not think he really cared very much about me in a
way I was beginning to feel was important. I started about then to
want something besides fucking. This change in my attitude
brought me two new boys, who were much older than my classmates.

Mikael and Olof were roommates at Uppsala University
when I met them at a holiday party in Stockholm. At first Mikael
was my favorite. He was very intelligent and full of talk about almost everything. Mikael and I had sex with each other the night of
this party. It was very bad for both of us the first time. It was
quite new to me to find a boy who could not have his penis become
hard. I think he was frightened that other people at the party might
see us while we were in one of the beds. I promised Mikael that
we could do it some other time, and I think he was very grateful.
When we met again in Uppsala after writing to each other, things
were much better. I enjoyed being with him very much. I also
began to like Olof very much and was disappointed when he could
not be with us. As I was staying with my aunt in Uppsala, it was
difficult to spend as much time with them as I would have liked.
So it was very nice to learn that Olof had an uncle with a farm near
my home, whom he visited occasionally. Mikael did not seem to

mind if he would stop to see me also.

   After a few weeks Olof did stop at my home. He wanted
to know if I could go with him to see his uncle. I knew immediately
that I wanted to go with him, and I was even hoping for more. It
was a wonderful spring day with warm, gentle winds blowing
through the fields. After meeting his uncle, we walked several
kilometers through a forest on the side of the fields. Finally we
stopped walking in the forest, and we kissed with great passion.
Before long, we were having wonderful sex with each other. I
was very hot. It was the only time I had made such love lying on
the floor of a forest. I felt the most wonderful feeling of romance
for these minutes. Olof was very complete in his way of giving me
satisfaction. He parted my legs and with his mouth for many long
minutes kissed my sex parts, and then with his tongue he entered
my vagina and stroked me until I had a very happy orgasm. Then
we fucked with great pleasure for both. This was one of the finest
times I have had with a man.

DISCUSSION   *With Eva we have a variety of experiences and relation-*
ships to evaluate. What psychological, social, and sexual
patterns do you see evolving through all these relation-
ships?

DORTHE   *Dorthe was raised in Copenhagen, and except for the*
influence of some summer vacations spent with relatives
in a farming community, she is very much a city girl. She
says that most of her experiences have been very
different from those of Jane. Dorthe describes the role of
the peer group in sexual socialization with some com-
pleteness. Relatively early in adolescence she has what
she feels were successful experiences with sexual inter-
course. There follows a period of casual sexual activism,
and then what seems to be a return to sexual behavior
that is relationship oriented. Dorthe has focused on some
psychological and moral issues that concern many young
people in both the United States and Scandinavia. Her
commentary makes especially clear the sexual values and
norms of a great many Danish young people today.

Jane's sex history leaves me with many questions and thoughts about her present life. It is very good for her that she has found this man who now gives her some sexual satisfaction and love, but I question how free that experience has made her. The way she talks about her sex life before this man seems very strange to me. It is as if sex is still unnatural to her. To me, Jane is interesting in all the ways she has hidden herself from understanding eyes.

Of course I, too, have problems. Maybe Jane is even a much better person than I, but I feel that my sexual feelings and things I have done with boys are better. It seems strange that I should come out to be so different from Jane in this respect, having had a mother who was no better in sexual matters than Jane's. I did not learn about babies from looking at a terrible scar across my mother's stomach, but in most matters about boys and having sex with them she was very strict and not very kind to either my sister or me. My father never gave these things any attention. He never did interfere with my mother's ideas about sex—or anything else, for that matter. I do not believe I ever heard my father use bad words like Jane says her father did. But I would have liked him to, just to see what my mother would have done about it.

DISCUSSION   *Dorthe's wife-mother dominated home is not the model of egalitarian sex roles. What kinds of conflicts might a child feel when the mother is very dominant and the father very passive? Do parental models for sex role learning have more impact in childhood or adolescence, in your estimation?*

I was born nineteen years ago in Copenhagen. Until this fall I lived at home, except for short visits to a farm during the summer holiday. I love Copenhagen and could never live in another city in the world. Both my girlfriend and I have very nice boyfriends. I think I am in love with the poorest boy in all of Copenhagen. It is fortunate that he is the best lover, or I would throw him away.

It was not forbidden to talk about sex with my mother, but it was not very often that I would ask her questions, because she always wanted to know why I was asking. At eight years old I read a book called How, Mother? which gave me quite enough to know for some time. Such knowledge came again when I was almost thirteen years old in a class about these things at school.

But I think this study was much too late for all of us. In the school
it was just technical talk, with no talk of feelings about sex. The
other learning I received from books I found for myself or was told
about by girlfriends in school.

My feeling about playing sexual games with other children
is quite different from Jane's. I have a sister two years younger
than myself. All through our early years of childhood we had a
neighbor boy to play doctor with. Claus was always the doctor,
and I was his nurse, with my sister having most of the fun being
the patient. Of course, sometimes the doctor would become sick,
and I would administer aid of various kinds to him. From seeing
and playing with Claus's penis I felt that it was a very funny thing
to be hanging there. I wondered if it would not get caught on
things while playing games or falling. I was happy not to have
such a thing.

When I was about nine years old, I had the first of many
experiences with a boy cousin in the country. Arne was only about
a half year older than I, but he knew much more about sexual feelings. He told me stories about how he would watch boys and girls
making love with each other in a forest near his house. I wanted
him to show me what they were doing with each other. Arne agreed
to do it if I would be the girl, which I was quite willing to do. I
wanted to see what Arne's penis looked like very much. We found
a very nice place in the forest to lie upon the grass. I was surprised to find that Arne's penis looked very different from Claus's.
It was stiff and straight out, with the end coming out of the skin.

Arne's instructions were quite simple. I was on my back
with my legs spread. I remember him lowering himself to put his
penis into me. It did not work at all. He could not find the opening,
and for some reason he did not try to find it with his fingers. I do
not remember becoming sexually excited from this. I was only
curious.

I do not think this game with Arne was at all bad for me.
Shortly after this time in the forest, I was able to find with my
finger the place he should have put his penis. I played with my
finger in this way many times that summer and was very pleased
to discover this pleasure and to reassure myself.

When I was eleven years old, I returned to the farm for
about a month. I was still completely undeveloped sexually, but
Arne was just beginning to grow taller—and perhaps even seemed
a little handsome to me. One day Arne asked me to go with him to

the forest for some fun. He thought we might be able to see some lovers, he said. Of course, again there were no lovers—only the two of us. After walking around the forest we stopped at the same place we had played two years before. I remember the very strange feeling that came to me as we stood in this spot. But it did not turn out to be the fun that I had hoped it might be. Arne's penis had grown a lot during the past two years. He had started to have some hairs around it, while I had not yet started such development. I think I was a little frightened by this bigger penis, which Arne tried unsuccessfully to push into me. He was a little disappointed. I wonder why neither of us thought to use our hands to give us some satisfaction. It is also funny that we never kissed. Now I love to kiss all the boys I am with very much.

That summer was my last with Arne at his farm because there was a big quarrel in the family, and my parents would not visit there ever again. When I was fourteen Arne's parents invited me to stay with them for several weeks, but my mother would not let me go, so instead I was with my first real boyfriend, Bo.

DISCUSSION   *Dorthe's interpretation of her experiences with Arne suggests that she did not feel guilt or fear as the result of this behavior. What are the social and psychological benefits of this? What were the risks of less desirable consequences?*

Although my mother was very strict about my being with a boy, it was not possible for her to watch me all the time. As soon as I had my first menstruation, my mother became very difficult about this sort of thing. She told me terrible stories about how girls are taken away by men and forced to have sex, and how the girls end up as whores on the street. I would listen to her talk but knew not to believe.

Bo was very popular in my earlier school. I would meet him during the day when my mother thought I was with a girlfriend. For a month when we first were together, we only walked with our hands together. There was not even any kissing between us, although I had become quite experienced with other boys from school at our parties, in kissing and even some petting. Oh, yes, by this summer my figure began to look quite good to many of the boys. I found it exciting to have a boy touch and feel my breasts from the outside of my blouse or sweater. And, while bathing, I had discovered the pleasure of caressing myself there.

One day Bo asked me to come to his house when his family was gone for the day. That was the day my virginity left me. While it was not the pleasure for me that it should have been, I think it was a much better time than it was for Jane. At least, Bo was not what she called a beer-bar dude—whatever that may be—it does not sound so good. I think a girl who is a virgin always wonders how it will be the first time with a boy's penis inside her. Bo was quite experienced in what we were going to do, and I worried about whether he would be careful. He knew that I was a virgin, and I had told him all about Arne and our times in the forest. When he told me his sex life, I was pleased to find out so much about how he would masturbate thinking about a girl, and finally me. We went into his bedroom, and for an hour we listened to his recordings sitting upon his bed only holding hands. I was finally kissed in a very romantic and passionate way by Bo, but I remember how much his hands were shaking, though it was not at all cold.

After some very exciting kisses, he began to feel my breasts, and then put his hand under my dress. I became very hot and moist from these beautiful caresses. I removed my pants to give Bo a free way. The fullness of his feeling me moved me to great passion. I had never felt this from doing it with myself. After some time at this we very quickly threw all our clothes on the floor, and then in these first naked moments together we pressed our bodies into one. I could feel his penis upon my stomach, and it seemed so nice and warm to my skin.

Unlike Jane's first man, Bo said absolutely nothing while we were making love. He was so beautiful, even not knowing anything about what to do. When I asked Bo to put his penis into me, it was because I wanted him very badly, and it did not seem to matter if it would hurt me for the first time. I tried to help Bo do it as much as I could. I spread my legs and held my knees in the way I had read it should be done for the first time, and then after he had placed a condom on his penis, I helped him to the opening of my vagina. At first he could not get through my virginity, but after a few moments at my entrance he pushed himself through. I can still remember the little bit of feeling from that moment, but as soon as he was through I felt such a beautiful fullness of his penis in my vagina. After only a few minutes Bo had an orgasm, which I could feel coming to me throughout his body. I was not to have an orgasm this first time. It all happened too quickly.

When Bo took his penis from me, I could see that I had given up some blood with my virginity. Bo looked a little scared about this, but I told him that it was all right, and I felt nothing from it. We had taken leave of virginity together, and while it was not the best time for me, without orgasm, I enjoyed it very much.

Bo and I did this many times during the summer. It was during our second time of sex together that I had an orgasm.   I almost always have orgasms with the boys I go to bed with. Sometimes it happens many times, if I am very excited and the boys are very good in what they do. My sexual passion for Bo began to change near the end of the summer. He began to think of other girls too much.

DISCUSSION   *What are some social and psychological implications of sexual intercourse at this age? Is there a difference in your view as to how this experience affects girls and boys, Americans and Scandinavians? How do you feel about this matter in your own life?*

I also met a very nice new boy named Nils, who was two years older than I and much more experienced than Bo in sexual matters. I went to bed with him twice, with very good results each time. After Nils there were many others for the next two years, most of them older boys from my school. I did not go to bed with all of them, only the ones who seemed very special to me in some way for a time. Many of my friends were quite full of envy because I was so popular.

My mother was terrible with me over my boyfriends. She did not lock me up in the house as she wanted to, but I could tell her nothing about what I was doing. When she found some condoms in my purse, she was almost out of her senses for a whole month. But I did not care. I was having a great deal of fun and enjoying all of my boyfriends. The parties I went to with boys now were different and freer, though I did not like all the drinking and did not want to do some of the things that happened later at the parties. This time of my life was very exciting, but I began to tire of having so many boys who were so meaningless to me.

DISCUSSION   *Dorthe's gradual disillusionment with her social acitivities and casual sexual affairs suggests that she was desiring a more serious kind of relationship with someone of the opposite sex. What social and psychological needs are not likely to be gratified in the kinds of experiences she has just been describing? Do you believe that men and women tend to be different in terms of these needs? Why?*

Finally there was Jakob, a boyfriend for almost two years. He was a class ahead of me. He did not seem to have too many friends at school and was very quiet, being interested only in music. Suddenly he became very popular, as he could sing and play his guitar in a most beautiful way. I think I was the first girl he had ever taken anywhere. He was so unlike any of my other boyfriends. I did not have to wait that long to satisfy my desire for sexual relations. Jakob learned very quickly how to satisfy me, and of course he was very pleased with these new sensations in his own body.

Jakob had never been to bed with a girl before me. Perhaps it would not have happened at all if his aunt hadn't left the city for several weeks and asked him to take care of her cat in her apartment. Jakob and I found ourselves together there much of the time. It was the first night I had stayed away from home all night without telling my mother and father. This night with Jakob was beautiful for both of us. I fell very much in love with the tenderness and gentleness of this boy. His fingers and then his penis were to find their way into me with much ecstasy for both of us. No one could have believed that this shy boy would be so good with a woman's body. I wanted to tell everyone about Jakob, but kept it all to myself. At this time I began to take pills to keep from becoming pregnant. I was relieved not to bother about the inconvenience of other ways.

I was heartbroken when it all ended last year during the winter. Jakob had graduated and had found some new musical friends at the university, whom I did not like at all.

Since I have begun my studies at the university, my own life has changed very much. I dated some boys from the institute, but they were quite meaningless. I also grew very bored going to the Disc Club every weekend, although it was there that I met my present boyfriend, Hans. My roommate and I saw him come into the club at the very same time. We decided that we would let him pick which of the two of us should have him. I do not know why he came to me rather than Britha, because I think she is much the prettier of the two of us, but has a way of looking too Swedish sometimes. After Hans had danced many dances with me, I knew

I was having some very strong love feelings for him. The very same night Britha met the boy she is still with, and the four of us went to our apartment. Britha and I had never brought any boys home to our rooms until this time, and we have now arranged the sleeping places so we can be alone if we wish. But that night the privacy was only the darkness of the room. I do not like the idea of how it happened for the first time all together, but perhaps I just say that because it was great fun, with a lot of giggling and laughter.

DISCUSSION   *How do you feel about privacy in your sexual behavior? How can you explain your feelings from psychological and sociological views?*

chapter 6

Larry, Björn, and Jørgen

LARRY

Larry, at nineteen, seems particularly aware of the learning experiences of late childhood and adolescence. Many of his comments can be developed into insights into the way many boys feel about their social relationships during adolescence, especially those who have not always been well integrated in the social networks of their peers. Larry's relationships with the opposite sex have not been so rewarding as he wanted. He was often confused, uncertain, and insecure. His description of the male peer group as a source for conceptualizations about sex indicates fairly typical American socialization patterns. His portrayal of the girl he hopes to marry is worthy of some attention, as this relationship can be used to illuminate certain social and sexual insecurities.

I am nineteen years old, and I live with my folks. At the same time I more or less live with a girlfriend. I enjoy having sex, and it doesn't matter where or when. I dig it! I have great fantasies of orgies and skinny dipping on the beach. Unfortunately most people close to me do not share my enthusiasm. I'm probably a sex nut, when I come to think of it. My girlfriend has terrible hang-ups about sex, and when it comes to trying new things she has been very hesitant because she had always associated sex with sin and filth, but fortunately I've begun to get her to realize that whatever is pleasurable to both of us is beautiful, not filth. Her mother and father unload such shit in her head you wouldn't believe it.

I led a pretty introverted life as a child. I had many crushes on girls, but I would rather have pulled a lunch sack over my head than reveal my feelings because of fear of being rejected. I was pretty quiet both at home and at school, especially when adults were around.

My parents are ordinary folks, who have lived since their marriage in Los Angeles county. My father is sort of a big gun in one of the aerospace companies. He got himself a good education as an engineer back in the Midwest, moved out here after the war, picked up my mother at a hamburger stand, and married her. Her education is something else, but she has been a good mother to both my sister and me. We have a hell of a nice house, which makes all of us feel pretty good. Dad got me a car when I was seventeen and helped fix it up. I used to spend a lot of time with my family, but now about the only thing we do together is go to church on Sunday, because I'm busy with my girl.

What I learned about sex in my childhood was not interesting at all. It all seemed to have something to do with the dirty parts of the body. The idea of a girl's wee-wee splitting open so a doctor could pull out a baby was really scary, and not my idea of excitement. Older boys at school made the basic facts of life into a lot of jokes I did not understand, and when my mother tried a couple of times to drop a few words on the subject, she almost choked up like she was talking about someone dying. Some of the words I picked up at school really blew her mind, so I learned to keep my mouth shut around home. In our home everyone was always very careful about showing himself. This has been a kind of hang up for me at times. My mother would always go into some sort of panic about my zipper being unzipped. Now I love being naked. Even running along the beach naked at night is a turn-on for me.

My first real girlfriend came in the seventh grade. She was a foot taller than I, broader, and weighed much more, but we were still attracted to each other. She invited me to a birthday party and then dinner with her folks. The party was okay, because there was a lot of kissing in one of the dark bedrooms when her folks left, and the food was really great.

Two things came about at this time that were important. I noticed that I got hard-ons from kissing my girl, even though the kisses were something like the pecks of a mother. The guys started to talk about their hard-ons with girls, and I was glad that I wasn't left out. Jokes about girls getting knocked up and a lot of wild rumors were the only sex education we got in school.

DISCUSSION   *How does Larry's formal sex education compare to that of other American males? What might critics of sex education programs in the schools say about his commentary? How would you evaluate their arguments?*

Before graduating from grade school I had become fully aware of my sex. I remember one day taking a bath and discovering the very sensual part of my body and how quickly I aroused myself by rubbing it with a little soap. Masturbation then became a part of my bathing routine. It seems quite possible that my regular fooling around in the bath caused me to associate sex and masturbation with cleanliness and helped me to develop a cleaner and healthier attitude toward sex.

DISCUSSION   *Is this an example of sexual rationalization?*

During the summer before my junior year, I had my first real make-out session. A friend and I had picked up on a couple of chicks on the beach. We kept dropping things down the tops of their bathing suits and then wrestling with them to remove them. At the beach it was mostly all talk and no action, but later that evening under some old bridge we made out. It was nothing more than kissing and light petting, but for me it was a great deal because it was the first time I had kissed with the deep French technique. This really pressed the button in my brain that said "hard-on," but anything more would have blown out my fuses. These girls must have figured that we were a little slow for them, because they wouldn't even talk with us after that. It didn't bother my friend and me too much, because they were really pigs.

DISCUSSION   *Is Larry again unconsciously rationalizing the frustration and anxiety he felt in being rejected? Does such a mechanism often work better if it can be shared with others and mutually reinforced?*

The rest of the summer was spent surfing and hanging around at the beach. At night a bunch of us would go down to the beach, make a fire, and just lie around until we had to go home. It was a damn good summer, but it didn't have much sex in it for me, although the other guys did a lot of bragging, which was mostly bullshit.

In my junior year I went out for sports. I worked hard at it, and for over a year and a half I never dated. I joined a surfing club and, except for a bunch of wild parties, did not have any close contact with the opposite sex. Most of the fun at these parties was getting puking drunk on cheap wine and stoned on grass before hitting the beach for a midnight swim. Unfortunately I never bothered to bring a chick to any of these parties, and the ones who were there were always with someone else.

It wasn't until the end of my senior year that I dated a few girls, but these never amounted to more than a movie, dinner, and a good-night kiss. Near the end of high school I wasn't so self-conscious, mainly because of the confidence I had built up playing football and working out with weights.

DISCUSSION   *Were Larry's football and weight-lifting an effort to compensate for his feelings of social and physical inferiority? How do you think success or failure in these male activities affect sex role development, social relationships with the opposite sex, and sexual behavior?*

During the summer following graduation I met my present girlfriend. We have been going together for the past year and hope to get married when we finish school. She never dated in high school, because her parents were afraid to let her. They are really crazy people. Talk about sex fears! Unfortunately, some of it has rubbed off on Charlene, but I love her enough to change her.

We met at a fund-raising dance at our church, and I really dug talking with her. From that time on she was the center of most of my activities. At first I took her out to dinner or a movie, brought her candy and flowers, and the whole bit. Gradually I was able to work her up to go to a drive-in, although her folks had forbidden her to. All we did was hold hands and eat a hell of a lot of popcorn. The good-night kiss was a car affair that lasted three seconds, so her folks wouldn't know. Her folks would always sit in the living room with the lights out watching out the windows.

I always tried to be a perfect gentleman when I went out on a date, though I didn't always succeed. A big problem I had was my wandering hands. But I never forced her. Her mother had always told her not to let anyone touch her, so she was afraid of sex and didn't know what to expect at first. I didn't know what to expect from sexual relationships either, but I was eager to find out and fear of doing it never entered my mind.

After several months certain barriers began to wear down. The thing that was really great about our relationship was that we could talk about what our standards of sexual behavior ought to be. She set the limits, and I adhered to them until she allowed them to change. I was gradually permitted to feel her breasts from the outside of her clothes, and after a while she did not object to my slipping my hand under her bra and then unsnapping it for a fuller feel. We had been dating over six months with a fair amount of heavy kissing and feeling of her breasts before I made my next move. All this time her mother had been pouring all kinds of stupid shit into her head about pregnancy and sin, and her father would give me quick little moral lectures about what can happen if "kids" lose control and such. I really hated picking her up at home. The only thing my father ever told me about sex was to "keep your zipper zipped."

DISCUSSION   *Is Larry's attitude typical of how boys at this point feel about parents and their role in sex education? Do you think Larry's role as a parent will be much different from that he reports for his own father?*

One night at a drive-in I reached down and put my hand on her knee and started to gradually work it up toward her womb. Finally my hand was so far up that she put her hand on top of mine through the dress, and I couldn't go any further, but she didn't push it away, either. This was really great, so I left my hand where it was and went back to work on her breasts with my free hook. After a while I got my lower hand moving again and got to the right place, where I could feel some hairs of her crotch. I was really wild with my feelings of accomplishment, but just when I was thinking "wait for next time," she put her hand on my cock. I reached further, and for the first time in my life my finger felt the warm, moist flesh of a girl's cunt. She did not object, and actually she started gently rubbing my cock inside my pants. We went no further, but we drove home without saying a word. There was no question that she was all ripped up over what we had done. When we got home, she didn't kiss me but instead went into the house alone with tears in her eyes. I felt a bit like a shit and didn't call her for several weeks. We started dating again although for several months we stayed out of the drive-in. Finally a movie we both wanted to see was playing only at a drive-in, and we repeated much the same activities, but this time it was much different. I had really gone to work on her brain to flush out some of the garbage her folks had dropped on her. This time she really enjoyed the heavy petting, and she trusted me in knowing that I would not do anything to make her pregnant. Little did she know that this meant I now had a pack of rubbers in the glove compartment.

DISCUSSION   *While Larry has remarked about how Charlene and he are open in their sexual communication, does this last comment suggest otherwise? To what extend does this relationship reflect traditional sex values and standards in American society?*

She had never seen a rubber in her whole life, and when I showed them to her later she became all unglued because they are against our faith. Her reaction was so extreme that I knew we could never use them. The episode almost ended the relationship, though I tried hard to explain that I had them only in case it got too heavy. The next date was better, and much to my surprise she started talking about the rhythm method of birth control. Somehow I half jokingly asked her where she was in her cycle, and again I could barely believe my ears. She said that the next week would be safe. For almost a week I was out of my mind in anticipation. We saw each other every day before the big night.

So there was dinner on the pier and then off to the drive-in. We got into one of the back spaces, and the show really began. After about an hour of very heavy petting, I unzipped my pants and put her hand on my penis. It had not occurred to me that she would be frightened by this, but it was the first time she had ever touched the raw flesh of the male organ. She said she didn't think she could do it, and she worried about its hurting the first time. I promised her that if it hurt we would stop, and she trusted me. After a short while I was able to kneel on the car floor and stroke her womb on the outside with the end of my penis. Gradually I tried pushing it up into her, but I only made it a third of the way when I had an orgasm. I really felt like a heel because it had hurt her so much for such little pleasure for me and none for her. After soothing words and many promises about the future, I was able to make her feel better about it.

About a month later we again tried to have sexual intercourse. I really worried about coming so fast, so I had masturbated several times before we went out. While I felt a bit dull and depressed over doing it again, the situation almost demanded that we try it, as her cycle was again right. We were both scared about where we were parked, but we went ahead. I was able to completely stick junior into her womb, and we had sex for about ten minutes before I had an orgasm. She did nothing but lie on the back seat of the car almost totally motionless. Her only words were for me to go slowly, and I know I was hurting her. When I finished, there were tears in her eyes. She felt very dirty and called herself a tramp.

DISCUSSION   *What may be some of the social and psychological outcomes of this kind of initiation to sexual intercourse? What elements of the American sexual culture have influenced Larry and Charlene to behave in the manner reported here?*

Since then we have had sexual intercourse several dozen times. She has told me many times that she does not enjoy sex. I don't know exactly what a girl is supposed to do when she has an orgasm, but I know that she has never had one with me.

I have read a lot of books about how to excite a girl, but none of it seems to do much good. I think until she leaves her parents and the brainwashing she gets from them after every date that our relationship is going to have a sex hang-up. We talk a lot about getting married as a solution to all the shit she has to take at home, but until then I shall treat Charlene with as much respect and tenderness as I can. I love life and sex beyond measure and don't intend to give up either, as long as I can help it. Perhaps Charlene is the beautiful kind of girl who can only fully love a man in marriage.

BJÖRN   *Björn is very critical of Larry. He is convinced that Larry is a victim of sexual patterns in American society. Some of his comments may seem rather abrasive and self-serving, but he is an individual who seems intent on always speaking frankly about sexual matters. Björn is the end product of Swedish sexual socialization. His*

*search for social and sexual intimacy, and the events he
describes at home, school, camp, and with peers seem
ordinary by Swedish standards.*

This story that **Larry** has told about himself is very sad,
even though he has tried to be amusing about his life and problems.
He still uses the same kind of expressions my friends and I used in
our younger years. A person who is so immature should not think
seriously of getting married. Of course the strange actions of his
girlfriend are so sick that someone as young and inexperienced as
Larry cannot help her. Larry would probably be thought in America
to be a very good boy with a fine heart for his girl, but in Sweden
most boys and girls would find him to be quite the fool and a victim
of bad traditions about sex matters. He thinks his attitudes are
kind and tender, but what he believes makes his problem with this
girl worse. It is not hard to see that his love for this girl is a
fake. He only feels guilt for her and does not have enough feeling
of security yet in his manhood. I wonder whether he is more concerned with Charlene's sexual satisfaction or in proving to himself
that he is enough of a man to give her satisfaction? He is too weak
to deal with this clever girl, who is trying to use her sex problem
to capture him in marriage.

Larry has treated girls all his life as if men and women
were very different in their sex desires. He thinks that girls are
to be tricked into fucking, so he can feel that he is a man. Swedish
girls would not like his attitude at all. If a Swedish girl fucks with
a boy, it is because she wants to do it with him. If she does not
want to do it, it is because she does not like him for such things.
Larry has spent too much time planning the seduction of this girl
for mere pleasures of his penis, and how he is trapped in his dis-
satisfaction and failure!

It is not possible to say very much in comparing my life
with Larry's, because he did not tell much about his family, which
I think is very important in understanding personality. He should
have examined his society more closely and seen how its traditions
have brought his state of mind and actions into being. The idea
that sex is sin is still in the back of his mind, even when he runs
naked on the beach. The problem he has with this girl in bed is a
sign of her attractiveness to him. She is so full of purity and
sweetness that it is natural that she would not like sex until after
marriage. Fortunately my family never taught me that sex was

anything but a natural activity between those who are old enough to be responsible for themselves. Not everyone in the countryside yet agrees with us, but everyone knows the old ideas will soon be completely gone.

I am twenty-two years old and a student in my second year at the University of Stockholm. I lived with my parents until two years ago. My younger brother and sister still live at home. We have always lived in the same house in a nearby suburb. Both my father and my mother are well thought of in their professional careers. My father is an accountant, and my mother has been a teacher for many years. The three of us children have taken good care of each other, although when we were very young we had some help at home from older women. My mother and father are a very good match for each other. Neither one interferes with other's interests and activities. My brother and I spent most of our summers away at a wonderful camp, which our parents and sister would visit on weekends.

There is nothing in my childhood that I should have feelings of shame about or hide from view. My activities with other children seem quite normal to me. My parents talked about sex quite openly with us, and they had no interest in not letting us understand grown-up sex relations. They would discuss sexual matters freely with us whenever we had a question or brought such topics into the conversation. Several good books about sex were available to us, but it was sometimes a problem to understand them. My friends would come home with me after school to read these books when I was about ten years old, and I remember being surprised that their parents did not like them to read about such things. One of them told me that we should hide such books from my sister, but that made little sense to me. I should say that my interest in sex was not very great at this time. How children are conceived was just an accepted fact, except it had not been made clear that fucking was the great pleasure that it is. What would I have done with such knowledge before I came into adolescence? I think I would have started masturbation earlier or, if I was lucky, had some interesting sexual experiments with girls. As you can tell now, I have none to report before I became an adolescent. I did not discover masturbation until I was at least fourteen.

Until adolescence all of my friends were other boys. I did not like girls too much. My interests in sports and science activities were better satisfied by doing things with my brother and other boys. I had a girlfriend when I was thirteen, like most of the other boys in my class, but it was an empty and meaningless

association of two disinterested persons. We went together only
when we were with other friends. I think children today are much
advanced in their sexual contacts because friendships between
boys and girls are strongly encouraged now. Teachers now watch
children to help them get over shyness with each other.

My interest in sex grew when I came into adolescence.
My voice changed at about fourteen or fifteen. I was then very
interested in my own body and others'. My cock, to my great
interest, began to grow to a fine length, and I became very proud
of the hair that grew full around it. I even thought that it was
good to exercise it by masturbation, just like all body muscles.
At the beginning I was a little worried about whether I was masturbating too often, but when I read that it was not dangerous at
all I was very comforted. My parents never said anything about
masturbation's being dangerous, but they never said that it was
good either. My friends sometimes talked about doing it, and we
all felt that it was a very normal thing to do when alone and thinking about girls.

DISCUSSION   *Björn's attitudes and behavior in connection with masturbation were apparently supported by the views of his
friends. Today Scandinavian sex education programs
stress its normality. How do you evaluate such learning?
What are the social and psychological implications of
masturbation? In what ways may attitudes favorable to
this practice contribute to healthy patterns of social and
sexual development? What do critics of this practice
believe about its consequences? Why?*

During this time I was aware that being sexually experienced
was of great value, but I did not fuck any girls until I was nineteen. I
was very shy with girls until my last year at high school. I had read
many books about sex, but I did not feel that I knew enough to be
successful with one in bed. The fucking stories my friends told
about themselves made it seem very easy to do, but it was very difficult for me to find girls the way they would. I was always too quiet
with girls to be successful in this. Until my last year at high school
I did not have a girl who was even a close friend. During the early
part of that year I got my first sexual contacts at school dances and
things like that. Such girls limited me to small kisses and careful
petting with our clothes on. Most of my friends who were fucking
did not do it with girls from our school but would find girls at the
dance clubs in the centrum. All the time I longed for sexual inter-

course, much like Larry. I had the feeling that the first sexual intercourse would change me a great deal.

DISCUSSION   *The initial experience in sexual intercourse is often perceived as a turning point in maturity, and is sometimes made into a test for social and sexual adequacy. How are such attitudes learned? What are the social and psychological implications of emphasizing the end of virginity? Do you think males and females perceive this event differently? What differences are there between American and Scandinavian attitudes toward first intercourse?*

Near the end of the school term I developed a very good friendship with a beautiful girl in my class. We would always walk home from school together, as she had recently moved near me. Her mother was also a teacher. After some time had gone by, we felt very much in love and began to talk freely about sexual matters between us. Although we had only kissed each other and petted with our clothes on, she had let me know that she wanted more. Also, it was quite obvious from her comments about her former boyfriend that she had fucked with him many times. This boy was often drunk on weekends, which had caused the end of their love affair. I did not like him at all and found it difficult to believe that my girl could have been attracted to him. He was always talking with other boys about all the girls he fucked.

One weekend her parents went on a holiday to Denmark and provided the opportunity for the lovemaking we desired. Her mother and father had known very well that we were going to spend much of our time in their apartment. Her mother had made a lot of food for us to eat, and her father, strangely enough, had left some condoms on his desk in the bedroom, which gave us a good laugh. Needless to say, we did not use his, for I had my own.

DISCUSSION   *How would most American parents react to this situation?*

All of my shyness left me. We were very much in love with one another, and everything we did with sex was very satisfying. It was exciting to be naked for the first time with a girl. We fucked many times the first night and afterward took our bath together. It was exciting to wash each other and play in the water. We were completely free with each other. Not only did we have much fucking, but we enjoyed her kissing and licking my penis, and I enjoyed doing the same with her sex parts and breasts. I remember surprising her when I told her after a while that she was the first girl I had been to bed with. I had led her to believe that I had gone to bed with another girl at school, but she understood my lie and was very pleased to understand the truth.

The only unfortunate thing about this very good time was that her father became upset that we had drunk all of his best wine. I had not thought that he would feel so furious about three bottles of wine and some spirits. I offered to pay for all of it and did so, but he was still very angry with both of us. He accused his daughter of having had a wild party with many guests because we had used so many towels taking baths. It did not seem reasonable to him that only his daughter should have needed so many. Finally she told her mother that it was true, and her mother quickly understood what we had done.

My love for this girl lasted the whole next year, although we never had sex in her apartment again. Several times we had sex in the storage room of her apartment building, but this was very cold and uncomfortable. After I went into the military service, she visited me several weekends during the summer. Then we always had sex in the forest near the military base. It was very beautiful to sleep with a girl in a sleeping bag. I remember falling asleep with my penis in her vagina and awakening with her gentle movements exciting me in the middle of the night. She had her birth control device then, and it was so good to feel the warm inside of her vagina with my penis while we would sleep, or pretend to sleep. We liked to sunbathe in the forest clearings, and again we would enjoy fucking. It was not all just sex for us, because we talked of many things, including our plans for the university when I was finished with my military service. We agreed that it would be wrong to get married until both of us had finished our educations.

It is too bad that her interest grew less and less with the passing of time. I think she became bored with my long letters. My letters grew longer, and hers became shorter and less frequent. Finally we met for the last time, just after I returned from military service. She told me that she had found a new boy, who had finished his first year in the medical school and who she was very much in love with. I told her I understood—in truth, I was very hurt, but not that surprised. She had been living with him for several months. I became very depressed by this event, and my parents became very upset with my new attitude toward life.

When I started at the university, I still lived with my parents because it was very costly to live comfortably alone. Because in the military service I had learned to drink too much beer when I was feeling lonely, I did not want to live by myself. So for my first year most of my time was spent at home or in the library. This was a very dull and boring year in all ways, including my sex life. To relieve my sexual tension, I only masturbated. Occasionally I would go to a porno shop and purchase some sex booklets.

My second year at the university went much better than the first in all ways. I had better relationships with other students and also became acquainted with a friendly professor who found a very interesting job for me in one of his research projects. The money from this work made it possible for me to move away from home and live in a small apartment, which I still share with another boy.

The girl I am now going with is in her first term at the university. While she is not as beautiful as my first love, she has a much deeper awareness of life and society. We love many of the same things and study in the same institute. Our sex life has included fewer romantic notions of love. But after all the first rush of our sexual instincts is over. Of course, it is good to be fucking again. Our only problem is that my girlfriend prefers to have me use a condom, but she has promised soon to get a device put in her to prevent pregnancy. She speaks of this as my birthday present next month, and nothing would please me more, for I dislike the condom.

To say much more about myself or Larry would probably not be very interesting. I think my life so far has been much better than Larry's in most ways. I feel very sorry for him living in a society so full of hate and violence that he must use sex to escape. But because Larry is only nineteen years old, he still has some time to learn better ways.

JØRGEN   *Jørgen's commentary shows the importance of peer group relationships in the formation of social and sexual attitudes. Jørgen goes into some detail to describe the impact of his friends during adolescence as he begins to develop an interest in heterosexual matters. While he has a number of experiences that give him frustration and anxiety, Jørgen seems able to solve these problems with a series of helpful girls. Many of his present attitudes and behavior are reflective of his experiences in late adolescence.*

I am twenty-two years old. Sex to me is something beautiful while it happens and while it lasts. However it does not occupy my thoughts very much these days unless I am with my girlfriend or other girls. There are many wonderful and happy things in the world besides the joy of fucking. Since coming to the university two years ago, I have discovered many good friends and enjoy living with them in all ways. I feel very free with my friends and truly believe that I do not have any problem or antagonisms about sex now. That is not to say that I did not have difficulties when I was a little younger than Larry is now. Like Larry, I was very shy about sexual matters. My parents and schools never gave me any education about sex, although I think the general attitude in Denmark is much freer than in the U.S.A. Such education in the home and school are very good, but for my classmates and me, less important than what we learned from each other. Parents and teachers were too frightened to tell much, but my parents' interest in me in other ways was very close and warm.

DISCUSSION   *When Jørgen was in elementary and secondary education sex education programs in Danish public schools were often nonexistent or very abbreviated academic encounters. However, since the mid-1960s there has been a vigorous effort to develop effective programs at all levels of public education. How does such an effort compare to what is happening in the United States in your estimation?*

At about eleven older friends who played in the woods told me my first stories about girls having sex with boys. I knew then that there was more to having a girlfriend than kissing. When I was with an older friend, we found a box of condoms in his father's drawer at home. I asked my friend what it was, and he told me rather coarsely how his father rolled them on his penis before he put it into his mother. I was quite shocked, although I did not tell him what my idea had been until that moment. I remembered seeing

used condoms under my father's bed one morning and how he had
told me that they were used to spit into at night. It had not dawned
on me that my mother and father had been doing such things together.
For a while this thought bothered me, and I would watch and listen at
home very carefully at night to see if I could hear anything, but
without success.

When I was about twelve or thirteen I heard some friends
discuss "how to make it stand." The stroking and pulling back and
forth of the penis seemed to be a pleasant enough idea, so I tried it
as soon as I heard about it. After this single attempt in vain and a
pause of several months, it had a result, I enjoyed this experience
very much, although it was some months later that I had my first
ejaculation. My other friends at this time used to talk a great deal
about the kinds of things that would give them pleasure as they masturbated, and I was always interested in trying out what they had
learned. We began to talk a great deal about girls and sex, but none
of us dared to try out such information upon the classmates. Masturbation was soon a very regular thing for me to do, both before
falling asleep at night and upon awakening in the morning. I have
always liked to masturbate for the wonderful pleasure it gives and
also because it helped me to avoid the unpleasant night ejaculations,
which were embarrassing to me in the first few years of my puberty.
My younger brother became very interested in what I was doing, and
I was proud to show him my maturity and how it worked. For a
short time we would masturbate together, but we stopped this after
a few weeks. For company in such matters I preferred another boy
in my class, until we also grew tired of doing it with each other.

*DISCUSSION   What factors not mentioned by Jørgen might account for
his growing tired of this sexual activity with his friend?*

At about fourteen I began to take a serious look at girls and
found myself very attracted to several in my class. I think my
friends in school were much more advanced in these matters than I.
They appeared to know an awful lot, but I was always very careful
not to show my ignorance. Soon it was my turn to expand my very
limited kissing experience. A well-developed girl in the class took
it upon herself to give her new boyfriends a good time. After a
couple of months it was my turn. I visited her one night she was
home alone, and then I received my first hot kisses and was encouraged to feel her breasts. This was very exciting, and I fell in
love with her immediately. We did much kissing and petting, but I
was not able to summon enough courage to do more. Other boys
had told me that they had put their fingers into her vagina, but such

an adventure was not yet for me. I think she became somewhat bored, so this relationship was over after a couple of months.

When I was fifteen, I moved to another school. It was very clear that my new classmates knew much more about sex than my experience with this girl had shown me. I wanted to fuck with a girl very much. I had seen many pictures of fucking and other aspects of the sex act, which were very exciting to me then. I thought a lot about finding a girl who would give me experience, but for a long time I was unsuccessful. My opportunity came when I least expected it.

Our class was on a trip to another country, as we belonged to a music group that had received many awards. My first fucking was to take place on the train. Well, it was almost a fucking. One of the girls I did not particularly know, or even like very much, had planned for me to go with her to her bed in the sleeping car. It was a tremendous experience, first of all because of the risk of being found by the teacher, and second because it was the first time I was in such a beautiful situation. We first kissed very deeply and petted with our clothes on. Then, without much encouragement from me, she suddenly began to take off her clothes while telling me how much she had always liked me. Finally she was completely naked, and there was nothing for me to do but remove my own clothes. I recall the beautiful sensation of placing my body upon hers and gently rubbing my penis between her legs. She had a wonderful warmth and softness, such as I had never felt before. I placed my finger in her vagina and was very surprised to discover how large this opening was in her body. When I removed my finger, she asked me not to stop. It was very exciting for me, as well. This was the first time a girl had fondled my penis. She did it ever so gently, in contrast to the way I had usually masturbated. After we were at this sort of thing for a while, she asked me whether I had a condom. With great pain and a feeling of stupidity I had to tell her that I had none. I had heard that if you take the penis out before ejaculation that this would prevent pregnancy, but the girl said that this way would not do. So there we were having this most beautiful thing happen, and because of my neglect the fucking could not be properly finished. The next best thing was her suggestion. I simply rubbed my penis across the entrance of her vagina, which she found less frustrating than I did. Finally I had an ejaculation by rubbing between her closed legs, which turned out to be quite messy.

As I entered high school, I met the girl who became my first great love. While we were very free with each other's bodies, we did not truly fuck with each other. There were many difficult times when our passion for each other was very hot, but our way of satisfying each other was not completely without event. In the last six months of our relationship we got a lot of pleasure with oral fucking. I found this to be especially exciting for myself. To be able to give pleasure to a girl this way has always seemed very pleasant to me. At the time, I thought it was not only a good substitute for regular fucking but also the safest. By the way, I had presented this girl to my parents as soon as we started to go steady. They liked her very much and in all wholesomeness she slept several times in my home with the approval of all our parents. She became in some ways like a sister in our house.

However, this relationship was not without its interruptions. I often grew tired of her and was keeping an eye out for other girls. It was during one of these breaks that I had my first complete fucking. I was about seventeen and a half. The girl was a boyfriend's girlfriend whom I had had an eye on. I knew her sexual ability from my friend. I knew she used a diaphragm, which was not very common among the girls I knew. It was at a friend's party that I met her rather casually. She had an argument with my friend over how drunk he had become, although she herself was very loud and drunk before the end of the night.

I would like to be able to say that this fucking was the great pleasure that I had hoped for, but the first time with this girl was almost a nothing.

After much dancing and much beer we went upstairs. It was quickly off with the clothes, a little kissing, a little feeling of her vagina, the rolling on of a stubborn, stuck-together condom, the clumsy leading of the penis into her vagina, a few inexperienced movements, and then fiasco! I was really much more drunk than I had thought. On with the clothes, back to the party, and then waiting half asleep to try again if possible, as she promised.

Finally the party was over, but many of us stayed overnight, sleeping on pillows on the floor. At daylight we tried again. This time it was not difficult at all. Finally I had an orgasm with ejaculation, and she gave me the beautiful excitement of an orgasm of her own. It was beautiful, very beautiful. We covered ourselves with a nice, soft blanket and went to sleep in each other's arms, to awaken to a beautiful sunlight that warmed our exhausted bodies. When we finally awoke alone, we both were silently wondering what my friend would say upon hearing what happened. As it turned out, my friend was not bothered at all, as he had gone off with a new girl that night to fuck. They were finished anyway.

I don't really think that the sexual profit from this night was very large—at least, not for me. But it was liberating to be able to tell myself that from now on there was nothing to be nervous about. For the next year or so I went with this girl to several events when I was not back with my other girl. However, these times did not make me want a serious relationship with her, and she felt the same. My steady girlfriend eventually heard something of the story at the party and so my two-year love came to an end with more disappointment for my parents than for me. At this time the thought of fucking many girls was much more alluring than being with only one. My friends became those who were older and much more experienced than I. I stayed away from home many nights with them at parties. There was much drinking of spirits, and I went to bed with many girls I did not know. My parents thought I was going straight to hell very soon, but very little was said except through my older brother, who had married a good neighbor girl. By the time I had completed my final exam at high school, I was very experienced in sex.

DISCUSSION   *Jørgen here reveals a rather typical Danish parent-child relationship in that even when the son is engaged in behavior the parents do not like, there appears to be little inclination to seek a direct confrontation. Jørgen's parents chose to try to use the older brother to change some of his behavior. How does this compare to middle-class American norms? What forms of control do American parents employ over the sexual behavior of their adolescent sons? With what results?*

The summer before coming to the university was the start of a very different relationship for me. A girl invited me to a party, without my knowing anything special about her beforehand. This was not the only time that I had received a tip that a girl was interested in me. I think I was becoming known to many girls for my sexual reputation, as they often would tell me what they had heard about me. I had learned a lot about how to please a girl, and myself as well. This new girl was the beginning of a love that lasted seven or eight months. We were on the dance floor almost all night, but there was no opportunity to make love, as we both wanted. I took her home, hoping that we could have a good fuck there, but bad luck was with us. Her mother was up. So a week later I had something of a party arranged, and we met at my room. Soon after she arrived, I had both of us ready for what was a good fuck.

During the summer we had a lot of fun together, and I did

not think much about having other girls. I could not begin to count the times we did it. The summer weather was very warm that year, and we spent much time at the beaches and in the woods running, playing, and fucking between the trees and upon the sand. I loved the beauty of her body, and no part of either of us was a stranger to the other. Her mother liked me very much, and much of the time I lived at her house.

In the fall I took a room in Copenhagen, and on weekends she would live with me. For many months I looked forward to the weekends with her. Living in the city with my own room gave me a wonderful feeling of freedom. However, near the end of my first term I began to feel that the sex and our whole situation together had become too routine. It had also become very difficult for me to study on weekends, as she could not share my studies and the other things I needed to do as a student. She saw little value in the things that I had begun to interest me.

One day, rather suddenly, I pulled myself together and finished us. She cried for a whole day, but I did not relent. Afterward I felt like a pig. I did not try to find a new girl for several months, and only took care of myself with my hand. Finally, in the last three months of the term I began to go to some parties with some new university friends. I also would go to the dance clubs and a few other places to try to find girls fairly often. Sometimes I was very successful in finding very good girls, who would come to my room to fuck, but I did not engage myself emotionally very much. I do not remember any of these girls as especially interesting, but all of them together made my attitude about sex more and more free.

The last few months have not been very good sexually to me. It is interesting now for me to think how my feelings about sex and love have split into two widely different branches. I can easily go to bed with a girl without knowing anything about her, not even her name, and still get a great night out of it. A couple of days later I have forgotten her absolutely. Every now and then I miss the cozy, the intimate, the confidential, which the good steady relationship brings about. At the same time I want to combine the free and steady relationships simply by finding a girl whom I can like for longer than a single night and with whom I can find something to share other than just the bed. But I do not want her to give me the feeling that I am caught in the net. I think Larry will also find the same winds of freedom roaring through his own spirit. He will not find freedom by staying with a girl who fucks like a dead woman.

chapter 7

Gloria, Ingela, and Maren

GLORIA

Gloria is twenty, but in some respects she seems in a social and psychological state of prolonged adolescence. Gloria reports in some detail her experiences of adolescence, and makes clear that she has been a popular and socially active girl among her peers. The effort to maintain her place in the dating game without exceeding her limits in sexual behavior has produced its problems, but she has managed to cope. Her discussion makes it possible to understand some of the values and norms that relate to sex role behavior and sexual expression. The popular and attractive adolescent girl can usually use sex to initiate and maintain desired social relationships. Gloria seems to have been very successful in this game, but now she wonders what it all means in finding more real social and sexual satisfaction in her relationships.

I can recall very few details of my childhood before the age of five or six. This is not because I am so old, but because I find it difficult to remember things that are important. Somehow I think that very few occurrences of a sexual nature took place during this time.

I was extremely close to both of my parents all through my childhood. I was an only child and very pampered. My parents got along reasonably well, even though they were quite different. My father was not very well educated, while my mother finished high school and became a secretary for a cement company before her marriage. My father was one of the drivers for the company, so you can see how they met and fell in love.

I can remember asking both my mother and my father when I was going to get a brother or sister. My curiosity about how babies were made was with me all the time. I was determined to find out exactly what took place. My parents wanted to tell me nothing except that it was "just something that happened." Of course, you had to be married to have one! My peers at this time were not much help in my search for the truth. I doubt that any of my playmates knew more than I did about it. For a long time I understood that when a man and woman married and waited for a time a "blessed event" would be sure to occur. How many times, or why, was a big mystery.

When I was first in grammar school, many of the boys were continually being scolded for the use of dirty words, especially fuck and tits. Some other words of this type were used, but I don't think I should repeat them here. Anyway, few of us girls ever used them with each other. Most of the boys had no idea what they were saying and couldn't explain themselves. Finally, in about the second grade, one of the older boys took some of the girls aside and explained what it was. He said the daddy put his "pecker" in the "mother's hole" and planted a seed that grew until the doctor pulled it out. I thought it was a big ugly, but saw no reason to believe that it was not true. I'm sure my parents were very careful in their sexual life, because I never saw or heard a thing between them. I only saw my father naked in the front once.

I gather from what I have read that masturbation among children is quite common, but I do not remember doing any such thing. Only once can I recall playing doctor, in the first or second grade, with an older boy, older by perhaps a year or two. He was the doctor, of course. The other girl and I took turns being his patient. We both peeked to see what he was doing with the other. I don't think I had as good a time from this as my girlfriend, because he tried to push a pencil into me, which hurt. I really did not care for this kind of play.

I can remember very clearly at the age of seven or so being shown a magazine with pictures of nude females in somewhat suggestive poses. These photographs seemed rather silly and meaningless, though intriguing. At this time my girlfriends and I were typically overconcerned as to whether our breasts would ever be as large as our mothers'.

In the fifth grade my sexual knowledge took a little jump. A new girl in our class was much older and more knowledgeable than the rest of us, and she told the story with wild new angles. She had the pecker getting hard before it went into the mother and told how parents enjoyed doing it with each other. I was impressed by her statement that mothers did not have to have their stomachs cut open every time a baby was to be born, something that had been very frightening to me until then. She also said that her mother and father were very sexy with each other and would fuck almost every night. I told her that perhaps her parents did it, but my parents would never think of doing such an ugly, filthy thing unless they were trying to have a baby for the family. (For a while I thought it was okay if we never had a baby in the family if it would hurt my mother in some way.)

In the sixth grade the most frequently used word was still fuck. We never used it with a boy at school. All the stories had finally sunk in. My problem was I didn't know any other word for what it meant. One day my mother decided to quiz me a bit on the facts of life. I explained to her that when a husband and wife wanted a baby, they would fuck. She got all red and flustered and explicitly told me such a word was very unladylike. I was told never to use it again. Since then I have never used the word with her. In the seventh grade I used screw, but this caused almost the same uproar with my father, who has always been fairly careful about his language, even though he drives a truck. My mother apparently knew that I had learned all I needed to know, so we never talked about sex until my junior year in high school.

DISCUSSION   *What are the implications of this language and communication problem? How does it affect her sexual feelings, attitudes, and behavior? What other styles of sexual communication commonly exist in American parent-child relationships? Problems of sexual communication between children and parents are often caused by the absence of a socially acceptable vocabulary to express sexual ideas and feelings. Is this the case here, or does the problem run deeper? If sexual ideas and feelings are felt to be evil, is a socially acceptable vocabulary even possible?*

In the seventh and eighth grades we learned to dance with boys and went to some parties. We also had slumber parties, where we would mostly talk about the boys we thought were cutest, but sometimes we would discuss what we thought about sex with a boy. Some of the girls would talk about how the boys would get hard in the crotch when they danced too close to them. Most of the girls were too embarrassed to talk about sex directly. This was also the beginning of the time to go steady. It didn't matter if one cared for the one who would ask her to go steady, so long as she could say that she was doing it with "so and so." I did not go steady until I was fifteen. It seemed to me to be mostly a status thing. Also, I don't think my parents would have liked me to become serious about a boy that young. Maybe I missed out on some fun, but I am sure that I am just as well off now.

The first time I was kissed by a boy I was thirteen, at a church dance. To my amazement I was pleased, even though I was somewhat fearful of the opposite sex, but I actually felt a bit guilty that I had met this boy away from home and that my mother did not know him, or even that I was with him.

Later I discovered that if I was going to have any real fun at all with boys, it would have to be far away from home. My father suddenly started teasing my friends, and me especially, about running after boys all the time and being wild, just because a couple of boys from the eighth grade class would come over and sit on their bicycles around our driveway at night.

DISCUSSION   *How effective is a father likely to be in preventing these types of social contact at this age? In your opinion what can be the unintended consequences of parental derision and ridicule in attempting to curb heterosexual interests at this age?*

I did become a little boy-crazy when I was fourteen. After graduating from grammar school, I went to a mountain resort with a friend and her family. We met several boys we especially liked. The two boys we ended up with were several years older; it was really my first big chance to be with a boy. This boy gave me quite an education, considering my age.

That summer I had started menstruation, and my mother and I had had just a bit of a talk about it. I knew that I could become pregnant, so everything with this boy had some control on it from me. Nevertheless, it was something new for me to take long walks at night with a boy. He wanted me to go to his cabin one day when his parents were out shopping, but fortunately I didn't give in to his desires. We had been doing many things that I had never done before. There was a lot of very passionate kissing and petting. This was the first time that I had ever let a boy put his hand on my breasts and feel them while kissing. It was as far as I cared to go.

During the heat of one of our sessions he told me he wanted to "make love to me." I didn't understand this statement, because I thought that making love was what we were already doing. When I asked what he meant, he told me he wanted to "go all the way." He showed me a condom he had with him, but I still couldn't even consider such an experience. To show me how safe it would be, he took out his penis and rolled the condom on. I was intrigued by what he had done, but very scared too. He moved my hand on it and asked me if I would hold it tight while we kissed each other. I did what he wanted me to do. In just a few minutes, while I just held it and he made a few movements with his body, he had an orgasm. As soon as he was through, he stopped kissing and fixed himself up. Then he suddenly wanted to go home with me, although it was early. He left me confused about his feelings. Perhaps he was ashamed of what he had me do.

DISCUSSION   *Has Gloria used the mechanisms of projection and rationalization here—focusing on the boy's responsibility and his sense of shame and guilt—to protect her sense of self worth?*

My first two years in high school were a lot of fun. Near the end of my sophomore year I went steady with my first boy. This boy was very strange. He would spend a great deal of money on me (we were fifteen at the time), but when it came to any demonstration of feelings or emotions he was quite cold. It's really rather odd because he was well known around high school as "the lover." Very little more than a few good-night kisses took place between us. We stopped going steady by mutual consent, and I didn't miss him at all after a day or two.

My junior year I had an odd talk with my mother about "running around" with boys and what "can happen." I didn't want to become known as a "cheap girl." Boys could only go so far with me before I would stop them.

At sixteen I had another summer romance. The boy was a surfer, and a senior at my high school, although I did not know him there. He had a car, which made an important difference. I could really go out and have fun like most of the older kids. I felt very grown-up in a lot of ways. We started going steady after two weeks.

Our relationship started off with the usual kissing and necking but soon spread to other regions. By the time I was sixteen I had become fully developed. I allowed him to kiss my breasts. This was a very erotic zone for me. I would always become very passionate when a boy did this with me after I knew him and loved him deeply.

This boy wanted to go further, but I just could not bring myself to let him feel me below. I was embarrassed because my panties would become so wet from all the other excitement. Nevertheless, I did my best to try to satisfy him. He would take his organ out of his pants and masturbate to a climax. It seemed strange to me, but I never objected, and he did not seem to be embarrassed. This affair went on at school for several months, but it ended when I lost his ring and he became very mad at me.

During the summer a friend's cousin came out from back East. We liked each other right from the beginning. He was about two years older than me, which I liked very much. Although we didn't go steady, we went everywhere in Los Angeles together. The only trouble was that he was not very handsome. All of my other boyfriends had real good looks. His mind was very good, but his personality was a little dull. After going out to a movie or something, we would park and neck some, but I feel that something was always missing between us. We never went very far. I never saw him again.

My senior year was a fairly pleasant experience. I did not have to worry about being left out of things, because boys were always asking me out. I didn't go steady with any of them, because I liked playing the field. I was fairly careful about my reputation, so most of the boys knew that I would let them go only so far, then that was it! The senior year had a lot of kissing and petting in it, but the only new thing that happened is that I let a boy massage my genitals for the first time. Except for rubbing myself against a boy at the beach a number of times before, I had had no idea of the kind of excitement that could come from this kind of contact with a boy.

It happened the week before the prom with the boy who had invited me to go with him. The week before the prom we went on a date and parked. Maybe I let him go so far because I was so happy he had invited me to the prom—I don't know. We became very excited with each other. I even did the unforgivable thing of reaching into his pants and taking out his organ after I had allowed him to put his fingers in my pants. We both had orgasms from feeling each other. Following the prom it all repeated itself at a party. I did this with a lot of regrets later, because I found out that he had told some of his friends about what we had done, and it got back to one of my girlfriends. That ended him. I felt really ruined for a long time. After the prom I didn't go out. I felt real ashamed and guilty.

DISCUSSION   *Was Gloria ashamed and guilty because of what she did with this boy or because of the social consequences? Why might the boy not feel ashamed and guilty? Do you feel that the determinants of sexual shame and guilt are different for the American female and male?*

I have concluded that sex is of major importance and is definitely not to be taken lightly. It has very dangerous aspects, like pregnancy and venereal disease. There is supposedly a sexual revolution in this country, but I am not sure that it has done much more than make me a nervous wreck. I would like to get in a romantic situation now in which I could have sex and not feel scared or guilty about it, but there are many difficulties in handling this type of relationship. Too many people are untruthful in order to achieve sex with another person. I have dated some thirty boys. Some were out for what they could get, and nothing more. I now know how difficult it can be to be deeply in love and how easy it is to be fooled.

INGELA   *Ingela appears to have followed a rather independent course through childhood and adolescence. She illuminates some of the problems of learning sex roles and behavior within the context of Swedish values and norms. Her description of her peer relationships during adolescence, particularly with the opposite sex, provides a view of many of the social and psychological stresses a girl in Sweden may confront. Her responses to Gloria's history are mostly sympathetic, probably partly because they have felt alike at times about the opposite sex and have had similar difficulties in correctly assessing male motivation.*

I feel a little sorry for Gloria. We are the same age, but so different. I am also an only child and am very close to my mother. It is too bad that the word fuck has so much feeling in it for Americans that a child should be severely punished for using it in front of their mothers. The question about how babies are made was answered quite clearly early in my life. At first I did not know anything about how the father participated, but I remember my mother's telling me that seed would come from my father's penis when they held each other at night. This seed would go into the mother only if they wished to have a baby. It had always been explained to me when I, too, wanted a baby sister or brother that there was no more room in our small apartment for another child.

Most of my playmates before and after I started school were like me, I believe. Nothing was hidden from us, but we knew it was something special and not for children for a long time. This did not prevent us from playing with each other.

When we were very young, my cousins and I would go to the beach. Playing naked in the sand with other children was quite natural. I don't think I paid any attention to the penises of boys, although I could see them all the time.

Before I went to school, two boys and another girl and I showed each other our genitalia. I am sure the boys were more frightened by what we did than the two of us were. We both laughed at how the penises looked and how they felt like large noodles from a soup. It was not an important sex experience for me. I had seen my father naked hundreds of times, and I went along for this sex play with the boys only because my friend wanted to feel what it would be like to hold a penis. I have always been very happy being a girl. I thought it would be wonderful to be a mother someday and have a child in my stomach. When I was very young, I would tie a doll to my stomach under my dress and pretend that I was pregnant and think of a classmate as the father who had given me his seed.

In school when I was about eleven, we were shown pictures of genitalia and given a simple talk about sex. "This is a man, and this is a woman." And then, "Here is the way the baby comes." The boys smiled and acted as though they had known such things when they were first born. Gloria does not tell of her school education in this subject. I wonder if she had any? Perhaps not, from what I have read about American schools and the fright and shame about telling children such things. It was not that we learned so very much from this sex teaching, it was that we knew it could be discussed if we wished.

During high school we had five or six lessons on sex. We were shown films about a birth of a baby and talked about preventive protections, the physical growth of boys and girls, and so on. I was especially interested in the birth of the baby. I was fifteen when these lessons were given. It should have been sooner, but some of the parents still feel traditional about such education for their children. Boys and girls should know how to prevent pregnancy as soon as they are old enough to have babies. Too many boys are careless about this, and even girls are to be blamed for permitting sex without contraceptives.

DISCUSSION   *Ingela is correct in noting the absence of formal sex education in Gloria's schooling. Do you think Gloria's basic attitudes and behavior would have been changed by the kind of sex education Ingela received? How influential do you think such sex education programs are in forming attitudes and behavior compared to what is learned from parents and peers? Why are Scandinavians more supportive of sex education than Americans, in your opinion?*

Like Gloria, I went steady with a boy at the age of fifteen. That meant holding hands, kissing, and hardly anything else. It was not a hot love in a romantic way like Gloria liked to have. It was nice just to be with him as a friend. We were this way for almost a year.

The next boy I went steady with was a little more sexy. We would go to parties with older students. There was much dancing, some drinking, and usually boys and girls having very physical activities with each other. Many of my friends were having sexual relations with boys they knew very well. It was assumed by almost everyone to be the correct thing to do in steady relationships. But I did not feel that I wanted to do it with this boy, and he did not ever demand that I should. I did not think it was right to make sex into a public display. Once I watched a couple make love with everyone standing around the bed watching. I wondered how drunk they must have been to put on such a show for their friends, who would laugh at them for a long time later. Seeing this lovemaking was good for my education. I thought, "I can easily do that and probably much better when I decide that it is my turn, with a much better boy who does not have a fat stomach like the boy in the bed."

DISCUSSION   *Ingela points out two different standards for sexual behavior among her peers: those who make sexual intercourse conditional on a meaningful social relationship, and those who experience sexual intercourse for pleasures not related to the quality of a relationship. Is there always a clear separation between the two?*

For the year and a half I was with this boy, I could feel from the erection of his penis that he enjoyed our intimate times together. He would tell me how he would go home from our dates to masturbate thinking of me. Of course, he told me so I would be persuaded that we should have sex together, but I was not. I was getting tired of him and the way he would get angry when I would talk to other nice boys at school.

When I was seventeen I went to bed with a boy after we had known each other for two months. I went steady with him for only a month after that. He was a very handsome and strong football player. I did not like him very much at first, but his smile and words were very exciting to me. One day after school we walked to his house and made love in his bedroom.

When I told him that I had not been with a boy before, he did not want to do it with me, and I had to urge him. We talked too much about it, and it was difficult for him to have an erection. But finally his penis became very hard and very big, to my surprise. When he put it into me, I felt a quick pain, which was my tearing, and then he pushed it further into me. It was not as good as I had hoped it would be. Such a big penis needed gentler movements, but perhaps he had no way of knowing. We made love for only a few minutes, and then he had his orgasm. The condom was covered with blood, and there was even some blood upon the hairs around us.

He looked frightened at this, but we talked more and held

each other in a nice way. He was so concerned that I should be thrilled by his manner with me that I could only lie and say that it was wonderful.

Whenever I could arrange to see him at his house after school, we would go there to have sex. The second time was much better than the first. I had an orgasm and felt wonderful. In the next month I went to bed with him about twelve times. I enjoyed these sex times with him very much, but soon I learned that I did not like him outside the bedroom. He was always looking for other girls. I also did not like his friends, who would do so much drinking that their minds would leave their bodies. He would also drink too much at parties and want to have sex in a way that would not be private.

DISCUSSION   *How has this relationship contributed to Ingela's social and sexual development? Does she express any frustration and anxiety over it? How might Gloria have reacted to Ingela's discussion of this relationship?*

After some months of being alone, I came across another football player who seemed to like me. We used to kick the ball around in the field after school. Finally we started to be with each other very regularly. It was not too long after our first kiss that we talked about sex. I told him that I had been in bed with a boy once, and he told me the same about himself. I knew from what he said that he was very free and open about his life and sex. After we were going steady, we went to his parents' apartment one weekend to have sex. I loved him then with all my heart in a silly schoolgirl way, just as Gloria must have felt about her boyfriends.

This boy was so considerate of all my feelings and so able to give me sexual excitement. The kisses all over my body were returned to him with my own lips. This was the first time a boy had put his tongue in my vagina and kissed and licked me in all these parts. I had orgasms that were almost overwhelming to my senses. It seemed natural and right, and we were so happy giving each other this happiness and pleasure. We had an enormous feeling of being one when we had our orgasms together.

This boy was very good for me in many other ways. He was very kind and generous, but it was not always easy between us. We both had strong opinions. We argued about whether to go together on a summer holiday and not tell our parents. I wanted to do it finally, but the fighting had destroyed us. The shock came when he went off with another girl for a time in Denmark. It was so unlike him to do this, that I still do not understand it.

DISCUSSION   How do you evaluate the quality of this relationship?

My third boy was not very good at all. I was eighteen then. I cannot understand how stupid I was to spend six months of my life with such an untrustworthy person. He is the only boy I have ever allowed to take advantage of me. I must have wanted to suffer for my disappointment in my last love. I know now that I was very confused during the summer. But he was so handsome, and he knew it so well from all the girls he had had before me. I met him during a summer holiday, in the mountains where my father liked to fish. There were no other young people around. I thought at first how lucky I must be to have him all to myself.

The third day we were together, we cycled into the forest and had sex. I had hoped to wait before doing it with him, but the choice was not mine. After only a little kissing, he pulled me to the ground and tore all my clothes from me like a wild animal. He bit at my neck and breasts and then thrust his penis into me without a condom. He seemed to care nothing about how his penis was hurting me. It was not that his penis was that much bigger than the other two boys I had known; it was the way he would do it that hurt so much. He was too quick to put it into me. We rolled on the dirty leaves in the forest like foxes fighting. When he had his orgasm in me, it was all over, except for the terrible worry about pregnancy. He did not hold me afterwards and seemed only interested in his own satisfaction. We came home looking like tired pigs. My parents asked what we had done, but it was not possible for me to tell them how foolish I had been. I refused to have sex with him again during the whole holiday, although he begged and begged that we should repeat what he called "our fun." But we would only walk and talk with each other. He knew of my worry about not using a condom. And he tried to tell me that it would be very unusual to have a baby from just one sexual time together, but I was not satisfied with such an irresponsible point of view.

DISCUSSION   What is your interpretation of the meaning of this sexual encounter as reported by Ingela? What did Ingela learn from this experience, in your opinion?

When we went back to Stockholm, I soon discovered that I

was not pregnant, and I was more grateful than I can tell. I called
this boy to tell him that my worry was over. Of course, he said
some things that were nice, but I am sure that his words were less
than sincere. He wanted to see me again. I gave in and agreed to
meet him secretly. He invited me to his house for a small party.
Afterward we had sex, but this time I forced him to use a condom.
He was gentler this time but still only interested in his own satisfaction. When his climax was over, he would just jump from the bed,
light a cigarette, and put on his clothes. I was at his house five
times during the next four months, and it was the same. I could
teach him nothing about what a girl would like with a boy. Every
time I would feel foolish for going back to him. Finally, I would
not see him any more. It was better not to have sex than to have it
this way.

The next boy and I went together after I came to the university. Fortunately his parents are rich, so I guess they will care for
him if he becomes a mental invalid. I do not know why I fell in love
with him. We met at a party, and he was very drunk and ugly with
everyone. I was like a mother, taking him home in a taxi. There
was something about him that I liked very much.

At first I thought I had been a fool to care for this boy, but
it was not long before he called me on the telephone to thank me for
it. I was excited beyond all thinking. I wanted to go to bed with him
from the very first. We met one night to go to a movie. That was
what I told my parents, but it was more than this. It was an exciting
sex time for me, but I was soon to learn that having a good time with
sex was not enough.

The very first night we went to a party together we had sex.
I did not want it to happen this way, but we both became very excited,
and it was possible to be private. It was a wonderful sex experience,
as he did everything to give me pleasure.

Three months later this romance was ended, when he told
me he had found a girl to marry. I could not believe it at first. I
was very hurt. I loved him, and I wondered how it was that he could
have found the time to find another girl while we had been sleeping
together. For the first time in my life it was the boy who thought
that I was not for him.

Finally I met a boy from the university who is two years
older than I. I fell in love with him almost immediately. He is very
handsome, and a wonderful person. I am a little ashamed of how I
chased him at first. I think he knew I was eager to meet him. We

have become very close. Our sex is very difficult to describe, because I think it is hard to say things about someone while you love them very much. What we do with each other is fully satisfying to us. I now do anything he wishes, and he does the same for me.

So this is my life. I live a little bit at home, but mostly with my lover in his apartment near the university. We study together much more than we make love, but I love him much more than I study. I am now very happy and hope that I shall always be able to say so.

MAREN   *Maren brings into focus some of the experiences of a Danish adolescence. Her childhood relationships with her parents appear to have been without major problems. By the age of eight Maren knew about the facts of reproduction and many aspects of sexual behavior. Her early adolescent years followed a rather typical pattern sexually. At the age of fifteen she began a serious love relationship. Concerning the rest of her commentary there is little question that this first relationship was very important to her.*

As far as I am concerned, I have always learned in my sexual development what I needed to know. I knew from what my mother told me that children came from the stomachs of their mothers after the man sent some small seeds with little tails to meet an egg inside of the mother. I am sure that I was always given this correct information, instead of some of the silly stories other children had from their parents.

I knew that the seeds came from the penis of the father. When I looked at my father naked once, he even explained the parts of his sex organ to me, and I thought it was a very natural thing to know. I was only six years old when he did that. But when I was eight I learned about its being stiff by accidently seeing my mother and father fucking.

After looking at them for some moments, I greatly shocked them by asking, "What are you doing, Papa"? They sent me away very quickly, and I knew from their voices it was not my place to be there. When I sat quietly at our table for breakfast, my mother and father talked very kindly about what I had seen. They told me that they were making love with each other and were not fighting as I told them I thought. I was so happy to learn that they were not fighting that I gave little attention to the importance of what I had seen as sexual knowledge. I understood them when they said that it was something that should only be done alone and that children should be nice and let their parents be in private. I know they would often do it in the mornings, especially on weekends, and I always remembered not to bother them.

DISCUSSION   *This parental behavior would not be approved by all parents, especially most American parents. How should parents handle a child who observes sexual intercourse between others? What do you think are the psychological consequences of such observation? What are some of the psychological consequences of various parental reactions?*

When I learned sexual knowledge in this way, I was brought to understand the natural feelings about fucking. Knowing all of these sexual explanations in some detail did not make me feel different from my classmates. Like Gloria's boy classmates, they would often tell sex stories and use the sex words the teachers did not like, but there was no mystique about such things for my girlfriends and me, and especially me. I knew about it all, but it did not lead to anything sexual in my life. I did not even play any sex games with other children.

Through all my childhood I was quite happy. Most of the boys and girls in my school were very nice with me. I did not have a brother or sister, so much of my time was spent with other children from my school. Until I was nine or ten years old, I would play a lot with my dolls and with other girls, who would come to my house for such games. My mother was always happy to be nice with my friends. I could talk with her about anything, and perhaps even some of my friends thought that she was nicer than some of their own mothers. She would take my friends and me to many places good for children.

When I was eleven, my mother and father got divorced. For my father it was another woman who brought an end to the marriage. He fell into the trap of romance and could not get out. Soon after he married this woman, they gave me a stepbrother. It was a tragedy in our lives, especially for my father, who divorced this woman after only two years to return to my mother. Only when I see my stepbrother at home on some weekends do I remember this bad time in my teen years. This woman was always bothering us and trying to get my father to return to her, and my poor stepbrother was used in a very unhappy way. I like him very much and just love to take care of him when he visits. He is such a sweet boy, with a very happy face, despite his troubles with his mother. About his sexual learning I can say nothing.

When I was twelve, I went to a party where there were boys. It was the custom that when you became that old the birthday party would have boys as well as girls. At the beginning it was just that. The boys would come to the parties, eat the cakes and candies, and make a great deal of noise. But by the time we were thirteen the parties began to change. Usually they were at night, and the parents would let us have music and low lights, and there would be dancing for those who liked. At some of these parties the parents would let us alone entirely, and then the kissing games would start. I had a very good time right from the very beginning. When it was time for my fourteenth birthday, I had already had six boyfriends, but it did not mean very much to say they were boyfriends. We were always together in groups and never did more than kissing and petting. The kissing was without much meaning then.

My fourteenth year was filled with new experiences. At the beginning, my menstruation came. It was a little after most of my girlfriends had begun. I was happy to have it begin, because it made me feel more mature. This year was also the time I had my first orgasm. It came from masturbation quite accidently while doing my schoolwork one night. I was in bed preparing for an examination when I put my hand down there and was fiddling a bit. I probably did not even know I was doing it at first, but suddenly there was the realization that I was feeling something especially nice, and even exciting, from touching myself with my hand in that way. I suddenly felt almost faint with pleasure and a pleasantness I had never known before. I wanted to find out what was happening to me, but it was difficult for me to discuss this very personal thing with my mother. I must have felt the sex taboo about this one thing. I did not know what to call masturbation until a little later, when I read a book about sex play in marriage.

When I was fifteen, I began to go with a boy from my school. Nils was a year older but had no more experience with girls than I

had with boys. We liked each other very much, and it was nice to
be with him. For our first six months together we only held hands
and kissed. We were always kissing and holding hands so much
that one of my classmates would call us funny names. But we liked
each other so much it was natural to want to tell our feelings to
each other in these touches and holdings, even at school. During
the summer we went to bed with each other, but there was no fucking between us that first time. It was something we both agreed to
do. The kissing and petting was very passionate. With our hands
and fingers we gave each other our first orgasm and was only stopped
by the mess upon my Nil's stomach at the end. My own orgasm was
much simpler, but yet more beautiful, from his fingers in me.

After this we made much the same kind of love through most
of the summer. We wanted to fuck with each other, but both of us
were scared of pregnancy. My fear was mostly because I understood
my father's misfortune so clearly. Finally it was to happen with Nils
just before we returned to school. We had sex on a blanket in a park
on a very warm night when it had gotten very late. He used a condom
and was very careful. For both of us it was the first time. I was
disappointed that I did not have an orgasm, but he was so quick it was
all over before I knew it. At least there was no painful tearing in
me, as I thought must take place. Perhaps my masturbation and our
sex play together had made me quite ready for his penis. In the next
four or five months we began to have sex with each other with much
more satisfaction for both of us. We could talk about what we did and
did not like to do.

DISCUSSION   *Usually Swedish and Danish students can freely discuss
with each other their sexual feelings and what is and is
not satisfying. Are American adolescents likely to communicate with each other with such frankness and
candor? What factors inhibit sexual communication
between some individuals?*

During the summer Nils and I did not see as much of each
other. He was away working for two months. Each time we met it
was to have sex, which I think we both missed very much. But I
also began to think about how good it would be to come to know some
other boys when he was away. I was of the mind that I had closed
myself off from other boys, with the result that I could not know
fully what human love could be. And so it was that Nils and I talked
some of coming out of our shell with each other and letting ourselves
be with others. We had a very good talk. I worried that Nils would
be hurt, but that was not the case at all. When he had been away, he

had gone dancing with another girl. Now he had become free to do
the other things, and I was feeling quite free to begin something
new for myself. When it came time for Nils to begin the university,
it was left between us as only a warm friendship, and so it is for
the present.

DISCUSSION   *How does Maren's experience compare with the more
casual dating behavior of Gloria in contributing to
emotional and social development? What are the advantages and disadvantages of so complete a heterosexual
relationship at this age?*

When Nils was gone, the boys in my school all seemed to
know what had changed. During my last year I was with many boys
of all kinds, but I went to bed with only two of them—Erik for the
winter, and Carl for the spring. Both of them were very nice. They
were good sports about everything and had much experience with
many of my friends. But with them there was not the same relationship as between Nils and myself. They were with many different
girls but did not do very much sexually with them, from what I could
learn. It is not very good to talk about boys together, as if they
were the same, but in many ways it is hard for me to see very much
difference in how we were together.

From the beginning of my time with Erik I was taking pills,
so I no longer had any fears of pregnancy. It was arranged with our
clinic as soon as Erik had invited me to go to a party with his friends.
I must admit that I was quite eager to go to bed with him. Since Nils,
there had been nothing for over two months. We went to bed with
each other at least every week for about four months. There were
always parties and gatherings of friends on the weekends. It seems
funny now how much of our concern went into planning how we were
going to find a nice place for sex when the parties were over. Not
once did we fail, but it was also not the very best situation.

Erik did not end suddenly for me, but then Carl came into
my life, in a very innocent way at first. Carl and I would occasionally study together at school. He was not only handsome, but very
proficient in mathematics. He and I were to go to a party together.
I told Erik, but it was of no consequence to him. I did not really
think that it would cause a serious change in my direction with Erik,
but it did. We went to bed with each other the very first night we
could arrange it.

As soon as I came to the university, I was through with
these boys from the town. During my first few months I was very
lonely in Copenhagen, but gradually I began to know some of my
classmates and fellow students better. I finally went with them to
parties and was asked to go dancing with them at the clubs. One
of the boys was Jon. I went to bed with him once when, again, I
had become very unsettled about not having had much luck in finding someone I could really like. It was a very good experience in
learning how meaningless such a contact with a man can be for me.
There was nothing wrong with Jon, except I did not feel very much
about him. But Jon was important for another reason. He was to
introduce me to Björn, who has been my lover ever since we met.

Björn and I have lived together for the past fourteen
months in a very good relationship. It seems very silly for me to
describe us in any sexual way. Of course, we get along fine. With
Björn sex is something very clever. He can joke and make light of
it, like no one else I know. He thinks Gloria is crazy, and it is
impossible, in his view, to compare healthy Danes with such people.
I do not believe Gloria is crazy at all, but I do feel that the comparison between us is difficult. She has locked herself in a box away
from sex. Until she lets herself out, who can say what she will
become? Our stories are not yet complete. For myself, I look
forward to many new relationships before I come to feel that I want
to spend my life with one person and perhaps have some children.
Björn understands this perfectly well. I feel we are very lucky to
be with each other for now.

chapter 8

Norman, Johan, and Erik

NORMAN

Norman's commentary provides an opportunity to examine some elements of male sexuality in American society psychologically and sociologically. In him it is possible to see something of social and sexual frustration and anxiety, and the ways that sexual defense mechanisms can rush into battle to snatch the self-concept from defeat. Many of Norman's sexual values and norms seem to be remarkably consistent from childhood to adulthood; the content of his experiences with the opposite sex is almost predictable. He embodies the double standard, attitudes of male supremacy, and the pattern of using sex to express hostility to enhance his masculinity. Norman is still far away from knowing how to use sexual feelings and behavior to fulfill needs for social intimacy. The fact that he is a little older than most of our other Americans provides an opportunity to see some of the more enduring consequences of the adolescent learning.

Although the idea of discussing my sex life is very unusual, I think I am going to have a ball doing it. I've never stopped to sort

it out before. I will try my best to bring out the events that have
made me so horny during my brief, but enjoyable, twenty-three
years of living and loving.

I was in the second or third grade when I started getting
the first flashes of turning on to girls. I remember my first female
friend, Tammy. Watching the older kids at school holding hands
and kissing made the two of us go off after school and do the same
thing. Although I had forgotten all about this until now, I feel I was
definitely aroused by her sexually. What I mean to say is that my
dick (that's what we called our cocks at that age) would get hard and
point straight out after kissing with her like the older kids were
doing. At that time I didn't know what caused the hardness, but
after a few experiences with her, I began to associate the girl with
my throbbing dick. The idea of being turned on by a girl in a sexual
way jelled in my mind even before I threw out the stork theory.
Part of the problem in understanding was that I had gotten used to
having my dick get hard for other reasons besides girls. Apparently
Mom had noticed the same thing, because I would get dirty looks
from her when she would see it hard. I remember her telling me
that I shouldn't play with myself.

At this age the stork theory went under, after kids at school
had made me curious where babies really came from. I don't know
that I really swallowed the idea of a bird's delivering a baby, but it
had been the only answer to my few questions about it at home. I
now figure that my belief in the stork was shaky, and the important
part of the story was that I shouldn't be interested in the whole business, because it was adult stuff. Only when I began to hear the
word fuck and some of the new theories about babies did I begin to
pay much attention to the topic. I was probably like most kids at
that age. When your parents told you what they thought was good
for you, you didn't press them further.

I was thrown a little off the track when I was nine or so. I
still remember very clearly a drawing in the rest room of our
neighborhood theater. There was a man with no clothes on and a
big dick. He was just standing there, and a woman was sucking on
the end of it. The thing that is so significant is that underneath the
drawing was the word fuck. For a long time I had the idea that this
is what fucking meant, that somehow from taking his dick in her
mouth the woman could have a baby. I was actually shocked by this,
as I could not imagine my parents' doing such a thing. It also
occurred to me that it could be the reason I never had any brothers

or sisters, if that was what they had to go through. I stopped asking about getting any right then and there. This picture was in the rest room for over a year, and I checked it out every time I went to see a movie.

Finally the facts about fucking were clarified by my friends at school. I don't think it made much difference to me to learn the true facts. It was still dirty, and I just could not see my parents willingly doing it with each other, except for the one time when they had decided that they wanted a baby.

Except for using the usual dirty words with my friends, nothing much of a sexual nature had happened to me since Tammy. Then came another significant phase of my homemade sex education. Although most of my friends were my same age, I had a few who were older. We were sitting around on the school playground, and they were talking about fucking girls. Then the talk shifted to talk about jacking off. It was part of a joke, and I didn't understand what the guy was talking about, so I asked him. The other guys laughed about my ignorance, but gradually explained. At first it sounded like something weird a guy would do to himself. But then it sounded like fucking, except you didn't need a girl to do it. All of these stories and jokes from the guys began to give me some new ideas about fucking. Not only was it dirty, but apparently it was a lot of fun for a guy.

A short time after hearing about masturbation I tried it a few times. When I would wake up in the morning with a stiff dick, I would just lie in bed and stroke it. It felt good, but it was a few more months before it resulted in anything. Soon I heard a few other things about jacking off from other friends. They all seemed to make fun of the practice and people who did it. I think the main thing was about how it makes a guy queer. Kids thought two of the teachers at my school were queer and jack-offs. After that shock and backlash had worn off, I got back to doing it again. The next thing to happen to me was the suffering of my first orgasm. The first time I ended with an ejaculation I thought I had broken something in me. I was really scared and wondered if I was going to die. Of course, I couldn't say a thing to my parents about it, and I didn't want my friends to know either, because they would think I was becoming queer. For about six months I didn't play around with myself at all. The guilt and fear were so big. Finally, one of my friends mentioned something about shooting your load. What a break. At last my ejaculation made sense, and I was back on it in no time. By then I was twelve and even more developed sexually. I tried not to do it as much as I would have liked. I practiced as much control as I could manage. The guilt was pretty heavy then.

Now that I had achieved orgasm, I needed to express it with the opposite sex. This is when I had my first urge to fuck a broad, but, to my displeasure, none was to be had. How could there have been, considering my shyness? What older girl was going to let a twelve-year-old ball her? The idea of doing it with girls in my class made me sick. I didn't like any of them, and there was no word out yet on any of them wanting to do more than dance and kiss, which was of little interest to me.

Near the end of the eighth grade, a girl named Kim started telephoning me. She was from another school nearby. I found out that she was a friend of a girl in my class, but a year older. Other guys had gotten the word about her, and some of them gave her the name Boobie Although my parents were pushed out of shape over the idea of an older girl's calling me, I agreed to meet her at the theater one Friday night. She was my first date. I figured with her reputation I had nothing to lose. She turned out to be okay for what I had in mind. I probably could have screwed her in the lobby but was satisfied with what I managed to get.

I slipped my hand under her blouse without a flinch from her. She seemed to want me to do this, so who was I to stop? I played with her bra, which contained her boobs, but didn't take it off. After all, we were in a theater with people all around trying to enjoy a movie, and here I was, thirteen years old, trying to make a chick. Also, I didn't know how to take a bra off.

Boobie and I met at the theater about four or five other times for much the same action. The last few times I got enough guts to call her on the phone. Getting past her mother was a big drag. Apparently she was strictly boy-crazy and had to be watched. The last few times in the theater I was able to work my hand under her dress and feel the edges inside of her panties. For the last date we had, I was determined to give her the finger if I could, but when I finally made it to my objective with my hand, I got turned off. Her panties were all wet. I thought she had urinated. For the rest of the movie I worried what people would say to us if it had gotten through her dress. I also couldn't wait to get to the John to wash my hand. I was even worried that I might get a disease. I sat through the movie hoping there would be soap at the washbasin. There wasn't, so I had to watch my hand for signs of infection. What a mind-blower! Kim went her own way after our last date. Probably older guys were balling with her that summer. I suppose she was as good as anyone to get me started with girls.

DISCUSSION   *What do you think accounts for Norman's disdainful attitude toward this girl? Does he reflect traditional American male sex values and norms here?*

During the summer between the eighth and ninth grades I went out with Mary. Her problem was that she was hung up on religion, the store-front variety, but despite this hang-up she loved to make out and be petted. From her I learned the skill of removing bras, so I could get to her hot titties. One night her youth group was having a beach party, and I was invited to go with her. The leader wasn't too excited until Mary told him that she was trying to save me. I didn't know what she was even talking about, but was glad to be able to go along. The beach party turned out to be dull and shitty. Instead of making out on the beach, there was a lot of praying and singing of religious songs. Mary wouldn't leave the group for a walk down the beach, but promised to make out later. Later turned out to be on the bus. It ended as one of the most embarrassing incidents of my life. When the lights in the bus were out and all the other kids were singing, we started some heavy necking. She put my hand under her blouse and wanted me to commence petting her. I was awfully leery of the whole thing because of all the people sitting around us, but went ahead anyway. After about twenty minutes of this heavy stuff, the lights in the bus suddenly went on at a stoplight. He caught us real good, and everyone could see my hand up the front of her blouse. He gave some cutting speech about how we were expected to act like Christians and then made sure he left the lights on for the rest of the trip, which made everyone pissed. I felt really low, but Mary was even lower, because she knew all the kids. This was our last date, because she probably felt too ashamed to go with me anywhere again. Actually I didn't mind, because there were other fish to fry.

After Mary came Betty. She was quite a girl, and I think I even had a little love for her. She was short, compact, and had a fantastic body for thirteen. She used to baby-sit a lot, and naturally I would help her. All of her baby-sitting was at one house, where the kids were quite young. After they were in bed, I would arrive. These people were always out very late, so there was time to have a lot of fun. Usually after watching TV for a while, we would make it to the bedroom and make out on the people's bed, on top of but not under the spread. I never balled her, but I had a terrific sexual time with her. After the first time, I managed to get her panties off. I had my first honest-to-goodness look at a girl's hairy cunt and could also feel it with my fingers, although I was able to only get one finger just part way into her. She rubbed my dick inside my

pants. For some reason I did not want to take it out, although now
I could shoot myself for that. Betty taught me that the wetness
between a girl's legs was normal when she got excited. Away went
the myth I had been harboring since feeling Boobie in the movie.
Cunts are not just hot, they're juicy. I found out from Betty what
made a girl hot but had to wait for another two years before I could
use my knowledge to its final advantage.

DISCUSSION   *Could Norman have been positively influenced at this age
by a Scandinavian program of sex education? Do his
attitudes and behavior suggest that sex education should
include social and psychological aspects of human sexuality as well as biological knowledge about reproduction
and sexual functioning?*

High school more or less separated me from Betty. She
was still in the eighth grade. During my first two years I dated
four girls, but none of them for very long. Betty had spoiled me.
None of the girls I dated during this time let me go as far as she
did. I might have gone further with Betty, but she started hanging
out with another stud. Other girls who had the hots and would let
guys get into them usually dated only the ones who drove cars. So
without a car you were out to lunch, as far as most of them went.
For this period of my life I had to be content with what I could get.
Until my junior year I just went to some parties, some school
dances, some concerts at the Bowl, and was left with some necking
and a few quick feels.

My sex life got quite a new shot when I started dating Joan
(remember that name!). I had turned seventeen, and we were both
juniors. We met in a typing class. She was kind of a weird chick
but had a nice body and seemed to have a lot of experience behind
her. I was still hearing stories about her two years after they
happened. She was probably a good example of what had happened
to a lot of girls from my class earlier in high school. While my
friends and I were waiting to turn sixteen, the girls our age were
balling all the older guys.

After a couple of years of playing it cool with the chicks,
it was good to find one who liked a good time with the skin. We
went together for the rest of my junior year. On our second date
we walked down to the beach after a movie and there started a great
sex relationship, which unfortunately always stopped short of fucking. She had balled with other guys but claimed to be reformed.
She had gotten a big scare out of nearly getting pregnant, so would

never let me get into it. But we did everything else. The last
three months she would go down on me, and I would do the same
for her after a while. I had given up trying to convince her to
ball, even though I had rubbers with me all the time. At the
beginning of the summer we called it quits because I wanted it
and she wouldn't. I'm not one who would rape a girl to get it.
During the summer she and her family moved to Indiana, and a
year later I got an invitation to her wedding.

During the summer I met Dorothy at a party. She was
an anxious chick sexually, so after a few dates we got going pretty
well. I finally got my own car near the end of the summer after
getting a job and paying my dad for the extra cost of the insurance.
The car was mine for only a week when it became the set for my
FIRST PIECE OF ASS! Making Dorothy was a very simple operation. We parked in the Manhattan Beach lot one night, with all the
other dudes who were making the scene. She was scared, but not
virgin. I was a bit nervous at first because I knew all along what
I was going to try to do with her. First the necking, then the next
stages of kissing her breasts, and with the fingering of her cunt I
knew she and I were on our way together. After my dick was out
of my pants, she really got hot. After a few front-seat gymnastics,
I pushed it into her. God! What have I been missing, I thought.
It was from here on out that I knew I would always need girls for
something, and this was it.

The summer following graduation produced one of the most
fantastic experiences of my life. It was a wild summer with three
of my classmates from school. We thought we knew it all. After
all the parties, the sex, and beer, there didn't seem to be much
more for us to learn. While I had had a lot of late nights with
Dorothy, I had never stayed out all night, so this was next on the
list of things to do.

By the way, my parents had been great to me all through
high school, except for hassles about the car. They pretty much
let me on my own. I'm glad I never got any sex education from
them, because it all would have been wrong. I respected their
curfew and stayed out of trouble, but after turning eighteen in the
summer, I felt free as a bird, so to speak. The far-out night I'm
going to describe really took place, and I don't think I'll ever forget it. So maybe it is important in my history.

Because some of the parents of the other guys were a little
uptight about staying out too late (two of them were still seventeen),
we worked out a story for them. I told my parents that I was staying

at Jim's house for the night, and Jim told his folks he was staying at my house. Dennis and Pete did the same.

We had no real plan except to drink a lot of beer and stay out all night and see what the action was in as many places as we could truck off to. An older guy bought three six-packs of beer for us. We drank all the cold beer that our bladders could hold in one of the beach parking lots. The rest we drank warm, as the night wore on.

After hitting all the spots in Hermosa and Manhattan, including a few drive-ins in Redondo, we decided to hit Hollywood and Sunset, to see what was happening. Needless to say, much to our displeasure, not a damn thing was going on, it being a week day. So far, at midnight there had been just a lot of driving, warm beer, and stopping every mile to piss. We stopped at two bars but were turned away at the door for being under age. Near two o'clock we were still driving around after stopping for some hamburgers at a coffee shop.

We drove down La Cienega Boulevard, now in Beverly Hills, with Jim riding shotgun and Pete and Dennis in the back. We were at a red light when Jim and Dennis started talking to this woman in a black Lincoln. It was crazy, but she looked interested in us, so at the next light the conversation continued. After the second light she agreed to pull over in the middle of the next block. I parked the car, and we all piled out to see just what we had landed. I think we were all bombed out of our minds.

By the time I had reached her car, Jim was getting into the front seat. In no time at all he had his arm around her, while the rest of us crowded around outside so as not to scare her too much. She was a little bombed herself. But she didn't look too bad for a woman in about the mid-thirties. She was blonde and big-busted. After a few minutes of quick planning, she agreed to drive with Jim to a side street nearby, where we parked both cars. Dennis, Pete, and I stayed in my car. It was dark, but we could see with our straining vision that Jim was balling her after about ten minutes. He must have finished her after only five minutes. When the light went on in her car, the three of us rushed up to see who was next. After Jim got out, there were a few words, and then Dennis got in to replace Jim. Another ten minutes or so, and the light went on again. Then she insisted on going but wanted to take all of us for some breakfast. It was a little after three o'clock before we landed in a coffee shop. In the bright lights we could all see that she really was in her thirties. But the whole scene was so wild we couldn't believe it and didn't want to end it.

When she went to the John, we decided to keep it going as long as we could. Unfortunately Pete had gotten sick from all the beer and had all but crashed. When we left the coffee shop, it was almost four o'clock. Jim and Dennis agreed to get her to take me on, if they could watch. The plan was to leave Pete in my car because he was sick and drive somewhere with her in hers where I could ball her. It worked out just that way, although I personally think she had almost had enough of us after she began to sober up a little. She paid the bill for the half-eaten breakfasts and was saying goodby when Plan X went into motion. After some weak excuses, she agreed to drive up into the Hollywood Hills for the final act of the night.

All the way up into the hills I was a wreck. All I could think about was that I'm going to be screwing a woman I didn't even know. When we found a dark section of street, she stopped. (1) She undid her bra and blouse. (2) She slipped off her panties and pulled her dress up around her waist. And (3) she reached over and took my dick out of my pants. None of the stuff about foreplay I later read applied to this case. Fortunately, I was as hard as a rock in seconds. With Jim and Dennis sitting in the back with their eyeballs popping out of their heads, I got on top of her and balled her. She must have had a lot of kids, because her cunt was really loose. Of course, maybe Jim and Dennis had made her a little slippery. After I came, she wanted to drive us back to my car, even though the other guys wanted to have "seconds." They had their dicks out in the back seat and were ready, but no dice. We got back to the car and thanked her for a great time. After she left, we realized we didn't even know her name. So the four of us called her Sweetie-Pie. I suppose I'll wonder the rest of my life whatever happened to her.

After this experience things more or less returned to normal for me. I met Sharon through a friend. We went with each other for about two months. From the beginning we got along real well sexually. She liked to ball as much as I did. She had a beautiful body, but absolutely nothing in her head. Comparing her with some of the girls at the college, I was forced to conclude that I was starting to torture myself with her around my neck. But I must say you could never criticize her body and shape.

After Sharon I had my first virgin. Joyce was in my history class, and, after a few weeks of talking with her about history, we got on with other things. I took her out to a movie, but for some

reason I decided to use a little class with this one. We worked
into it gradually, mostly by just talking about sex. When she told
me she was a virgin, I was a little surprised because of her talk.
On our next date she invited me to her house after going to a movie
in Hollywood. Her parents were gone for the night, but she was
supposed to be staying with a girlfriend, who agreed to cover for her.

Balling with a virgin turned out to be a little more than I
expected. After some heavy preliminaries, I finally put it to her.
She wasn't fooling when she said she was a virgin. She bled all over
the sheets, and it was even rough on me. Unlike Sweetie-Pie, or
even the others, she was as tight as a keyhole. I got off finally. It
was a month before we tried again. Fortunately, it was much better
for both of us. After the second time our sex relations became
regular, whenever we could arrange it. She refused to do it in the
car with me, which sort of pissed me, because I think balling in a
car is its own trip, in a way.

The end of the first semester in college brought me my
first setback in school. I got a load of Ds and an F. Then I decided
to join the army for three years. Joyce stayed in school. We talked
of getting married, but I couldn't get serious about it. While I was
in basic training, she got her own apartment, so we could be together
when I could come home on leaves. That move began to get me a
little pissed off, because it assumed that I was really that serious
about her, which I wasn't. Actually, my joining the army may have
been my way to get away from her. There wasn't that much wrong
with her and the way we got along, now that I think about it. But I
do know that I did not want to get married. Within the next four
months we drifted apart—less writing between us and less time
spent at her apartment when I was home on leaves. I also found
that other guys were coming over when I was not there, so the end
came without feeling a loss.

During the next three years I grew up pretty fast, like all
guys in the service. After finishing my special school at Fort Ord
I went to Europe for eighteen months. I had probably two dozen
whores in Germany, not counting the repeats. It was just a way for
sexual release. Fortunately I escaped from the rape of VD. I can't
say I particularly enjoyed the whore scene. The girls were usually
so mechanical and phony. All those faked orgasms from them make
me laugh. As for the army, I was just putting in my time. Europe
was a ball, but I was glad to get stationed back in the States for the
end of my duty. The chicks here are a lot more fun.

When I returned from the army, I got a full-time job and

just waited to begin college again in the fall. I was amazed how the beach crowd had changed. Half of my buddies had gotten married and even started families.

Remember the name Joan (I told you not to forget)? Once again, after more than four years, I met up with her. She was back from Indiana and divorced from the guy she had married out there. I was cordial enough to her and made it clear that I didn't have any resentment. I took her phone number and knew she was really excited about the prospects of a date sometime. Finally we went out. Dinner, a movie, the whole bit. Because I was back living with my folks and she was staying with relatives, we went to the Blue Pacific Motel and stayed for the night. The whole night went beautifully. Her husband had trained her very well from the point I had left her. Her vagina seemed to suck on my penis. It was outstanding. In the morning she told me how much she really loved me and how she had missed me through all those years. That was great, and I was hot to begin the whole relationship all over. But then the blow came. She told me she had two kids staying with her ex-husband's parents. That finished it. I'm sorry, but that trip was not mine. I never saw her again or even made an attempt to. I think she understood how I felt when I told her that morning that I didn't think it would work out.

Shortly after this I met Kitty, a very striking, good-looking girl. I was immediately infatuated with her. I have been seeing her on and off since then. The first few times we went to bed, I didn't even screw her. I wanted to test myself to see if I could still get emotionally involved with someone. All of my whoring in Europe and then the rerun with Joan were making me think a little about the fact that I might have some problems in relating to girls in an emotional way. They had all become just hunks of pussy to wrap around my dick. Finally we became physically intimate in the usual way, but I discovered that she was really a bum piece. Kitty is a wonderful person now as a friend, but balling her is like doing it with the dead. I've tried to get her head straightened out, but now I have learned to stay away from the topic. She thinks I'm a sex maniac, but I know I'm not much different in my sex drive from most of the guys I know, and certainly those I knew in the army. Ass was all you talked about overseas.

DISCUSSION   *Does Norman's sexual identification with his army buddies help him rationalize his sexual behavior and feelings about this girl? Does she probably threaten his image of himself as a normal and virile male? Do you think Norman would tend to project his sexual inadequacies onto others if he could? To what extent may his army experience have reinforced his earlier social and sexual development? What are some of his problems in testing his ability to become "emotionally involved with someone"? What may have caused him to express this objective?*

When my relationship with Kitty went sour, I went on the bar circuit. I'll tell you, the pickups practically have to be beaten away from your car with sticks. At "last call" some of these places look like a scramble for the last screw, as if the world was going to end the next day. The only thing that saves me is that I'm staying with my folks and the girls usually turn to ice when they find out it's either their apartment or none. I don't dig the idea of checking into motels for just screwing a chick. It's all over too soon, and what you have left is the memory of the tab.

This past year back at the studies has been the best academic showing of my life. I must be drinking the right beer. Actually, I have been studying hard and just taking the girls as they come along. I have started to mature a little and see some things in life besides sex, but I know a lot of soul-searching is still needed. I feel my sex life thus far has been very normal, except for my army experience. I am just about ready to get into something a little far out. A buddy of mine at the bar thinks he may have a little group sex figured out for us. I don't know that I really care to try that scene, but I sort of figure if it comes along I might give it a little whirl. What the hell do any of us have to lose if it doesn't work out? By now I can probably handle anything. Right?

DISCUSSION   *Or wrong?*

JOHAN   *Johan's appraisal of Norman is unusually temperate. He seems to have been entertained by Norman to some extent, but he is also moved to evaluate what Norman was really saying about himself. The differences between Johan and Norman are many of the differences between the Swedish and American sexual cultures, especially the male outlooks. Johan points out how adolescence has been important in providing opportunities for learning adult sex roles and expressing mature forms of sexual behavior. His heterosexual relationships have been reported along lines that seem very typically Swedish.*

My first reaction to Norman is that I feel much more healthy and free in my sexual attitudes and behavior than this American boy. I can see that we are very different. My life at twenty-one seems much more mature than his, though he is several years older. His friends and most of the girls he has fucked seem very boring to me. It is hard for me to believe that such a childish person could be studying in an American university. But perhaps that is the way it is, having seen many films about your country. He does not care about women, except to fuck them without concern for their feelings. Perhaps such behavior is not too unusual when one is quite young and very excited about learning about sex, but it should begin to change when you get older.

I don't think Norman has been to bed with more women than I, as I count them up, but I am sure that my experiences were quite different in their meaning to me and my girlfriends. This does not mean that I was always happy with a girl. Both of us would sometimes become very sad, but we always knew this was happening together and would discuss our need for a change of relationship. Norman seems to be very impressed with his ability to move from bed to bed without feeling for the girls he has fucked. Girls, to him, are little more than a substitute for his hand as he jacks off, except he seems to have more guilt about his hand than about the girls he throws on the junk heap. I am not some kind of Swedish angel, for I have also done many wrong things with girls I have known, and they to me, but I am sure of one difference between Norman and me: I am not proud of my mistakes, as he is.

I cannot remember my earliest years very much. My family has always lived in the same part of Stockholm, although we moved several times to better apartments. My sister and I were always well cared for in every way. Both my mother and my father were very kind and took great interest in our schooling and play. My father always encouraged me in sports, and I became quite good in both hockey and basketball because of his help. My mother always worked outside the home as a secretary in a bank, but there was never any feeling of her being missed, as my sister was older and did much of the housework after school and looked after me until I was older and had my own housekey, beginning in the second grade.

About my first sex experiences, I do remember when I was five or six that some small boys in our yard, where I was playing, were talking about how babies came. They said that they came from their mother's stomachs after their father put their cocks into their mother's cunts and pissed into them. I didn't believe that and probably thought that it was too stupid to ask my parents about. I didn't understand how it could be done, and I also felt that piss was ugly. My mother had told me that there were a lot of germs in piss, so I could not see the connection between that and making babies. But fortunately I never did have to hear anything so silly as a stork's bringing babies.

I do not remember exactly when I began to become interested in sexual things again. I was not particularly interested in any sexual way with my sex organs or those of my parents or sister. We freely let each other see each other without clothes at home, especially until my sister became older, when she started to cover herself more from my view. I knew most of the basic facts about how children were born and what fucking was from what my playmates were able to tell me about the time I began school. Also, my sister, who was four years older, taught me a great deal. I learned a lot from several sex education books my parents gave my sister when she was about eleven. My sister helped me understand this material, although I learned a lot from the pictures without her help. When I was about nine I could read these books quite well, so what I was taught in school about sex seemed rather childish and incomplete. I do not remember asking my parents about sexual matters, although I can recall my parents' asking me questions to see what I knew. I remember my sister's telling my parents at dinner that it was not necessary for them to ask me anything because she had given me her books and answered all of my questions. That ended my sex schooling at home. It is unfortunate that things about human sex were not taught better in school. It is foolish to think that children cannot understand these things as part of life. Is it better to think that babies come from piss?

One morning, when I was eight years old, I awoke and had an erection. I was surprised about it and did not understand. I did nothing about it. I never tried to jack off until much later, although I soon understood from my sister's books that my erection was the result of being sexually excited somehow. Other times my cock would get hard from fondling it or having tight clothes press against it, but I did little but look at it and think how nice it was to see it getting bigger and longer like my father's. This was enough for me then.

I was about twelve one day when I was home from school alone. I remember the day because my feelings about my cock suddenly changed. This was the day it became especially pleasurable to jack off. I remember that the harder I grabbed my cock, the more pleasurable it was. I kept jacking off all morning, and suddenly it was just enormously pleasurable. I felt my body strain, and some wet thing came out from my cock. I thought that this was absolutely marvelous, and from that day I have been jacking off regularly, with a couple of days between times, although each time I usually do it several times. Today I'll do it without thinking of my other sex life—even though my girlfriend and I have many good times petting and fucking with each other. I never have had any guilt about it, as Norman seems to have. Perhaps this is because it is not only harmless but even useful to jack off, as I have often read in very good books.

DISCUSSION   *Johan appears to have interpreted masturbation as a normal and pleasurable experience, one that does not cause guilt feelings. To what extent does this experience, as learned and defined by Johan, contribute to positive sexual feelings and the capacity to enjoy sexual behavior with others later, and give the adolescent a safe and satisfying means for fulfilling the needs of the sex drive? How may the same discovery lead to negative social and sexual outcomes for less fortunate individuals?*

When I was about thirteen and fourteen, I was able to get myself some pornographic books and pictures, which I used to read and look at while jacking off. My friends and I would exchange them, and among us all we had quite a collection. One of my friends had an older brother who would buy them for us, although we did not have much money for such things. All of my friends were jacking off, and we thought it was quite natural to do so. We even showed some of this to girls in our class who liked to look at it with us. Even later I bought some porno books called Love, which my girlfriend and I would read together. It was very exciting for both of us to do this, although we would only kiss and pet afterwards. It was very pleasant to feel her cunt while she stroked my cock.

Having this experience was frustrating for both of us, but we were too shy to do more. One of our older friends had gotten a girl in our class pregnant, and we were very frightened about this for ourselves. I was very unsure about using a condom, although we talked about it several times. Each time she convinced me that it would not be safe enough, and I respected her feelings in this matter.

We seemed always to be together at parties and at school when I was not in sports. All of our friends regarded us as lovers, although some of our quarrels made it seem otherwise at times. For fun we would meet after school with other students at a coffee bar near our homes. Listening to all the new juke box music, eating, and telling jokes was a very popular pastime. We would often go at night to the centrum to see a film. And of course we always had a very good time at parties. Unlike Norman it never occurred to me to try to ask a girl I did not know well to go anywhere with me. While it is true that I was satisfied with the girl I was in love with, I did not know anyone then who would think seriously of looking for a girl to just fuck. Most Swedish girls would probably think that Norman had just escaped from a lunatic hospital.

At a basketball training camp I met the first girl I fucked. She was twenty, and I was seventeen. Perhaps I was too hard on Norman, considering this experience, for it did not have the kinds of things about it that I feel are important for a good love relationship. Some love for this girl developed after I had fucked with her. Perhaps I even forced some of my feeling for her. I thought I should love her because we had fucked.

I remember that night well. We had been dancing after basketball training. Birgitta followed me to my room, where we spent the whole night together. After lying for a long time on my bed hugging and kissing, I surprised myself by saying that we should take our clothes off. It was not long before she took hold of my cock and pushed it into her cunt. I thought it was wonderful to fuck and come inside her. She had been taking birth-control pills and was very experienced, from what she told me.

Each night she came to my room, and we did it. As a physical experience it was a very beautiful awakening of a desire I had felt for a long time. However the relationship was not a very good one because I knew that the difference in our ages would not permit us to have much in common at that time. Also, my friends knew that we had been going to bed, and I worried what they might say to girls back at school. I tried very much to like this girl and wrote many letters to her in which I almost falsely told her how much I liked her. I tried very hard to love her, but finally realized that I was just being sentimental over the fact that she had been my first girl for fucking. After a few months her letters stopped, and then I became tired of writing.

Playing basketball was a very good way to meet girls. They would often come to the games, and after showering the boys would often be invited to parties at the homes of girls whose parents were away. During my last two years in high school I got to know many girls. When I was not with a girl, I would spend most of my time with my friends. Sitting and talking with them in restaurants became very enjoyable and a very common way of passing the time. We often talked about girls and were always eager to have them join us. For some reason it became less important for me to get a girl to fuck. I think I had finished proving to myself that I could be all right in bed. As I mentioned before, I do not have any bad feelings about jacking off when I feel it will be pleasant. For these two years I was content to go to school parties and dances. Much of my interest at this time was in sports. I learned nothing new about sex until the summer after I graduated.

DISCUSSION   *Would the social and sexual patterns of behavior Johan has described thus far indicate that he and Norman were basically different in the biological intensity of their sex drives, or are the differences between them the result of social and psychological influences that can be identified in their commentaries?*

For three months I was in the military service. While this was not a very satisfying time, I met a very beautiful girl at a party while home on a leave. It soon became possible to see her every weekend, as the base was only thirty kilometers from her home. After my term of service we both started studying at the university. We are now living together in a small apartment, which is old, but quite pleasant in comparison to the places most student couples we know live. It is very quiet here, and there is no one to bother us. Occasionally friends will telephone, and we will sometimes invite them to visit. Most of our time is used for study, although other interests at the university sometimes attract us. Both of us have found our studies very difficult, as the professors give us much more work than we can possibly do well.

Our sex life is very good. We fuck a lot and have learned to be very free with each other. Each of us knows the other's body as well as our own. Whatever is pleasant for the other is what we do. My girl and I laughed when Norman had to announce finally in his statement that he now likes oral sex. He sounds so childish, as if he thinks that he has gone on to a new stage of being. It is probably wrong to laugh at Norman, because his life may turn out to be very unhappy in the end. Certainly he has made others sad and dissatisfied. He seems too happy going from girl to girl to ever stay with a single girl for long. Such a person would find it too difficult to make one girl happy. He is too busy trying to prove that he is a big guy to satisfy a normal woman. Such a small boy should grow up.

ERIK

Erik has lived most of his life in a small, tradition-oriented farming community in Jutland. His commentary shows clearly that not all areas of Scandinavia have been supportive of change in sexual values and norms. Erik's family and community are very conservative in their religious beliefs and practices, which inevitably has impact on sexual learning and behavior. His parents were stern and often unforgiving. Erik's initial encounters with sex all seem to have resulted in frustration or anxiety, but as a university student he finds much social and sexual satisfaction in an intimate relationship. This relationship contrasts starkly with his adolescence, which was apparently characterized by loneliness, feelings of unworthiness, and guilt. His reactions to Norman are often different from those expressed by Johan.

After reading Norman's sexual autobiography, which I enjoyed very much, I find my own life quite dull and uninteresting. I was raised on a small farm near the sea in northern Jutland with four older brothers and two younger sisters. Life was very simple compared to life in the city, and we had few luxuries, although food was always good and plentiful. All of us learned quite young

to work hard and contribute as much as we could to the family.
Both my mother and father were very religious and demanded that
we spend a lot of time reading the Bible, which I did not like to do.
I was often punished by my father, because I think he did not like
me as much as the other children. Even my mother often punished
me for things I could not do as well as my older brothers. The
ideas my parents had about sex until my sisters grew older could
have come only from the Bible.

        Of the years one to six I do not remember much. I recall
that I played with a girl from a neighbor farm whose name was
Jytte. She was my age, or perhaps a little older. Both of us were
punished often for being away from home too long. Once when we
were whipped, we were going to run away and even had bread
hidden away to take with us. But fortunately we never did go very
far, out of fear of our mothers.

        Jytte and I thought we both understood how babies were
made, as we had both watched animals fucking many times and had
seen them born. Also, I had often heard older boys talking about
going to bed with girls. I had seen the word for <u>fucking</u> written in
lonely places, and, although I could not read other words, I knew
what it meant because there were pictures of sex with it. I understood very fast that this word was one which I should not use at
home, for my mother punished me for asking her what it meant.

        One day when Jytte and I had been playing in the fields,
we agreed to try it. We found a big haystack, and there she pulled
down her pants. She had a tiny hole between her legs, and from
the hole I understood that this was where I should advance, but I
was not at all sexually excited. I remember her telling me to
make my cock stick out as soon as I had dropped my pants. She
could not understand why I could not make it straight by willing it
so. It was not embarrassing to me, but it was somewhat of a
puzzle for both of us. This was the first time in my life that I
ever wanted it to become hard. She pulled it very hard several
times, but nothing happened. While we were lying there having a
messy time of it, someone came, and before we could get on our
clothes we were surprised by Jytte's mother, who became
absolutely beside herself over what she had seen. I was dragged
home with Jytte, while she was being beaten with a thin stick her
mother found along the roadside. I was told to go home and tell
my mother exactly what we had been doing. I sat in a field for
several hours but finally walked home very slowly, full of re-
pentance and not too brave. By the time I had gotten home, our
sin was known. My mother also beat me, and I was forbidden to

play with Jytte for a fortnight.

Later that summer Jytte and I tried to do it again. This time I had discovered a very good hiding place, a very old building, that we called our house. Jytte and I would often go there when it rained. During one rainstorm we took off all our clothes and had fun running out of the building to see how wet we could get. When we tired of this, we agreed to try to fuck again. Again I did not have an erection, so we put on our clothes, but before we could leave, Jytte's father surprised us and forced us to confess our wrongdoing. He had seen us running in and out of the building without our clothes. He did not beat us but bawled us out, telling us not to do it again. Finally, after all of this trouble, we stopped having this kind of interest in one another.

When I was about twelve, I started to masturbate. I took a big interest in the obscenities that were written on the walls at school. I enjoyed using sex words in as much of my talk with other boys as I could. We had a lot of fun in our music class that year. While we were supposed to be singing very serious and solemn fatherland songs, we would substitute all kinds of dirty words in the texts. But this did not last long, as the teacher soon found out from the girls why they were giggling. Also, we grew tired of that and turned to other kinds of fun.

During this time another boy and I would go to his house to play around with each other's cocks. I had learned by this time that I could make mine hard by massaging it and looking at dirty pictures. Neither of us ever reached climax by playing with each other, but it was still very satisfying. I was always worried about being found out, but never so concerned that I missed a chance to do it. This homosexual activity with this boy stopped when he moved to Copenhagen.

I then heard from another friend that he knew a man who had some dirty pictures he would let us see. After my friend had made arrangements, we went to see him. He got his album out soon after we arrived and showed us the pictures. Most of them were of women who were naked except for ski boots. The man unbuttoned and got out a penis of great dimensions. He began to move it back and forth in fast tempo, and after a while some white stuff came out. I was rather surprised by what the man had done but was also a bit scared about the whole visit.

I was very curious about whether I could have an orgasm like his. The man had encouraged us to also take out our penises,

but we were both afraid. However at the first good opportunity to
be alone, I tried to have an orgasm by masturbation. The first
time I got a little bit afraid over my orgasm, with its cramp-like
pulls, but a desire to experience the enjoyment of it again got me
to continue masturbating rather regularly, even though I had a
strong feeling of guilt. During this period I had a few other sexual
times with other boys who were my friends. Such activities did not
last long, since we found them dull. Also, we worried what the
older boys would say if they knew about us.

DISCUSSION   *How do Erik's experiences and attitudes about masturbation compare to those of the other Scandinavian cases?
What factors do you feel account for these differences?*

    When I was thirteen, I was sent to a church summer camp.
Before long I was making little trips to one of the girls at night.
We used to walk away from the camp a little bit and find some good
bushes, and there we would lie kissing and hugging and having a
good time. I would steal my hand under her blouse, massaging
her tiny breasts. But neither of us wanted it to turn into more.
Every night that there was a chance to run away like this, we did.
I was so happy and excited with her, and she was with me, also, I
think. I did not know then that I would have one of the most terrible
experiences of my life doing this.

    The night before we went home, I was found by the camp
leader's wife with this girl. She had come to our bushes with a
lamp, which she suddenly shined upon us. She had seen my hands
on my girlfriend's naked breasts and had seen that my pants were
not zipped, although the girl had not yet touched my penis through
my underwear. My girlfriend became hysterical and cried for forgiveness and begged her not to tell the camp leader. I was sent
back to the boy's dormitory after she bawled me out. After I was
in bed, the camp leader came and bawled me out again and told all
the other boys what had happened. He took me from the dormitory
and made me stand in the cold for an hour in my pajamas and demanded that I pray to God for forgiveness. When he returned, I
was very cold, and I had been crying because of the trouble I had
caused my girlfriend. He then told me to take out my penis and
hold it before God and promise Him that I would never use it to
sin again. I was so frightened and sick inside that I did this, but
afterward I wished this man down into the blackest of hells.

    The following morning at breakfast the camp leader

addressed the whole camp very emotionally about sins of the flesh, and then he touched on our episode of the night before. My girlfriend and several other girls at her table began to cry, while all the boys and I sat in fear of the power of his words. He told how the Devil had visited his camp in the body of a young boy and girl the night before, how he had aroused sex feelings in us because we had let our feelings for God grow weak. The whole camp was asked to pray for our forgiveness.

DISCUSSION   *How would you evaluate the impact of this type of experience on the formation of sexual and social attitudes for different children?*

After this experience I returned to my old self. I masturbated and afterwards asked God for forgiveness. I would try very hard to go as long as I could without doing it. I would get new dirty pictures and then would burn them after masturbating with them. However by the time I was sixteen I had begun to question my religion. Boys and girls around me were having fun with each other, and I wanted to join them very much. I took several girls to parties and dances at school but for some reason could not become interested in any particular girl enough to make it exciting. Much of my time was spent reading and studying. Most of the boys I had known had girls, so I was alone much of the time, with only my parents and two younger sisters to do things with. My mother and father did not encourage me to be with girls, because they said such nonsense would interfere with my studies. I think I fell behind my friends as a person wanted by girls. One girl refused to go out with me, and I did not ask another for a whole year. I used to think very crazy things like maybe the girl had known that I was masturbating. I also found it very difficult to even talk with my old boyfriends because I thought they were laughing at me. At the end of high school I was quite lonely and unhappy. The only good thing about this time was that I had finally done very well at school and was looking forward to the university.

DISCUSSION   *Would you say that Erik's abandonment of religion eliminated its effect on his social and sexual development? What could have contributed to his relative social isolation with his peers and his reluctance to be interested in any particular girl at this time?*

At nineteen I left home and came to the university, where I lived in a small room alone. During my first month here I was

invited to a party and met Lisbeth, a stout and very shapely girl.
We danced and immediately liked each other. I felt very good
about her interest in me and would try to find time to look for her
in the study rooms. But she was often busy with other boys.
With great courage, I asked her to go to a party with me. It was
a very open and free party, and I became very drunk from wine.
I remember getting her to come into one of the dark bedrooms.
She made no protest when I began touching her sexual parts. I
got her bikini pants off and began stroking her cunt. She enjoyed
this, and I tried to push a finger in her vagina. It was wet and
warm, and it exerted a soft but firm and elastic pressure against
my finger. This is going to be it, I thought, and I hastily rolled
on a condom. But as I was going to enter her, she did not help
me and generally appeared reluctant. She said that she would not
get anything out of it. The fault was undoubtedly mine. I did not
know anything about her clitoris, and it did not even occur to me
to work her cunt up to passion. I got up somewhat grudgingly,
and we put on our clothes and returned to the party, where everyone probably thought we had had sex relations until they could see
my sad face. We agreed to meet the next weekend, but when I
called for her, she had gone off. Then I realized that it was over,
and I had made another terrible mistake.

I met other girls during this year but did not try to get
them to fuck with me. I was too afraid of what would happen. The
ways to excite a girl became very interesting to me. I began to
go to some of the porno movie clubs, which showed excellent fucking films. I would see the films and then return to my room and
dream about them while I would masturbate. I was very excited
by the way the girls in the films would masturbate and suck the
men's cocks. I also began to buy more of the fucking picture
books, but I always tired of these very quickly and felt very bad
about wasting my parents' money.

When I became twenty, I made up my mind that I had
waited long enough to go to bed with a girl. My experience with
Lisbeth had let me down all through the year. I thought I now
knew what to do to make a girl hot, but I needed some experience.
So one night I went to a bar near the central train station, drank
a lot of spirits, and found a girl who would do it for 100 krone.
She was eighteen and had a nice body and a lively manner. We
took a taxi to my room, and as soon as we were inside we quickly
undressed. When she saw my naked body, she said, "Hey, man,
you're good-looking!" She must have believed that I had some
physical disadvantage that I had to pay a girl to go to bed with me.
I lay on top of her, trying to find her vagina, but she did not make

any attempt to help. Finally, after much fumbling, I was able to push my cock inside her cunt. At last, after twenty years, I was fucking, I thought. Before long, she gave the impression of an orgasm, and it did not take me long to finish. We parted with the best of understandings, but something was lacking. I was disappointed, but still very glad that I had finally done it.

DISCUSSION   *What are some social and psychological differences between Norman and Erik in facing the problems of sexual intimacy? Are there any similarities?*

This year at the university has been very pleasant. I have many new friends and do not feel so much the stranger. A month ago I met a girl named Sussanne at a party. We enjoyed dancing with each other and talking about our terrible experiences with religion. It seems that she went to a church camp for many summers and had even worse things to tell me than I could report to her. I think we fell in love almost instantly. I took her home in a taxi the very first night. She had made it clear that she was a girl with some sexual experience, which gave me enough courage to suggest it to her. For a long time we just lay next to each other on my bed. Suddenly, she said that she loved me and wanted to sleep with me. We got each other undressed, and after we had fondled each other a little, I rubbed my fingers between her legs. I found a point which was a little harder than the rest and figured that this must be her clitoris. I could hear that it was, for she was humming. I knew that it was time to put my sixty-five kilos in motion. Sussanne said when I was rolling on a condom that she was sure that I had tried that with many other girls because I knew how to make a girl very hot. I really preened at that remark but said nothing. Very soon we were ready to fuck. And now the female assistance that I had so often needed was right there. It was a fantastic experience. During the whole fucking, we both worked with full power. She was rolling and swaying her hips under me, and I twisted and drove my cock into her as deeply as I dared. And at last it went all beautiful for both of us together.

part three

young adulthood

introduction

The adolescent typically looks forward to adult status, when he will be allowed gratifications he was denied earlier because of his assumed immaturity, lack of judgment, and inexperience. Some young people manage to work around these limitations, but recognition as an adult in one's social group and society usually produces some important changes. Several cultural indicators of adulthood may signal the advent of adulthood: when the legal rights of adult status are granted, when secondary education is completed, when an individual becomes self-supporting, when an individual leaves the family and moves into a separate living unit, or when marriage takes place. All of the young people in this book have met one or more of these conditions.

Adult status usually means much more than just new personal freedom. There are also new expectations. Some of these involve sex role behavior and even changes in how to meet sexual needs. Obviously for most young people not all of the social and sexual realities of adulthood are confronted in childhood and adolescence. Those who do not have a continuity in experience and learning to prepare them for adult status can be frustrated and anxious trying to fit into adult relationships. Young men and women who persist in acting like children and adolescents in circumstances that require more mature responses may find themselves in difficulty. Thus for some young people adulthood can be a time of social and sexual unlearning as well as learning.

The problems of preparing young people for adult roles and relationships raise certain questions about the ability of modern societies to socialize individuals for present and future social orders. Can we really make valid predictions about the future and the kinds of human relationships that will prevail in it? Given the diversity in contemporary life styles, can we agree on what parents, teachers, and others should do to prepare young people? For a great many young people the movement from adolescence to adulthood is not the same social process that is familiar to older generations, because they want something different from life, though they may be bewildered by the options and choices available. Of course not all young people are confused about where they are heading and why. The cases in this

181

part provide a view of the range of this experience and differences in attitude. Within this material there are several social and psychological themes of young adulthood: changes in attitudes and behavior concerning sex roles; changes in social and sexual intimacy; ideas, feelings, and responses to sexual difficulties; and changes in attitude toward sexual and social values, norms, and institutions. Let us look at these areas.

Changes in Sex Role Behavior and Patterns of Masculinity and Femininity

The young person usually discovers that the expectations of others in adult social and sexual situations are different from those that characterized adolescent relationships. Those who do not perceive these changes usually have some problems in relating successfully to others. Usually awareness of the problem is the basis for changing behavior to conform to more mature expectations. In other instances, adolescent social and sexual behavior can go on for years, especially if it is reinforced by others. The development of more sophisticated patterns of relating to others has many cultural variations, but the changes in expressions of masculinity and femininity can be easily generalized.

Male behavior in young adulthood tends to be less of a matter of meeting a test of manhood. In adolescence the male typically assumes a stance to defend against threats directed at his masculinity, but the use of defense mechanisms becomes less frequent as frustration and anxiety are lessened. Success in filling the male sex role seems to be the key to this pattern of change. Security as a young man can become a reality with the support of adult status and with some preparation for the change. Manhood is usually no longer a matter of pretense or "playing a role." Adolescent males are almost expected to act impulsively and emotionally, but young adults are expected and learn to act more rationally and not to succumb to childish responses. The adult male is also expected to act with more social responsibility, have more concern for the rights and needs of others, be serious in planning the future, and behave more independently of his family and peers. Adolescent rebellion against adults should be over. This social expectation for adulthood includes direct and subtle pressure upon the young male adult. Consider the cultural contrasts in these changes in role behavior in the following cases, but keep in mind that these young men and women may not represent all the social and psychological characteristics of the three nations.

A female's transition from adolescence to adulthood is usually not marked by major changes in the expression of sex roles. The changes we observe today are less rooted in the conditions of normal social development but more likely concern cultural changes from traditional sex roles to those that emphasize equal status for women. Many contemporary women find traditional female sex roles highly offensive. Traditional sex roles for the adult female, especially those in American society, have been an extension of normal child behavior. The American female traditionally has learned to feel dependent, passive, and weak. Adolescent and adult socialization directs her to become efficient in this subordinate status. Social skills are learned to enhance dependency and receptivity in forms that do not threaten male dominance and claims to superiority. The female following this pattern may further refine her femininity with sophisticated mannerisms of daintiness and helplessness and appearances of gentleness, restraint, and submissiveness; she may learn socially and sexually enticing skills to generate and maintain male interests. Such activities obviously complement the traditional male sex role and patterns of masculinity. Moreover, in the United States special schools and commercial programs impart these skills, and the American mass media relentlessly focus on female problems that can be solved cosmetically. Obviously American women who are no longer happy with the traditional sex roles reject much of this.

The Scandinavian woman is not totally immune to all this, but as you will note from many of the Swedish and Danish cases, cultural conditions have supported for a longer period a model of femininity that emphasizes egalitarian sex relationships instead of dependency and subordination to the male. Women are expected to equal men in resourcefulness, independence, and almost all skills that do not require strenuous physical labor. The Scandinavian girl is often in direct competition with or cooperatively related to boys throughout childhood and adolescence without experiencing sociosexual rejection or condescension, so she is not likely to shrink from competition with males in adult relationships, forfeit her independence and self-esteem, or even ask for unfair advantage on the basis of her sex to satisfy the male ego. (There are many exceptions to this model, some of which have been included in this book. Hopefully you may find some of the expressions of Scandinavian opinion useful for drawing comparisons to contemporary American trends in the women's liberation movement.)

Changes in Social and Sexual Intimacy

Among the significant developments at this age is the formation of relatively stable and meaningful relationships. With increased heterosexual experience, people learn to avoid some of the disappointments, frustration, and anxiety that arise from involvements with incompatible persons. Of course not everyone is prepared to make good choices and to experience social and sexual intimacy. Some unfortunate young people spend adolescence in loneliness and relative social isolation, without learning how to gratify needs in the social contexts of dating, romance, love, friendship, and companionship.

These differences in preparation for adult intimacy are represented in our cases on both sides of the sea. Fortunately the experiences of adolescence do not always set the dye. The popular and socially active teenager is not necessarily the person who ultimately is able to put it all together in a stable and satisfying relationship; nor is the inhibited and socially withdrawn individual destined for a life alone. As some of the cases show, the period of young adulthood can be a time of much change.

Adulthood brings changes in the ways sexual behavior fits into people's lives. Mature individuals can no longer be deprived of sexual knowledge. Social controls on sexual behavior for adults change, although individuals are expected to act with greater responsibility and self-control compared to what may be expected or tolerated for adolescents. Furthermore, the adult tends to perceive sex as a medium for expressing love toward another person. The blending of sexual intimacy and social intimacy in a love relationship is, in both American and Scandinavian societies, the cultural pattern for meeting adult social and sexual needs. For most young adults this model of social and sexual relationships becomes the basis of a serious search for a mate. In American society early marriage often ends the search very soon, but Swedish and Danish young people are not so eager to affirm their choices for marriage until they have tested their relationship rather thoroughly, often by living together. Sexual expression in intimate relationships is not one of the most problem-free areas of human interaction. The erotic experience is sometimes plagued by frustrations and anxieties. Let us note some of these difficulties, especially those that appear in the case histories.

Sexual Problems in the Individual and Society

Sexual expression is usually a source of much pleasure, but not for everyone. Human sexuality is not merely a biological phenomenon; there are also many social and psychological elements, as well as cultural variations. This all makes human sexuality a very complex subject.

Sexual difficulties experienced by men and women may be different but are often similar in cause. Lack of sexual knowledge, negative attitudes, interpersonal conflicts, sexual apathy, social inhibition, and failure to internalize appropriate sex roles are factors that can affect functioning in heterosexual relationships. For the male there may be a problem of impotency (inability to have or maintain an erection), premature ejaculation (ejaculation that occurs too quickly for a normal woman to experience her climax), failure to arouse and excite the sex partner, and the more diffuse problem of not feeling satisfaction in the sex act. Female sexual dysfunctions tend to be less understood and are commonly lumped together under the icy word frigidity. Some of the difficulty in recognizing and understanding female sexual functioning and problems is because most of the physical aspects are not so evident visually. Female sexual dysfunctions include: failure to feel sexually stimulated, insufficient vaginal lubrication, difficulty or discomfort receiving the penis, discomfort or pain during or after intercourse, inability to reach orgasm or a satisfying climax, and failure to stimulate the sex partner (assuming a desired and functioning male). The sex act can be unsatisfactory to one or both partners for many reasons that do not involve clinical description. All human sexuality consists of very complex interworkings of biological, psychological, and social factors. Fortunately most of the American and Scandinavian young people included here have been able to work through these problems to their satisfaction.

Not all the problems perceived by our American, Swedish, and Danish students are personal. Scandinavians especially have commented on the way sex is handled in society, in order to compare themselves and the Americans. Much of the commentary may seem overly opinionated (many Scandinavians are unimpressed with the ways American society deals with sex), but their remarks should generate critical thought about the serious problems young people face as sexual values and norms change.

chapter 9

Mary, Ingrid, and Lisbeth

MARY

Mary comes from an American working-class family with serious religious beliefs and practices. Much of her social and sexual behavior is a matter of conforming to traditional values and norms, but she is not in this sense a subjugated, totally dependent, and helpless type of girl. Mary has found a man she thinks she is going to marry, and their relationship included sexual intercourse as it became more serious. Mary's evaluation of their sexual relationship reflects in many ways the feelings and attitudes she learned in childhood and adolescence.

I am nineteen years old and about to start my second year in college. If all my plans come true, I shall be a college graduate and married to the most wonderful boy there is. I never thought college could be so much fun and I would be able to learn so much in such a short time. I can't help the way I think about some things. Right is right, and wrong is wrong, and we shouldn't forget that. The morals of some kids make me sick! I suppose I should feel sorry for them because they have nothing like my boyfriend, who will be marrying me next summer.

My family is extremely close and tight, and this was a great influence in my life. I always wanted my father to be the dominant person, but my mother took over most of the time. I saw a kind of love between my mother and father, with a lot of feeling being expressed openly. Even when they yelled at each other, you could tell that they were in love. I never saw them having sexual intercourse at night, but there was no doubt that something was going on, from all the noise.

I learned the meaning of love very early. Being handled and cuddled so often accustomed me to my present need for it. When my younger brother was born, I was no longer the baby, and it was necessary for me to give up my selfish ways.

My early experiences with other children were mostly with my older sister and my brother. We became very dependent on each other. We played all of the usual children games, including doctor and house when our mother wasn't around. I can remember undressing my brother and slapping his hand when he touched himself, just like our mother used to do. "Showing it" was a kind of game all our own. I recall mother's finding the two of us in the garage doing it. We were yelled at, and my brother was beaten, because he had his pants all the way off.

School introduced me to more peers—and, more important, peers of the opposite sex. Until then my brother was the only male I had played with. I don't think I really liked playing with boys very much, because they were a little too wild for me, especially as I later found out in my big trauma. Most of my friends were girls, although I had a real strong need for an adult male. When I was about seven, I had a picture of a real handsome man cut out from a magazine, which I kept hidden in my dresser. I would take him out and tell him my problems. Somehow I got the idea that he really loved me very much and I could tell him anything. Sometimes I think I even liked him more than my father, who was often sleeping whenever I wanted to talk with him. Also, my father would often go off on a toot with some of his drinking pals at work. He's an AA now, but those were some bad years. Finally, when all of us accepted Christ as our personal savior, the drinking and yelling stopped.

Throughout grade school I grew more dependent on my peer relationships, although the love of my parents continued to be the greatest influence. My mother and father were both very strict with me. They had a big strap they would use when I stepped out of line. I always knew they really cared for me, though I didn't like that strap very much.

    In about the third grade probably the worst thing that happened to me as a little girl occurred. I was playing cowboys and Indians, with the girls being the cowboys and boys being the Indians. After being captured, the only way you could be released was to kiss your captor. This game gave me my first funny feeling about boys. One day I was playing this game with just one other boy. Denny captured me and got me to go under the crawl space of his house, where he had his "tepee." There he tied me up, which he did rather easily, as he was about a year older and much stronger. I got a very sexy feeling from this, and I even eagerly looked forward to kissing him. But there was to be no kiss for Denny. He told me I was his prisoner and had to be stripped to keep me from running away. He went under my dress and pulled off my pants, although I tried to kick and scratch him. I finally gave in when he told me that he had trained the spiders to bite if I didn't give up.

    Denny took off his pants and underwear and made me lie quietly while he examined my private place with his fingers. This really scared me, and I started to cry. He made me feel his penis, which got very hard and long. Finally I grabbed his penis very hard and told him I would break it off if he didn't let me go. That really got him, and he let me go.

    Needless to say, I didn't waste any time getting home to report. My mother woke up my father, who tore over to Denny's house with me. The next thing I remember was Denny's mother chasing him around the house with a belt, and right before our eyes she pulled his pants down and gave him a terrific thrashing on his bare behind. He screamed and screamed and threatened to kill all of us. He kept telling my father and mother that I had wanted to do it and I was making up a lot of lies. This was a very terrible day for me, and a lot of the kids at school heard about what happened because Denny had told them how he had gotten my pants off. From that day on I think some of the boys had the wrong idea. I became more and more determined to save myself for marriage! Also, my folks became stricter with me.

    At about eleven I was becoming more and more aware of boys. All of my girlfriends started to go steady, and I finally got a good-looking boy in my class to be my steady too. But the day came when we were walking home from school and he wanted a kiss. We stopped to rest in a house that was being built. Without any warning, he pulled me down and began kissing my entire face. Screaming

and crying, I ran home, but this time I was too embarrassed and
scared to tell my parents. I worried that they would not believe
that happened, as they had started to call me boy-crazy because
of some of the phone calls they had listened in on. They had started
asking me where I was all the time. I had to come right home from
school. I couldn't go to any parties where there were boys. My
mother kept reminding me about Denny and what boys will do to you
if you give them a chance. Boys are boys, and they're out to get as
much as they can off you, if you let them.

In the seventh grade I had two steady boyfriends. I always
had to meet them on the sly because of my parents. I gradually
overcame my fear of kissing with boys, although it wasn't until the
eighth grade that I let a boy really touch me. I never did like boys
who tried to paw me. Once I knocked a guy's glasses clean off his
head when he tried to feel my leg at school. The teacher told me
I was in the right and made this boy stay after school for a whole
week.

At the onset of adolescence, I developed much more curiosity about sex. My girlfriends and I shared many ideas about
babies, boys, and love. My mother was one of those parents who
explained nothing, so I depended heavily on my peers for information. Even my older sister wouldn't talk with me. We had no sex
education at all in grade school. When I started my menstruation
near the end of grade school, I knew only what my friends had told
me about it. The first time was a terrible shock, although my girlfriend helped me some. I remember the two of us going to the
store to buy a box of sanitary napkins on the way home from school.
My mother was furious that I had not told her that I had started
bleeding in school, and she accused me of playing around and maybe
injuring myself.

During school hours my friends and I tried finding some
answers to our questions, but our teacher just thought we had dirty
minds to ask those questions.

In a lot of ways I started to run pretty wild, with boys on
my mind most of the time. The thing that always kept me in line
was my religious background. About this time I discovered that I
could have very pleasurable sensations from touching myself. I
never told anyone about this, even my girlfriend.

When I was fourteen there were new discoveries. My
body had matured rather quickly, and many boys had started to
notice me, which gave my parents fits. No boy could call me on

the phone, and I still could not go out. My first high school year
was filled with problems at home because of this. I got myself a
boyfriend and had to sneak out of the house to see him. This made
me feel very bad because of my religion. Also, my father would
get in his car and come looking for me if I wasn't home by dark.
At first my boyfriend and I would just participate in hard kissing,
and at times he would try to feel me up. I enjoyed the kissing but
would not let his hands roam any further than my waist. Once he
asked me to feel his penis in his pants, but I refused. At the end
of my first year of high school he drifted away, because he knew
that I was no easy make. On our last date he tried to go all the
way with me, but I was determined to avoid it.

       During my sophomore and junior years I got a little more
freedom at home. My older sister had run away from home with a
boy for two weeks, and my folks may have been scared that I might
try the same thing if they didn't let me go to school dances and
some parties. I dated many boys. I was afraid to get involved
with just one person because of the sex. The guys I dated knew
through the grapevine that I was a virgin. We had a lot of fun anyway. I would park, unless I just felt the guy was a creep or if the
date turned out to be a complete bummer. I sneaked in a couple of
drive-in movies near the end of my junior year, but I soon found out
that if a guy invited me to a drive-in I was not going to see a movie
but a fight to save my virginity. One double date was really bad.
My so-called girlfriend and her date actually had sexual intercourse
in the front seat. Her boyfriend even borrowed the contraceptive
from my date in the middle of their lovemaking. The three of them
had become very drunk. This boy was very popular in school, and
I was shocked by what he tried to do on a first date. I felt very
guilty about what I was forced to do. Both boys had taken off their
pants, although my date at least kept his underwear on. He forced
me to play with his penis while he tried to get into me. He left me
very disgusted when he finally masturbated himself to an orgasm.
After that he didn't talk with me at all and left me off at home without even taking me to the door. The next several months I didn't
date at all and vowed that I would never give in to a boy.

       My next affair happened at the beginning of my senior year
with a very nice boy whom my mother didn't like because his car
had too fancy a paint job. He was not really my type because he
was not very dominant, but he was nice. We only did some heavy

kissing, but my mother was almost out of her mind about our dating. One morning she accused me of having sex with him the night before because she said that she had smelled something in my panties. This almost floored me. I prayed every night that my mother would believe the truth, but she told me she did not want to hear any more and I should make my peace with God and not her.

I think some of the closeness of our family started to disappear then. I am sure that she told my father her suspicions, because even he mentioned some things that were embarrassing. I even offered to go to our family doctor, so he could prove that I was a virgin still. The only thing that saved us was our church. At one service I received the call to come forward, and I confessed the sin of the drive-in when I had touched the penis of the boy. For a time I felt much better, and so did my mother and father.

DISCUSSION   *What sexual defense mechanisms are usually embraced in the course of alleviating guilt feelings about forbidden sex acts through the medium of religious confession? Does nonreligious confession to others sometimes accomplish the same results?*

During the spring vacation of my senior year I met the boy I am now going to marry at a beach party. It was a very disgusting spectacle. There were a lot of college kids drunk and stoned having sex all over the place—in the bedrooms, in the living room, and even on the floor in a bathroom. One girl was in bed with three guys at once, and she was doing something with each one at the same time. It was horrible to see. It was really good to leave that party with Fred and just walk down to the beach and hold hands.

Fred and I have known each other for over a year now. He still has a lot of bad habits to change, but both of us now have the same faith, and with God's help I am sure we can make it. I need a man who is dominant, so I don't try and run things too much. Increasing his dominance is a big struggle, because his mother still runs his life too much. I think he will increase his self-confidence when he decides to go back to college in the fall. He now knows that to get ahead you need an education, and his present job isn't going to get him anywhere.

*DISCUSSION   Mary's is a typical American pattern of sex role conflict.
She needs to manipulate in social relationships, but she
seeks a subordinate role as a matter of social acceptability,
which is reflective of traditional female norms. In your
judgment has she picked the right kind of mate? What
problems of compatibility do you anticipate on the basis
of Mary's commentary thus far?*

When I look at what some of my girlfriends now have for
husbands, I feel very lucky. Most of them had to get married as
the result of their folly. My getting Fred as innocent as he was is
a good thing for both of us. Our own sexual relationship never
went to the final stage until after I got my ring, and this is the way
we both wanted it. Giving him the love I felt for him after I got
the ring was something I felt I had to do.

Like other couples in our situation, we became very intimate and progressed from light kissing to heavy petting. He would
find my weaker spots, and soon we were both very excited with
each other. His playing with my ears and biting my neck really
aroused me in a way I never felt before. He is the only boy I have
ever wanted to touch in his private parts, and he has told me the
same.

Our first intercourse happened in a very natural way,
while parking. The only thing that scared us was that we used
nothing to prevent me from getting pregnant. I guess I was just
a little scared because I respected my parents and knew it would
hurt them if they found out. For some reason we both felt that
God would understand our true love for each other.

*DISCUSSION   Is this an example of both religious faith and sexual
rationalization?*

The intercourse itself went very easy, as Fred was
very gentle. I had no pain, and there was no bleeding, as I
thought there would be. Of course, we had spent almost two
hours of very heavy petting before the act was started with his
penis put in my vagina. I know Fred enjoyed this very much.
His words of love had a very special, deep, and spiritual meaning. This was his very first intercourse as well.

Since this first time we have had intercourse when it

has been convenient. I do not yet have an orgasm, but I am sure
that when I am fitted with a diaphragm and have the opportunity to
experience the other pleasures outlined in our marital guide I,
too, will be able to reach a climax. Now it is enough to give
pleasure to Fred. Later sex will become even more important
for both of us when we have our own apartment and can work on
the other aspects of our love for each other.

DISCUSSION   *Assess Mary's expression of hope.*

     As we make plans to start a family (I want at least four
children), I know that all these matters will work themselves out
so we can have a life full of comfort and happiness together.

INGRID   *Ingrid is less typical of the Swedish norm than most of
the other Swedish girls whose stories are included here.
Her family life seems to have suffered from emotional
detachment and social inhibition in the relationships
between her parents and their children. Her encounters
with the opposite sex outside of the family were not
encouraging. She developed a rather inward and negative
approach to sexual needs in the form of fear. Since she
has become a young adult, however, a great deal has
changed for Ingrid. She is now much more autonomous
without being so lonely and detached, and she seems to
feel relatively comfortable in her female role in relationships with the opposite sex.*

     It is especially bad for me to know that Mary and I have
shared some of the same kinds of fears and troubled times. Now I
wonder just how much we are the same. Both of us have very
strange parents, even though they are not much alike. It is difficult
for me to compare my life with hers because I am three years older
than Mary and have had many experiences she will probably never
have if she becomes Fred's bride.

During my early childhood I also had a strong relationship with my parents, especially my mother. My feelings toward my father were that I should also show him love, but that he did not like such play around him. He would even push me away when I tried to kiss him, but I always knew that he adored me even more than my brother and sister. Everyone said that I looked the most like him. Unlike Mary, I never noticed any love between my parents, because I am sure that they felt they must never show this to us children. While we liked each other very much, we did not ever say it or show it to each other.

It is interesting that Mary's parents would yell at each other in conflict. Such a thing never happened in my house. There was never any physical contact among any of us. I suppose this is the basis of my later difficulties in sexual contacts. I had great fears of physical contact until I was older. My family has never attended church, and none of us believe the things Mary mentions. The fear I had about any boy's penis was bad enough, without thinking that it was controlled by a devil in hell.

When I started school at about seven, I naturally found many new friends. My younger brother was left alone much of the time then. I remember wanting to hurry home from school so we could play, because I knew that he was lonely and was waiting for me. I liked my brother very much, and I would worry that he might have an accident and die. I sometimes thought that I would like to die with him if he had an accident. I never had any sex thoughts about him.

DISCUSSION   *Are the psychological and emotional patterns of Ingrid's family life compatible with certain values of Scandinavian society as Ingrid and others have described it? Would parents who are like Ingrid's father and mother be likely to model these emotional patterns for children to follow?*

It was in my twelfth year that I had my first experience with erotic matters. And this was a very brief encounter at a summer camp with other children my age. Some of us girls examined each other to see how we looked. It was very thrilling to look at those who had their first pubic hair and breasts. But I felt sorry for them, and I wanted to be undeveloped for a very long time. I felt the things about sex were frightening, without knowing why. At the camp we also played a sexual game, which was to answer embarrassing questions. If a girl would not answer a question, the boy had to put his hand under her dress and feel her, and if a boy would not answer, the girl was to kiss him. I was shocked by this game and thought some of the girls were bad. Playing it made me feel afraid and regretful. But I had to take part, or I would become an outsider.

When I was thirteen, I became interested in a boy in my class. He became my very first love, although I never told him. When he tried to kiss me, I became very frightened and did not know what to do. It was almost the same kind of feeling that Mary may have had, except I did not beat the boy. I was only scared that he might have some idea of our having sexual intercourse. Such a thought was unnatural then. This boy tired of my coldness, since other girls were doing much more with boys, and found a new girl-friend very quickly. The first love ended because of my fear.

When I was fourteen, I had a boyfriend for about three months. His name was Kristofer, and he was very handsome and tall for his age. One night when Kristofer and I had been to a school party, he walked with me to a very dark park near my home. It was very cold this springtime, and there was no place for us to lie down to kiss and pet. Kristofer became very excited by our kissing, and after some time I reached down to feel his penis. This did not excite me at all, but I was curious to feel it and see what it was like. After a lot of this, Kristofer took his penis from his pants. I remember my cold hand touching this warm thing. I was terribly scared of it.

When Kristofer pulled my pants down away from my dress, I was still more scared but did nothing to stop him, as his kisses had put me into a helpless trance of pleasure and fright. He put his warm penis against my stomach and tried to rub it near my opening. I felt nauseated and fearful at the thought of him trying to force it into me, so I began to push him away and refused to feel his penis when he put it into my hand to help him. I became very mixed in my feelings and fears.

Kristofer was very kind after he finally put away his penis. He kissed me very gently and said he was sorry for what he had tried to do. I knew that it was not his fault, because I had first felt his penis, and he could not have known that I would be so afraid. My next boyfriend was not so nice, but at least I would not be so afraid of having a boy touch me, although I again would be very scared about trying to have sexual intercourse.

Next came Viktor. Viktor was about a year older than I.

He invited me to a party at his house when his parents were gone.
He did not really like me at all, I am sure. It was only a kind of
chance that I was invited to a party with older boys. Perhaps his
real girlfriend could not come, or something like that. Many of
the boys and girls were drinking beer, which I did not like at all.
Viktor and I only kissed and danced some. I thought I liked him
then but did not want him to know this, as I was afraid that he
would think that we should have sexual intercourse. Again, I felt
very afraid when Viktor pressed his hard penis against me while
we were dancing very close. Because my mother did not know
that I was at this party, I went home early, but promised Viktor
that I would return to help him fix his house before his parents returned from their holiday the next day.

The next day Viktor was very excited to see me, or at
least he acted so. I helped to clean the house, and then we started
to dance. Again I noticed that his penis became hard. It was not
long before we had danced into his bedroom. He covered me with
hot kisses. Very quickly he had pulled my pants from my body and
kissed my stomach. Since my experience with Kristofer, I had
experimented by putting my finger in my vagina. But still I could
not see how it would be possible for a penis to enter without hurting me very much. I hurt a lot when Viktor pushed his finger in
my vagina as I had done for myself.

When I asked Viktor to stop because he was so rough, he
became almost enraged by my protest. I began to think that all he
wanted was to push his penis into me. When he threw me on his
bed and pulled off his pants, I knew that it would be a terrible thing.
His penis was even larger and more forceful looking than Kristofer's.
He grabbed my breasts and tried to bite them. It was plain to me
that he was out of his head, and I did not know what to do to stop him.
When I told him that I was a virgin, he told me of his love for me,
which I did not believe.

We stopped this lovemaking for a short time so he could
tell me how to do it for the first time. But it was all so frightening
I thought, "What is the sense of this"? It seemed like pleasure
only for Viktor and not for me at all. Again he started to push his
fingers into my vagina, while with his other hand he pulled his
penis back and forth as if he were masturbating. I watched this
through my tears.

Viktor seemed very pleased when he was able to get his
fingers into me. He said, "Now I am going to give you a good fuck!"
He took his fingers from my vagina, and then while I covered my

eyes he tried to push his penis into me. My opening was almost
forced closed by my fear and hurt. Again he pushed his fingers
in, and then again he tried with his penis. Finally his penis found
the way, and I could feel this boy inside of me, with almost nothing but pain on my mind. He carried on this intercourse for only
a minute, and then, to my surprise, he pulled his penis from my
vagina and a lot of sperm shot from his organ. It was very nause-
ating. I had never seen male seed, and I thought that perhaps
Viktor had something wrong with him. He then fell upon me and
tried to give me gentle kisses and words, but such were not for
me. I left his home as soon as I could be rid of his sperm. I only
saw Viktor again at some school parties. I think he was ashamed
at what we had done.

Several weeks after Kristofer and I had been in the park,
I had had what I think was the beginning of my menstruation, but
there was very little to it. Most of the girls in my class had already begun, so I knew from what they had reported to me that it
was to be expected. My mother had never said anything to me.
After Viktor and I had done the sex act, I became very frightened
that I was fertilized, as my periods had not continued after the
first time. This fear caused me so much unhappiness that no one
can really know how terrible it was for me. I could not talk to
anyone about what was almost driving me to madness. I was sure
that I was pregnant. I thought that my stomach grew. I felt my
breasts every morning and night to see if they were becoming full.
I often thought I needed to throw up in the mornings but held back
so my mother would not suspect. I wanted only to kill myself and
be rid of this terrible life. I could not even talk with Viktor, for
he had a new girl from his class. After three months my menstruation returned, and it was the only time in my life that I thanked God
for something. Then I told my mother I had blood in my pants, and
she gave me some cotton pads but said almost nothing about it. It
was as if I had accidently cut myself on a kitchen knife cutting
carrots for the family dinner. It was as though some shame was
connected with it, and I could understand this idea because I felt
very guilty. The whole next year I did nothing with boys, and
many of my friends at school left me alone.

DISCUSSION   *The Swedes are noted for their sexual candor but there
                  are exceptions, as evidenced by Ingrid's experience. Her
                  withdrawal from her peers, particularly those of the
                  opposite sex, may be identified as the defense mechan-
                  isms of sexual denial and insulation.* (Sexual denial *is the*

*refusal to acknowledge sexual matters and to reject the
reality of sexual feelings and needs.* Sexual insulation *is
the overt withdrawal because of fear or guilt from social
and sexual interaction.) What factors would cause an
individual to use these mechanisms? What are the
implications if these mechanisms are continued into
adulthood?*

At sixteen I met a boy whom I loved very much. It was a
platonic love that was to last for three years until I left high school.
Since I did not dare to have a sexual life with a boy, I was very
satisfied with this friendship. Only once during these three years
did I go with another boy, but when I discovered that he wished to
have sexual intercourse with me, I returned to my platonic friend.
All of my girlfriends were having sexual intercourse with their
boyfriends. They would often talk about how they did it, and what
could I say?

My boyfriend and I had decided not to have sex with each
other. He thought that I was a virgin who wanted to wait until
marriage. But I also think that he was never interested in girls
in any sexual way. We would sometimes kiss each other, but that
was all. We would mostly talk about our problems at home. While
my relationship with this boy, Markus, was very good sometimes
for my loneliness, he was very bad to be with all the time because
of his depression. I think now that it is very good that he never
had any worries about being fertilized, for I am sure that he would
have killed himself right away. We had fun sometimes, but it was
mostly a sad kind of love for me. He is now at another university
to become a doctor of medicine, and I only get very short letters
from him.

DISCUSSION   *Ingrid has brought into focus several distinctly Swedish
patterns of how to feel lonely, alienated, depressed. Her
search for love has been a search for someone who can
share her melancholia. Social isolation and emotional
detachment are serious negative conditions in Swedish
life. Some associate the problem with Swedish communication norms: talk should be frank, to the point, and
quickly over so people can be left alone with their
thoughts. Such inwardness is related to other cultural
variables as well. What could be some of these factors for
Ingrid?*

After I graduated from high school, I moved to an apartment on the other side of the city. My mother and father said nothing. I think we could all move away from each other without causing much interest in each other. As soon as I had my apartment, I started writing to Hans, and I could tell quickly from his letters that he was as much in love with me as I was with him. I invited him to visit me in Stockholm. He said that he would come before returning to his university at Basel. I could never tell from his letters whether he planned to stay with me, but I suspected this was how he wanted it. And then I did not know if he should sleep in my bed or if I should try to get another for him. Again I was becoming scared to death about the thought of sexual intercourse; however, I had found since Viktor that I could sometimes have an orgasm from masturbation. I had also discovered from my doctor that my vagina was quite normal and that even a large penis would not hurt me if the boy was careful at first. I must have been looking forward to going to bed with Hans because I purchased a box of condoms.

The first night Hans put out the lights and came to my bed without any clothes. I was surprised to discover he had so much hair all over his body. It was a great relief to find that his penis was not big enough to cause me pain. After we had been in bed about a half an hour, kissing and petting with much excitement, he placed his penis in a condom and entered my vagina. I became very hot, and soon I had an orgasm. All during the night he tried to make love to me. This was at last my first real intercourse. I could think of nothing but love for Hans. He was so gentle and tender. It was as if he had known all about my troubles over sex and was sent by fate to help me.

During the week that Hans stayed with me, I kept him hidden from my parents, for I did not know what I could tell them. After he left, I cried and cried and cried. After one letter he told me that he could not love me because he was going to marry a girl from Basel. I immediately stopped crying and began to look for a new boy.

DISCUSSION   *Has Ingrid moved to more secure ground as the result of her relationship with Hans? Does Ingrid seem pleased by some of the results of this experience now?*

The memory of beautiful sexual intercourse with Hans was very good for me. My fears disappeared. I had even begun to enjoy touching and feeling his very fine penis. I remember being rather amazed by the way in which it could be so little and yet get

so big. We would lie in bed for many hours in the night and morning, just feeling each other with our hands. I loved the male body
for the first time in all the ways that a woman should love it. I
even learned the excitement of kissing his penis and putting it into
my mouth. Hans was very tender with me as well, and he did the
same with me.

It is now over a year since I began living in an apartment
away from my parents. I have some very good friends, and my
telephone is always busy when I am not seeing them. I am no
longer the shy and frightened schoolgirl with boys. When I go to
bed with a boy, I can give him real pleasure, but I also expect him
to satisfy me. There are many boys interested in me now, so I do
not have to be alone when I want some fun and excitement.

LISBETH

*Lisbeth's life embraces very liberal patterns of sexual
behavior, but not without some limits. Her parents,
especially her mother, played important roles in developing her liberal attitudes toward sexual matters. The home
environment features many learning experiences that will
undoubtedly seem very strange and unrealistic to most
Americans. Lisbeth seems to be looking forward to a very
different life from the one that Mary anticipates. She has
little interest in marriage and does not seem insecure in
her present style of meeting her social and sexual needs.*

I can't help pitying Mary a bit. She has had so many
troubles about things that have always gone quite easily for me.
Her difficulties with her parents about sexual matters and the very
strange way she behaved with some of her boyfriends are sad. Her
story and the conclusion with this inexperienced boy whom she is
planning to marry are almost heartbreaking. I wonder how she
has been able to fool herself into believing some things?

So much of what Mary thinks about life is wrong, from
my point of view, but I am sure that she could not start to think
differently. She has rigid attitudes toward life, just as her mother

and father have. She would probably never consider any living
arrangement other than the traditional family. She wants only to
be married. She has his ring. She has his promise. And she
has had her sexual intercourse with him. He has fallen into a net
and has only a little time left to swim away. Perhaps I pity Fred
more than Mary. But what kind of man would not see this? Does
he have some handicap Mary hasn't mentioned?

The traditional ideas this girl holds seem almost funny to
me, but I know these are important ways of life to some people in
the U.S.A. She believes that there is only one man she really
loves. And this person must be nice and all the other ones wrong.
This is a very traditional view of the man-woman relationship. It
might give her some troubles later, when she finds disappointment
in this boy and sees some things in other boys that are better.
She wants four children before she has even one orgasm. Her
unrealistic dream of what marriage will do for her is probably
going to crush her.

From her upbringing, you can understand that she has
many things to fight off. Her home life and education seem much
different from my own. Both of my parents were academic, and I
think much better educated than Mary's mother and father. Both
of my parents felt that they should be equal in all things. I never
expected my father or my mother to be dominant over the other.
What a silly thing to want, if both a mother and father are intelligent and either can do things as well as the other. Our home life
was always filled with joy and good times. I have always been
able to say anything to them, and they have never been authoritarian
with me. We have always been close to each other, and I really
love to tell them things. I love my parents more than I can say.
Mary has so many bad things in her relationship with her parents
that I cannot find in mine. It has always been impossible to hide
anything from them. It would be terrible if I could not tell them
what I might want to tell them. I feel strongly that my parents
are more understanding than Mary's are. This is very important
to me. Also, my parents have always had great respect for my
privacy. They would never have thought to tease me about something that worried me, and they would not ask about things I felt
might be personal and part of my own life away from the family.
If I needed their help, they knew I could ask without embarrassment
or fear.

My mother and father have always lived in Copenhagen
because of the family business and some work that my father does
with an institute at the university. I am twenty, and have a

brother two years older. I still live at home with my parents, but many times each month I stay with my boyfriend in his apartment.

Concerning my childhood I know that I always enjoyed playing with other children, including my older brother. We could talk freely about out problems in school or about difficulties with other children. We were very close until he left home three years ago to begin his studies at the university.

As for sexual things between us, we were quite old as children, and still we enjoyed taking baths together. We would wash each other and play without shame. Once, when I was perhaps seven, my father came into the bathroom to ask how we were doing. He showed my brother how to wash under the skin of his penis. I remember doing this thing for him the next time.

Because of my close relationship to my parents and brother, I did not have very many friends in school. I think this part of my childhood was bad. The games at school often seemed childish to me, and I was never very good at athletics. Perhaps I was a little shy until I entered adolescence. I did not really want to be with other children if I could be with older people. I read quite a lot from when I was eight until I was seventeen.

Near the end of my eleventh year I had some very sexual feelings. I was developed quite early for my age. The older boys teased me some, but I began to like it. I started to have sex feelings about several of these boys. At night I would have rather exciting dreams about what I hoped we would do with each other.

By the time my first menstrual period had come when I was twelve, I was very able to satisfy my sex feelings at night by myself. I think at first a good dream about a boy would come to my head, and I would think of being in bed with him naked. I have liked to sleep without nightclothes since I was about twelve. To warm my body with my hands has always been exciting, and to sleep with a warm and tender boy with his flesh next to mine is even better.

When I was thirteen and fourteen I went with many different boys to parties. I did a lot of kissing and petting with these boys. Perhaps my most interesting boyfriend was Thorkild, who took me to the beach. I teased him about how he liked to go to the beach to see the naked girls sunning themselves on the piers. Probably the most exciting time would come on our way home, when we would stop in a nice place in the forest to kiss and pet.

Sometime during the previous year my mother had showed me one of my father's condoms and talked about how it was used and the kinds of care that must be taken. She knew quite a bit about these things for a woman, I thought. I passed on some of this information to Thorkild, in the hope that he might purchase some, but I think he was much too scared. Finally, at the end of the summer I said goodbye to this boy because of some of the dullness of our being together. One of my girlfriends had confided in me that she was having sexual relations with a boy in our class. I was a little envious because of my own lack of experience. Although I was only fourteen, I became quite determined that I should also have sexual intercourse.

Just before I was to begin school, I met a twenty-year-old student. I fell in love with him right away. He was not shy at all with me. I had to promise him that I would not tell anyone of our meeting each other, but this seemed to be a small price for the pleasure of doing things with him. We would take short drives into the country. It was in his car that I had my first sexual intercourse. I liked the way he did it very much, and I had orgasms with him quite soon. He was always very careful about using a condom. It was a very exciting time of my life, discovering the beautiful feeling of having a man inside of me and being able to satisfy each other in this way. He would always tell me how much he loved me, but I think I knew after a few times that he was just mostly excited about making love with a young girl.

After less than two months I began to feel that I did not like him very much. I wanted to talk with my parents about him, but instead I talked with my brother, who felt that I should give him up. Later he gave me several packages of condoms to keep in case it should happen that a boy did not have any. I don't think he talked with my mother about this, but about the same time my mother asked me to be sure to tell her when I started to have sexual relations with boys, so she could arrange to have a doctor give me a contraceptive device or pills.

I really loved to talk with her about this, and she was very kind and tender in her thoughts. I soon told her that I had had sex relations with a boy, and he had used a condom. It was not something she felt was unnatural for me. She even asked me if the first time was good, and I think she was very happy for me. It was not until I was sixteen that I went with my mother to be fitted with a contraceptive device.

From the time I was fifteen to the time I graduated from

high school, I had many boyfriends. I preferred quiet times to the loud and crowded party activities. Many of the boys would drink too much and spoil the fun for everyone. I would drink some but found that after a little I would become sleepy. Then I would think more about going home to read a good book than having a good time with my boyfriend.

During this time I went to bed with many boys. After the first three or four, I began to pick and choose more carefully. I wanted to feel in love with a boy before I had sex with him. My mother was very busy with her work, but she always had time to talk with me about my feelings and these boys. For some reason I could tell her things I would not dare to tell my best friend. I think my mother's sex life has been even more interesting than my own in some ways. Perhaps my own choice of a lover has been influenced by what I have seen in my parents' relationship. They have both had sex outside of their marriage, and I think my mother is right when she says that it has been good for both of them. I think it is natural that people find others to be sexually exciting while still being in love with a husband or wife. I think my relationship with a boy named Jørn in my last year of the high school was much like this for me.

DISCUSSION   *Lisbeth's story shows the importance of parental models and some patterns of the parent-child relationship which results in very liberal and permissive kinds of behavior for a child. On the basis of other cases, does she seem typical of Danish sexual socialization? How might she have reacted to Ingrid's story?*

Jørn was a very handsome boy and quite friendly with the girls. We met at a school party, and we liked each other very much after only one dance. I know that I fell in love with him because he was so free and easy to be with. After we had known each other for only a few weeks, Jørn came home with me after school, and several times my mother and father remarked on how nice he was. I was quite excited about the thought of having sex with him, but there was no place to do it. The way we were able to discuss the matter was very good. Finally we decided to take a hotel room for a night. When I told my mother what we were going to do, so that my parents would not worry, my parents told us that we could stay together in my bedroom if we wished. Jørn was very surprised at this attitude, but he agreed. From that time, my parents have respected my privacy with boys in my room. Jørn and I had many fine times

together at home. Of course his parents thought that he was staying in my brother's room, as did some of our own relatives and
family friends.

This was a wonderful year of growing up for both Jørn and
me. We did a lot of reading together, although I still enjoyed many
more books alone. We enjoyed music and television with my parents. In many ways he became a complete substitute for my brother,
who had left home. My brother also liked Jørn very much.

The sexual life we had together was also very nice. I loved
to sleep with him naked, no matter how cold it was outside. We always had sexual intercourse whenever he stayed with me. Even
during my menstruation, we would do it in one way or another. I
learned with Jørn about making love with his penis in my mouth.
Jørn liked this very much, and he was also quite happy I think to
kiss me there as well.

I liked the freedom of pills. Unfortunately his parents soon
objected to his staying overnight at my house. I think his mother became very jealous of our relationship, and his father, who was a very
weak and shy man, had little to say. His mother spoke very angrily
to my mother. My mother no longer denied that we had been having
sexual relations in my bedroom. Finally she threatened to report
the matter to the school authorities. At this point we decided that
we should make no trouble and that he would not see me at home
any longer.

Until I graduated from high school, Jørn and I would find
other places to make love, but in the last few months we began to
see each other less and less. We started to go to parties with each
other again, but we would dance with others and even go off to kiss
and pet with them. It was something we talked about, and both of
us told each other that it was a good thing to do. We were always
fond of each other and I can truthfully say I was not jealous when I
found him with other girls. The first time he went to bed with
another girl, I was very sad for several days, but now it would not
be of more than passing interest. I went to bed with a boy soon
after Jørn went with this other girl, so I did not have a lonely time
of it. When I graduated, Jørn and I went many times to the beach.
This was how we ended it, before his family sent him to Switzerland
to college. Jørn wrote me last year that he had married a French
girl, despite his mother's objections. I know that he will be a good
husband if she is a good wife, and I also know that when we see each
other we shall probably have beautiful sex again.

DISCUSSION   *Lisbeth reveals a rather free approach to sexual behavior in her relationships with the opposite sex. Much of this behavior is on the fringe of Danish norms, but permissive patterns of response to individual sexual behavior would hardly manifest the kind of negative reactions that might be likely in other cultural settings. How would American men and women react to Lisbeth, in your opinion?*

My first year at the university has not been all that difficult. I am home quite a bit, with the house all to myself most of the time. My latest boyfriend often comes to the house during the day, but he will not stay during the night when my parents are here. He is the most traditional person I have ever had for a boyfriend. I sometimes think he is a Puritan dressed like a hippie. I do not know why I really like him sometimes. Perhaps it is because he is so independent and strong in ways I think Jørn was weak. Our sex life takes place only in his apartment.

Stig seems to get special pleasure out of sex because, I think, he still feels it is a bit dirty. Of course his home was terrible in the ways he learned about sex. He was often beaten by a crazy mother for doing very ordinary things with himself. Stig has in his confusion wanted the two of us to go to bed with other couples at the same time. I cannot get myself to do this, but I have told him that he may do so with another girl if he wishes. I do not feel that I wish to go to bed with just anyone. I must feel something good inside about the person I make love with; otherwise I choose to use my hand.

DISCUSSION   *How well does Lisbeth understand Stig's sexual motivation here? How well does she understand her own? What is your evaluation of Lisbeth's criterion for having sexual intimacy with others? How do you compare her with Mary in this respect?*

Unlike Mary, I cannot say that I shall be willing to look at one man for the next fifty years. I know that Stig will only be a friend soon, and that will be fine. There will be many new boys who will be lovers and then friends.

chapter 10

Bruce, Alf, and Tage

BRUCE

On the brink of his twentieth birthday Bruce looks forward to his future with a confidence and self-assurance that many others might envy. He traces much of his sense of well-being to his family life and the influence of his parents. Bruce's family background is stable, middle-class, affluent, suburban. He seems pleased with his success with girls on both the social and sexual level of interaction. His attitude toward girls shows many traditional American underpinnings. His description of current relationships suggests a style of social maturity that would appeal to many middle-class American parents for their sons.

My father and mother are in their late forties; we get along beautifully now. I guess we are typical middle class: four-bedroom house, three cars (including mine), two color TVs, a family room with pool table, and a fourteen-foot runabout. The whole scene is in a good neighborhood, and no one is much different from us. We have great neighbors.

My sex life was probably very normal for a kid. In my

early childhood I was almost unaware of sex, probably because of my lack of exposure to it and my preoccupation with other things. What I did know about it I usually learned from my brother. He taught me that girls were supposed to be "wanted" by boys, and that they had body parts different from boys'. Because of how my parents and society had reared me, I felt that all of this was nasty and that I would never want to engage in such experiences. At this early age I behaved as if I feared sex, because I was unsure of the complete nature of sex and thought it was wrong for a little boy to do these bad things.

Going to school and associating with different kids made an impression upon me. After the first few grades my dad began to take more interest in my social development with other kids. We got into Indian guides together and did a lot of stuff that had a good effect on my character. Of course, none of this had anything to do with sex or girls. Nevertheless, I was beginning to have some impressions about girls and sex, despite my all-male associations and activities. When I was about seven years old, I started to learn a little of the true meaning of sex. My brother, five years older than I, had now reached adolescence and was beginning to learn about sex, and he relayed this information to me in a very frank way. I also began discussing sex more frequently with friends, who now included both males and females. Our understanding was still quite vague, but we were beginning to know much more about sex.

I still felt that sex was something dirty and somewhat abnormal because of parental advice and teachers. Even so, I knew that sex was a reality because of my exposure to it on television and in movies; I could relate some of this visual experience to my own knowledge. The magazines that I was exposed to showed me what I was supposed to be attracted to. I saw Playboy and a few other magazines that showed nude women, and I was probably excited because I was supposed to be.

By the time I was ten or eleven my attitude toward sex had changed: I now felt that sex was all right for older people, but for us kids it was dirty or nasty. The thing I recall the most about sex during this time was my fear of kissing a girl. My parents were starting to be more open about it, and I was learning a lot. My brother was still living at home and was dating. His experiences were very informative.

I was becoming attracted more and more to the opposite sex. For the first time I had a feeling that came upon me each time I saw, or even thought about, certain girls. The more I thought about these girls, the more I thought how it would be to be alone with them or to do something with them. I now had the inner desire to go out with a girl. Although I wanted to date, I was not old enough to drive; so dates were almost out of the question. Eventually I arranged meeting places near home where girlfriends and I could engage in such advanced sexual actions as kissing and holding hands.

My behavior was beginning to change drastically. Instead of being afraid of sex with girls, I turned into an aggressive sexual maniac, who could never be satisfied. This lack of satisfaction was caused by my fantasies about the kind of sexual activity that could really take place.

Although I personally did not believe that there was anything wrong with masturbation, I did not go out of my way to let everybody know that I did it. I wasn't embarrassed about it, but I just didn't feel that it was something to be talked about all the time, and on top of this, most of my peers made fun of it because they did not understand the sexual drives behind masturbation.

When I started the ninth grade, I probably had a lot going for me. I was fairly popular in my classes. I hate to brag, but I think most people like me. I probably picked up a lot of the social traits of my folks, especially my dad, who is a successful salesman. High school made a big difference for me. I was becoming what society often terms a young man, and at this new stage my sexual drives were becoming much more intense and mature. I had started to date very frequently and was acquiring much more knowledge on the subject of sex. During this time I felt that sex was acceptable and enjoyed participating in sexual activities. During my dating I often petted very heavily. I had truly become the aggressor in heterosexual relationships.

On dates I tried to get whatever I could, and it was often very difficult for a girl to tell me no. I knew exactly what I wanted, and I expected to receive it. I don't mean to give the impression that I always wished to engage in sexual intercourse with my girlfriends, but I did expect something from them. I did not feel that sex was wrong, and if I had the opportunity to engage in sexual intercourse, I normally would do so with no guilt feelings whatsoever. I did not, however, try to get a piece of ass from any girl I saw, because after doing it once I was not psychologically satisfied by such a relationship. I often had to resort to masturbation for my sexual releases if I could not make it with someone of my choosing.

DISCUSSION   *What social and psychological factors would lead an individual like Bruce to prefer masturbation to other readily available opportunities for sexual expression?*

My parents were encouraging me to date. Dad gave me all the bread I needed for this purpose. I do not think that they had any idea how far I was going with many of the girls I dated. They were very interested in my dates and often wished to meet them. They weren't trying to select the "right girl" for me, or anything like that; they were just concerned with what I did.

My peers were probably almost the opposite of my parents. They tried to influence my choice of dates, and I often resented it very much. I was in a clique in high school because of my participation in athletics. Those guys were very social-minded individuals; unfortunately they often thought they were superior to most of the other people around the school. I was expected to date girls within the same group, and I really resented this. When I dated girls who were not in the group I was ridiculed by my friends. I would get pissed off at this because I felt these people were trying to judge others when they had problems of their own.

As I grew older and more mature, I began to get a much greater feeling out of my dates. When I became attached to a certain girl, I would be truly concerned about her. I started to be much more aware of people's outlooks on life and how they thought about things. If I did not like a girl, I would not prolong the relationship in an attempt to change my feelings about her. I would simply not go out with her again, and I would search for someone else to date. For instance, if I found out that a girl was "cheap" or had poor morals, I was rarely attracted to her, which was unlike me at the first part of my dating career.

I felt that sex was not the main goal of a date, but that having a good time was more important. If sex did happen, I tried to take it as something natural in a mature relationship. I was not down on sex by any means, but it became less important in my dates. The selection of my dates often was based upon physical attraction. The other basis for dating a girl was the way she acted.

I was also changing the things that I did on dates. At the beginning I would almost always go to a drive-in movie, because then I was looking for sex. Now that sex had taken a step down, I tried to go places where my partner and I could just have an enjoyable time.

If I dated a girl quite a bit, I would often go steady with her. This type of relationship was much different from the usual date. To go steady with a girl I had to be physically attracted to her and to like her personality. I also had to feel that we were at least somewhat compatible. Steady relationships changed my normal routines. I was not trying to impress the girl or put on a phony act. I simply tried to be myself and expected her to do the same. Since we spent more time together, we learned much more about each other. Such a relationship often provided more sex, but the sex occurred a much smaller percentage of the time we spent together, because we enjoyed each others' company. Parents also stepped into these relationships, because of the time we would spend at one another's homes.

I really grew into a fairly mature person during high school, though my grades probably would have been better if I had not spent so much of my time dating. For my graduation my folks gave me a new Chevy Camaro. It really blew my mind; I hadn't expected anything like that at all.

My post-high school sex experiences are numerous, but they involve a short time span. At this point I have almost reached the ultimate in knowledge and confidence in my sexual relations with the opposite sex. My attitude toward sex has been, I am sure, totally set for my future life, because it has not changed at all for the past two years.

DISCUSSION   *What do you feel about Bruce's prediction? Does it allow for changes in his own personality, the social and psychological characteristics of his sex partner(s), or the emergence of problems that will enter into his sexual behavior?*

I am still living with my parents, and my relationship with them is very close. My parents are always frank with me when sex is discussed, and I am very happy about this. They still show the same concern about my girls as they did during my adolescent years. This is beginning to please me. Once in a while they will ask me to go somewhere with them and bring a girl along with me. I feel that this is a good thing, because it makes me feel more in the adult class.

My brother is now married, and we are still very close. His relationship with his wife helps show me some of the good and bad points concerning marriage. At this time I do not want to get married. I feel that there have been a couple of girls with whom I could be very happy, but only at the right time. I would like to get most of my schooling completed before marriage and be somewhat stable economically.

My present behavior in sexual situations is quite natural and calm. I behave as if I am very sure of myself, and I think I am. I act as mature as possible by trying to be myself—not phony or put on any acts—and behave in a sane manner. I should stress that my relations with girls are now much closer. I will not go out with a girl unless I feel that we have some interests or share some feeling in common. I try to become much more mentally involved with my dates and to learn as much as possible. Sex is not the main goal of my relationships, but it is a very welcome extra. My steady relations in the past year have almost always ended in intercourse, even though it was not overly pushed from either side. I feel that this is largely because girls no longer try to protect their reputations. Their parents now are not quite as protective, and the girls do what they feel like doing. This is a thought based on experience with post-high school females.

DISCUSSION   *How correct do you feel Bruce's analysis of contemporary female sexual attitudes and behavior is? Is Bruce psychologically able to accept women as equals in sexual motivation and behavior, or is he likely to still be more in tune with the double standard than he is prepared to acknowledge?*

My male peers are now falling into much the same pattern as I am, and therefore my friends and I can still communicate quite adequately. We do not discuss sex as often as before, and when it is discussed it is more as one giving the other advice rather than answering questions.

In summary, I feel I am now fully mature in my attitudes. I feel that sex is fine as long as it is used in the right way and with the right people. I now do not wish to make it with girls I do not care for. When I engage in sexual intercourse, I feel that my mate and I ought to gain a closeness to each other. From my discussions with the girls, they tend to agree with this statement almost 100 percent of the time.

ALF   *Alf does not seem to be afraid to acknowledge his own*
                         troubles and problems in the context of a broken family
                         unit and the economic strains that accompanied it. His
                         comments show some of the conditions and experiences
                         not usually thought of in connection with modern
                         Swedish family life. His sexual learning did not unfold
                         with all the smoothness Bruce reported. His conception
                         about adult sexual behavior, like that of many Swedish
                         young people, tends to emphasize the problem of finding
                         social intimacy in relationships.

I was rather disappointed in Bruce's history. He makes
no impression upon me of having grown up in the U.S.A., with the
difficulties that that would give an ordinary person. Bruce is very
clever in his discussion. He writes a happy ending for himself,
but I doubt that life works out so smoothly for most of his friends.
I became bored with the way he always solved his problems and
came out smelling like flowers.

I am glad that I did not have to suffer from life in American society, just to have all the "fun" with girls that Bruce describes over and over again. I see too clearly the pressures of
sex on the individual in America. I wonder whatever would have
happened to me if I had had to go through all the pressures that
were always on Bruce. All of that dating with meaningless contact!
What becomes of the individual who is not handsome or beautiful,
who is too thin or too fat, or who is shy and afraid? It is obvious
that sex is regarded as something of utmost importance in American society, and the whole value of an individual is measured in
those terms. In Sweden it is just fucking.

I cannot give you as nice a picture of myself as Bruce
was able to paint of himself, but I shall honestly try to compare
the important aspects of my life with his. First there is the disadvantage of my family life. My mother and father became divorced
when I was four. My mother went to work in a factory, while my
grandmother came to live with us and take care of us. My brother
is eight years older, and my sister is one year younger than I—an
unusual pattern, I suppose. While my mother worked, my grandmother was in the mother's role. Also, my older brother was very
dominant over my sister and me. My grandmother educated us
with old principles. Thus, perhaps my family was not a normal
Swedish one.

During my first years of school my life was not unusual.
I often played with my classmates after school. I was mainly interested in playing soccer and hockey. I thought nothing about girls
and sexual matters. Perhaps girls were of little interest to me
because I disliked some of the restraints put on me by my mother
and grandmother. Playing all the time with male classmates may
have been a substitute for not having a father in our home. These
years were very difficult for all of us in the family. I was ashamed
that we were poorer than the families of my friends, so I would not
have them come to see where we lived. Only in sports was I equal
to or better than the other children.

When my older brother became sixteen, he moved out to
live with a girl in the city. Actually he was pushed out because my
grandmother discovered he had been drinking. It was a tragedy for
me, because I really liked my brother and could not understand how
liquor could be the cause of so much trouble. Yet it was because
of liquor that my parents had divorced and that, before I was born,
my grandfather had had a fatal accident. Thus, there was always
a lot of preaching about drinking to my sister and me. But almost
nothing was ever said about sex.

When I was about eleven, I felt some awakening of interest
in girls, but it was in a strange way. We boys began to notice how
the breasts of some of the girls were beginning to grow. Several of
us tried to grab and squeeze them if we could catch them. Sometimes my friends and I would talk of sex, but it was only to make
use of the words we knew and to have a few laughs about it all.
Listening to the older boys talk about such things also interested us,
but we did nothing with our knowledge.

When I was beginning my teenage years, I discovered that
some changes were taking place in my body. Hair began to grow
around my cock and under my arms, and my sex organ began to
grow in size. I became proud of my cock, especially when I noticed
that it was larger than those of the other boys. While taking a bath
I would make it hard and measure it. I had seen porno pictures in
books, and I knew that I was as mature as the older men in the
pictures. I had regularly played with myself in the bath during my
younger years, but not with much sexual interest.

I had my first orgasm when I was thirteen. It was a very
bad experience. I was simply lying in the bathtub rubbing myself
with some soap around my cock, and suddenly, without warning, an
immense amount of sperm shot out. It was as if it would never
stop. It went all over me and into the bath water. Not only was it

a mess to confront, but there was actually a very sickening feeling inside of me when it happened. I have not heard of other boys having this feeling about their first orgasm, so perhaps it was just different for me. For several months it worried me quite a bit. The thought of sperm floating all around in the bath water made me worry that my sister might become pregnant from bathing in the same tub.

It was several months before I masturbated again, and when I did I really tried to avoid orgasm. This time I felt immense pleasure and satisfaction. My sex education in school and from my friends had not taught me what to expect. I firmly believe that the schools should teach, as they now do, about masturbation in order to avoid the problems I felt. Unfortunately there are those who would object to messages that describe the pleasure from masturbation.

I began to masturbate more and more often, and by the time I was fifteen I was doing it almost every night. To my knowledge my practice was not detected by my family. I did not discuss it with friends, either. Like Bruce, I felt it was a natural thing to do until you could start fucking girls—which at that point was still a few years away for me.

My life at home had become quite dull. My grandmother became hopelessly ill and required much attention from both my sister and me. When I was fifteen, we moved to a better apartment in Stockholm. This took me away from all of my old friends, leaving me quite shy and lonely. The students in my new school already knew each other, and I was the stranger.

An improvement came when my class went on a camping trip. My first real contact with a girl came on the bus. After a couple of hours we sat with our chosen girls, and some hours later my girl and I sat together holding hands and then kissing. This camping trip was almost a week long, and we traveled through much of Sweden and Norway. The boys would always try to make plans to meet the girls at night so we could have some fun, but the teacher was wise to such plans. All of us were very innocent in our experiences with each other at this time.

At sixteen I was much more on my own. My grandmother died, thus leaving my sister and me more control over our own lives. I began to spend some time with my brother, who lived in Stockholm with his wife and little baby son. My relationship with my sister also became much stronger during these years.

Unfortunately, my mother has never been close to us, and I now see how my father found it difficult to love her fully. She is quite cold, and not at all like my sister. She has not had any interest in finding another husband. Sometimes I would think that my father could return to our mother, but when I was nine years old he married another woman. I believe my father is quite happy, and we children respect his role in our lives.

My friends in high school and I were happy just talking with each other. It was quite enough if girls were among us. Two girls were important to me as good friends, but the idea of a romance like Bruce would have wanted could not have occurred with us.

I read many books about the biological facts and then more books on fucking, but for many years I was quite content only to imagine what a fuck with a girl would be like. The girls I knew did not encourage me to use my knowledge. Not until my last year in high school did I have my first fuck. We were both nineteen and felt quite a lot for each other. It was the first time for both of us. I understand that the first time for many is not too good, so I do not think it too important now that it was somewhat of a disappointment to me.

Eva and I often studied together at her home, and I believe her family liked me very much. Her father, a doctor, was like a father to me. We had some very good talks with each other. He even said that he hoped I could always be with his daughter and that I could have his help to study medicine at the university. This closeness with her family was very significant to me for the two years I was with this girl. It even controlled our sex life to some extent. For the first six months of our relationship there was only some kissing and caressing.

When Eva and I finally had our first fuck together, it was a nervous experience for both of us. I think we both knew exactly what was going to happen. We were alone at her apartment, because her parents were on a holiday. We drank some brandy with some beer. Then we lay down in the same bed and caressed each other. I was really excited, but she seemed to be quite dizzy from the brandy and beer. After some time we felt our total nakedness. Naturally all of this resulted in our first fuck. I had an orgasm immediately after breaking her virginity. She did not understand why it happened so quickly, and was hurt by not having been given more by the experience. So we just lay in bed together for a long time while she cried. I was disappointed in how quickly it was over myself.

This problem of coming too quickly was heavy on my mind for the next few times, so each time I masturbated before being with her. This perhaps kept the pressure from ending our loving too soon. Eva, though, had no problem. After our first time she always had orgasms. She really liked to have sex and would get very hot. I view our sexual relationship as the least important part of our friendship with each other.

Unfortunately the relationship was interrupted by my military service. After some months I was able to come to Stockholm almost every other week to be with Eva. I usually stayed with her family. It was common for me to sleep in the living room on a guest bed. Sometimes we would come home after drinking a little more beer than we should have had, and we would often have a nice fuck. Because Eva was at the university now and I was in the military service, I think her parents looked upon our sexual interests with an accepting view. Her father had even made sure that she was using the latest birth-control device, a special plastic coil. This beautiful relationship came to an end because she began to feel too lonely when I was away. I am sure that if I had been with her she would not have fallen in love with another student at the university.

DISCUSSION   *Is this an example of rationalization? Does Alf's inter-pretation soften his feelings of failure? If he becomes aware of his use of this mechanism, is he likely to change his perception of these events? If eventually he no longer believes in his rationalization but continues to use the explanation with others for social reasons, would you say then that he is only "making an excuse" for himself? When people become conscious of their use of these mechanisms what do they do to replace those that no longer work, in your opinion?*

The end came when she refused to see me during one of my visits. She was then going with Ulf, an older student who had attractions I could not offer her. He was from a wealthy family and often spent holidays with his girls in Switzerland and Germany. The thing between Eva and me ended when she went to Bayreuth with him.

As you can imagine, I was deeply hurt at losing Eva. I did a lot of drinking in town with the other unhappy souls around me. The only thing that finally seemed to lift my spirits was the end of my military training. When I returned to Stockholm, I picked up the pieces of my life and began my studies at the university.

DISCUSSION   *On the basis of other Scandinavian cases, was Alf's retreat into social isolation and the use of alcohol as a response to his frustration unusual? Can you use this and other case material to identify what may be regarded as Swedish ways of dealing with frustration and anxiety in love affairs? How do American males tend to react under similar circumstances?*

This is now my second year in the school of education. During my first months I made some very good friends. The restaurant across the street was almost like a home for many of us.

Among our group was a very beautiful girl named Judit. I would often walk her to the subway station after lectures or meetings. Because the station had an RFSU sex shop inside, we talked about sex as a matter of conversation. She made it quite clear that she was not conservative in her attitude about sex, but was certainly not one to go off fucking in a meaningless way. Judit and I became very good friends before we were to have the joy of fucking with each other.

It happened four months after we met. It had been so long since Eva that I was afraid that I would be too fast at the beginning again, but nothing marred this beautiful experience. We had dozens of good fucks and quickly adjusted to each other's desires. Judit had been to bed with two other boys when she was in high school but she had had no sexual experience with boys at the university. Of course, many of the students were very interested in her, but it was not her nature to oblige them, especially when we began to develop our relationship.

Judit is very experimental in her view of sex. Her attitudes were much more advanced than my own. She bought several very good books on how to get the utmost satisfaction from fucking, and we did many of these things. Sometimes we would even have a few laughs at ourselves. I really think such books are ridiculous for people to follow seriously.

DISCUSSION   *Do the attitudes and behavior Alf has attributed to Judit resemble the kinds of femininity and sexual interests Bruce or other American males would like to see in the opposite sex?*

Judit and I are still with each other. In the last few months we have fucked only a few times, because of the inconvenience of finding a place to do it. We always wait eagerly for her family to have a short holiday. Our sex relationship is good but would be nothing if there was not true love and respect.

In a few weeks I shall be twenty-two years old. I do not plan to marry for many years, although I believe in the importance of living together. I think marriage is only for those who have become absolutely sure about each other and who want children.

I only wish that I could meet Bruce, and then I wish that I could have you see us both ten years from now, to see what the realities of life have turned out to be for us. But, even more important to see, will be the differences between Sweden and what's left of the U.S.A.

TAGE

Tage, a serious Danish student, has given much thought to the place of sex in human relationships. Much of his commentary may seem rather opinionated, but it is likely to generate interest in the issues of sexual change in both Scandinavia and the United States. Following his effort at societal analysis, Tage gets around to discussing his own life. His childhood and adolescence seem to be related with honesty and candor. One gets the impression that a great deal has changed for Tage in the last several years that could not have been predicted for him earlier.

For introduction I would like to speak about sex in a rather abstract way. First, I believe that we are truly having a sexual revolution among the young people of the world. The old need to understand the importance of the new—the erotic—concept of sex of my generation. The issue is not whether there should be sexual freedom for lovers, but whether there should be erotic freedom for those who do not love each other in a meaningful way. Until now the idea was that sex was only for lovers. In Denmark there has been a long, culturally accepted tradition of sex before marriage, except among those who were very religious in the countryside; but sex without love is the sexual revolution in my land.

DISCUSSION   *Do you feel that Tage has accurately portrayed the meaning of sexual revolution here?*

I think young people in America are still wondering whether lovers should begin their fucking before marriage. For them sex still causes fear, shame, and guilt, even in love. Of course sex without love is the lowest form of dirt and evil, much worse than murder and genocide. Most moral preachments seem to be about sex in your country, not about the inhumanity and insanity of exploiting, starving, and killing fellow humans. That the young in America often protest this carnage causes me to pay tribute to them. But I think that the erotic concept of sex is still not the view of most young Americans.

The erotic concept is that it is healthy to express sexual feelings toward other people in ways that are satisfying to those involved. Some people think such an attitude is like turning the mind into a porno shop, but the porno only describes what is possible, as a cookbook shows how to make many kinds of food. You do not become a glutton because of cookbooks. Should we burn cookbooks because some fat people eat too much? The flourishing of the erotic concept in my country is due not only to the belief that people should be free to choose what is sexually right, but also to the belief that sex is a wonderful part of living to be available even to those who are without love. Since most people are without true love, we are discussing the predicament of modern man. Surely sexual frustration need not be added to his loneliness and alienation, which are frightful enough.

This does not imply that I see no place for faithful sex between lovers, if that is what both of them prefer. It is wonderful, I think, if two people can be happy and satisfied with each other all their lives. However, such people are probably unusual. I think we all come to be sexual bores with the same person eventually. Of course we need much more from life than sex. To give love to others and receive some for ourselves is the purpose of the best life. But fucking is something the individual must be able to put in its place and not confuse with more important human relationships.

We learned from our parents, the school, and our friends that sex was good only if it happened with strong and proved love for another, that without such a feeling you were supposed to feel shame and guilt. From my view the sexual revolution is the throwing over of the bad sex laws of the capitalist society and of the traditions from the old church.

DISCUSSION   *Tage's view is probably not representative of most Danish students. They would likely acknowledge his right to such sexual experience, but many would feel that certain kinds of sexual behavior are not emotionally gratifying, and so would not do what they are willing to permit others to do. In the final analysis, the sexual values and norms of a society are what the people actually do. Do you think most Americans perceive the erotic experience as separate from or part of other emotional needs and expressions?*

My friends and I do not live in perpetual eroticism, at the expense of other values and the more important social goals. On the contrary, we are much freer in our ability to work toward goals that are not sexual, because we can satisfy our needs for erotic pleasure and not confuse them with more serious ventures. We can truly feel love for people without turning them or ourselves into sex objects. Most of us can find erotic satisfaction outside of love relationships, and thus not feel frustration. A communistic state based upon love cannot have sex disrupting the love relationships, because these must hold it together if it is to work. The separation of love from sex is probably the goal we must work toward if we are to improve human life. The Danish erotic concept is the important beginning for the Western nations.

The capitalist world is founded on making people battle each other, not only for the benefits of human productivity, but also for sexual satisfaction. It is the interest of the capitalist society to turn people into sex objects within the system of marriage, the institution in which people become each other's private property. Marriage as we know it is sexual capitalism. It is especially sick in America, is it not? Why expect to find freedom in this bourgeois prison, which gives you only one other person to love out of all the billions of people? Why expect a healthy person to desire only one cellmate in the psychological prison of marriage? Sex can happen without owning people like pieces of property.

DISCUSSION   *Do you find any evidence of sexual defense mechanisms in Tage's analysis, or would such a judgment require evidence of frustration and anxiety on his part?*

I like Bruce very much, but I hardly think he is typical of Americans. He seems much too intelligent and gentle. Most of the Americans I have seen come to Copenhagen as if they were on a sex safari, here to shoot game with their frustrated little-boy cocks. A noisy and loud group they surely are. They have their fun at the movies, the exhibitions, the sex massages, and then they leave, missing the point of it all entirely. For them it is all Danish dirt. Listen to this now: it is Danish freedom they have tried to buy but are not healthy enough to enjoy. They are hypocrites, who crazily love and hate the erotic nature of sex.

Bruce seems much different. He is like me when I was fifteen or sixteen years old, all through fucking around with girls for a sex trip. He has moved from the sex trip to the love trip, fucks only when he likes a girl very much. To get his cock the girl must show love for him in the way he approves, I suppose by giving herself to him completely, like private property given to another for safekeeping. All of this is familiar to me, for I was much like Bruce in my first love affairs. I now regard this as a time of emotional insecurity.

About the way Bruce learned the biological information about reproduction, I can only feel the backwardness of American institutions. Such information has nothing to do with the nature of sex. Not to give complete knowledge to children about how babies begin and are born shows the extent of the unhealthiness of the American mind.

To finish my remarks about Bruce, I am very glad that he has been able to become so happy in his life. It would be quite interesting to hear what all his girlfriends say about him.

As for my own life, I am twenty-one. I was born and grew up in Copenhagen. My family is very bourgeois and would not be expected to produce a son with my views on sex, not to mention my support for communism. All of this did not come from an unhappy family life. It came from rational awareness of life and the foolishness I came to see in the world.

My sexual education at home was just a natural teaching about it. I clearly remember my parents telling me about how babies grew in the mother from the sperm and egg coming together. I remember seeing a dog give birth to pups when I was about six and not yet in school. I also remember seeing my parents naked. And, of course, when my younger sister and brother were born, there was no mystery about our sex organs, because we would often bathe together.

The sex education of my day was not good in school, but it was better than nothing for those children who had parents who would not discuss it. It was in about the third grade that our teacher explained the way children were formed and born. When I was about ten I noticed then that my brother, who was three years younger than I, would often have his cock stand in the morning. We both would practice making our cocks hard by rubbing and pulling them. Occasionally we would do it for each other. I believed we stopped doing it because it did not seem to lead to anything. I was about twelve when I was to rediscover the pleasure, after waking with a night dream. Soon masturbation was nightly habit.

I must have thought something was wrong with masturbation because I was careful not to let my parents or friends know. I did not care about my brother's knowing, but he did not seem to have much interest. In fact my own erotic interest was very low until a year or two later.

When I was thirteen we played a game called bottleneck at a party for the first time. It was just a way to get you to kiss a girl. I liked to play the game, but it was embarrassing to find all the girls wanting to kiss me.

When I was fourteen, I had my first homosexual experience. I see nothing wrong in homosexuality for those who prefer it for their erotic satisfaction. My best friend and I masturbated each other for about five or six months in various places, but I think we became bored with it as soon as we began to have sex with girls.

The same year my friend and I went with girls to a party. It was the first time I saw anyone fucking. My girl and I went into a bedroom, and while we were kissing we saw the older boy and girl fucking on the bed. I was very excited to see and hear them. The girl was very passionate, and I was surprised to see a girl be so aggressive in pulling the man into her. I think my girlfriend was rather shocked, but later she told me that she thought it was not a bad thing after all.

We went to bed with each other soon after this discussion, at her flat when her parents were not home. It went very well for us the first time, considering we knew so little. It was done with some fear by both of us. I remember that not wanting to hurt her was uppermost in my mind. I think I hurt her some, because my skills were so few for an inexperienced girl, but she was very brave. She said she was so happy not to be a virgin anymore, but I think she wondered whether it was all that good to have sex. It was not until the fourth or fifth time together that she was to have orgasm.

For almost a year we had sex whenever it was convenient, and sometimes when it was almost impossible. Fucking had become a very important part of our lives. Both of us talked a lot about our feelings, especially about how natural it was if you really loved each other—and we surely did! The main thing was to protect from pregnancy. We always used condoms. I did not mind them then, but now I prefer the girl to care for the protection in other ways. I enjoy the very sensuous feelings that come from having my uncovered member inside a warm and moist vagina.

With this girl I did not give much thought to what was happening between us in the physical relationship. It was like learning a sport and not knowing fully what the body should do, so one stays quite elementary, out of fear of making mistakes. It was usually over much too soon, and sometimes it was before I could satisfy her. Today I would use my mouth and tongue to give her orgasm if I could not stop myself from coming early. Not to give a girl her orgasm when she wishes it shows a terrible lack of care for her.

After my first love was finished, I started looking at other girls. I enjoyed talking with my friends about which ones were good for loving and which ones for fucking. When a friend would fall in love with a girl, he would usually keep his mouth closed about having sex with her.

It was almost a year before I got a new girl. During this time I was masturbating a lot. I enjoyed reading porno books. The picture books were much too expensive, and they soon became tiring, but reading about good fucking could be quite stimulating. My parents did not object to my masturbating, if they knew.

The next girl lived in another section of the city. We met in the summer. We were both ripe for delusional romance. Within two weeks we were deeply in love, as in an American romantic movie. Soon we were in bed. I did not know how experienced she was with boys until she told me. She was quite surprised that I had only been with one other girl in my life. Truly, we had wonderful times together, making the most passionate love possible between a man and woman. I liked the discovery of using our mouths and tongues upon each other's sex parts. It was almost as good as the best of our fucking together. To give a girl an orgasm with the tongue is a real thrill for me—more than for the girl to do the same with me, when I always think about how nice it is to be all the way at the end of her vagina.

This girl and I were together until I finished high school. It was a typical bourgeois love affair. It had the approval of our parents, although I did not like her father at all. One night he discovered us fucking on the floor in their parlor. We thought her family was sleeping, as it was quite late. When he turned on the light, he saw everything and ordered me out of the house. It was two months before we spoke to each other. At least her mother had known, because she had been told by my girl.

My family was happy for us to be together. She was often at my home. Most of the time we would be in my room only to listen to music, to talk, and to do some studying together. When we wanted our privacy, we would simply close the door. We had many sexual satisfactions, but spending so much time together was also boring me some. I began to think it was like a marriage.

After high school it ended. One night I had found a very beautiful Norwegian girl waiting alone outside the cinema. I walked her to the apartment building where she was staying. We were together every night while she was in Copenhagen. Because of my other girlfriend, I could not bring her home. She was a secret love for almost a full month. We would often go to Tivoli or just walk and sit in the botanical garden. When it got dark, we would fuck on the grass in the park. It was very good for me to know such a happy person. She was very spirited and full of fun and laughter. My conscience told me to inform my other girl that I had fallen in love with someone else. This was not easy for me to do. She cried and cried. I felt terrible for her, but what could I do? As it turned out, when my Norwegian girl returned to Bergen I had no one. My other girlfriend was typically bourgeoise about it at the very end. I had been unfaithful and was not repentant enough to suit her. The main trouble was to explain to my family that it was finished. They really loved her like a daughter, even though we had been together only one year.

My first year at the university I found many new friends and began to have some new interests, especially in political matters. The students were very active in trying to change society. At last I found a real purpose, in the study of government and ideology. It was not all work for me. I was often at parties with my friends, but now the talk was almost always about serious social and political issues, and there was little dancing and loving. There were some very beautiful and interesting girls among us, but it was difficult to get them interested in sex.

In my first year I went to bed with only one girl, a music student, but the affair was without much seriousness.

DISCUSSION   *Considering Tage's penchant for analysis, what may account for his inability to discuss this relationship? Could the failure of this affair have caused him to question the need for social intimacy in sexual relationships?*

In the fall I found several other girls to be with for both friendship and sex. With two of them I began to see more fully the value of the erotic concept. I found that sexual satisfaction could come without all the involvement. These last two were very intelligent and free about sex. Our friendships were very simple.

In the last year I have been to bed with fourteen girls. Some were very good in all the ways I like, and some of them meant very little to me, even sexually. The excitement I have had with all of these girls is very important to my way of thinking about sex now. I feel that I have almost completely explored all the sexual paths to enjoyment with girls. Now I am becoming more routine in my pleasure, but this is not from lack of desire for new adventure. I think that with much experience it develops that what remains to be new is only new people and their personalities. So perhaps I am looking more at the person than the fucking. The erotic concept is fully developed in my life now, and I doubt that I could ever want to change. Needless to say, the bourgeois institution of marriage cannot have a future for those who love the freedom of life.

DISCUSSION   *How do you feel about Tage's analysis of sex and the institution of marriage? Do you think Tage has discovered "the freedom of life"?*

chapter II

Elaine, Margareta, and Gurli

ELAINE

Elaine is one of seven children. The parents took many precautions to ensure that the children learned to conform to their traditional and conservative values and norms. Religious beliefs and practices reinforced this parental socialization. Until late adolescence Elaine has described herself in a manner that would suggest she was a willing captive of this environment. Following graduation from high school she undergoes rather remarkable changes in both social and sexual behavior. Her behavior takes on the characteristics of an intelligently planned and fearlessly executed assault on what her parents and church had tried to teach her concerning sexual values.

      I can recall little of my early childhood sex molding and experiences, especially about the first seven years of my life. Maybe it is because I wish to suppress the memories, but after conscientious reflection, I've ruled this out for specific reasons: (1) I'm too far into sex now for coy reserve, (2) I've had a couple of psych courses, which show that suppression never does anyone any good, and (3) I'm very curious as to where this sex research into myself will take me.

I come from a large family. There were seven of us, and
I was number three in line. One boy and one girl had preceded me.
Until four years ago we lived in an eastern university town, where
my father was a professor of biological sciences. He married his
lab assistant. If you are thinking this was a perfect setup for a
child's being clued in to the body and its mechanics—you lose! Dad
surely did try, but Mom is Victorian all the way.

There was never one talk from Mother to any of us girls
about sex, feeling, moods, and so forth. I can recall hearing from
a school acquaintance some words about sex when I was in the fourth
grade, but I honestly couldn't understand what she was talking about.
To think of asking Mom or Dad about it was beyond me. My sisters
and I (two of them quite close to my own age) shared and enjoyed
one another, but we never had an intimate conversation about sex or
boys, or even love.

Another big factor in my early childhood was religion. During my childhood and youth there was a constant stream of priests
and nuns, who were also cousins, aunts, and uncles. I think these
influences kept me stunted and incapable of anything even remotely
related to sex or knowledge about it. I never had any sexual experiences with other kids until I was in my last year of high school.

I was twelve when my menses began. This first day is still
vivid in my memory. I remember waking up in the morning with
blood on my thighs and bedcovers and vomiting on the floor when I
saw the mess. I was so frightened I couldn't even call to my sister.
My noise finally awakened her, and of course she ran to get Mom.
Mom did her best to clean me up quickly, but hardly said a word
when I asked what was wrong with me. She only gave me detailed
instruction about how to dispose of the soiled Kotex, then left me
in bed to ponder the mystery of my "wound."

I was scared and almost hysterical until my father came
in later in the morning with a large bottle of cough medicine,
which I learned was to be used for cramps each month. It was
Dad who told me what was happening to my body, what to expect
each month, and how a woman keeps a calendar. I was glad to
know that I was normal and that what was happening to me was
happening all over the earth to all women.

This day was important to me in a couple of other respects.
First, I had taken a hand mirror from the bathroom to try and see

how I had cut myself to make me bleed like that. Because of the
mess, I started to vomit again. Since then I have never been curious to handle or explore my vagina. It also probably caused me
never to feel any interest in masturbation. I never objected to my
later boyfriends feeling me or putting their fingers in me, but I
could never do it for myself—not for sexual pleasure anyway.

I was not quite thirteen when I started the small Catholic
high school for girls that my parents had selected. I was surrounded
by nuns constantly. My activity with classmates was quite limited.
The wildest talk was about who sneaked a smoke.

In high school I never had a date that was not arranged by
my parents or some of the nuns, and those dates were always chap-
eroned. At school the girls would discuss the boys who came to our
parties, but one of my school friends, while she played the role of
sweet and innocent for the nuns, was having sexual intercourse with
her boyfriend. I would beg her to tell me all the sinful details. The
act of sexual intercourse was still a bit of a blur in my mind. I did
not even know until she told me that a man had an erection.

Usually my mother would call an acceptable mother who had
an acceptable son, and then the "children" would be allowed to go out
to the places she thought were acceptable, usually the local theater,
an ice cream shop, and then home. The first time I said I'd prefer
not going again with a particular boy my mother became pale and
nearly had a fainting spell, which was one of her favorite stunts under
stress. She took me in the bathroom, locked the door, and wanted to
know WHY?—"Did he touch you anyplace"? Only one boy touched me
"anyplace" while I was still in high school. With him I had two dates.
(I always had to have things end after two dances at school or two
dates at home. To go on with a boy any further would have made it
"too serious.") I let this boy kiss me, feel my breasts, and even
let his hand wander up my dress. But the struggle I put up when he
tried to make it into my panties called it all off.

The year after high school I sure as hell matured. The
nuns and my mother would not let me start college because they considered that I was too immature. They decided I should go to a
religion-oriented business school for a year. To get to this school
I had to walk past a bunch of sex and "art" theaters. There were a
few girls in my class who decided that since my mother was such a
problem in sex education they would share what they knew with me.
I could hardly wait to get to school in the morning, to get my real
education. After a month or so, one of them suggested that we all
go to one of the movie houses. Her older brother bought the tickets.

There were five of us girls and him. We stayed from 8:00 A.M.
to 3:00 P.M., when school was out. I knew then what it took to
make love with a man. My attitudes about dates and boys were
very different after that, but I was a long way from the sexual
revolution.

After these explicit sex films I sought the advice of some
of my educated classmates on how to get out of the rut I was in. I
began to believe that my life was really unbearable, partly because
I was now intensely aware of sexual feelings and yearnings. I was
quite ready to do almost anything to be a little more free. The
advice they had was simple: clue my dates that I really could be a
normal girl and enjoy doing some physical things with them.

When my next date showed up, he had his dad's car. We
went to the usual movie, and at first there was the usual polite trash
talking. But soon I broke the ice. I rolled out a few outrageous
"movie lines" on him, which completely turned off the home controls
in him. He later laughed about how his folks had given him a set of
rules to follow—no holding, kissing, or parking on the first date. On
our first date we kissed and cuddled in the car for over an hour.

When I wanted to date only this one boy, Mom became in-
furiated and even went through her fainting routine. Fortunately
Dad was on my side, so I dated him for the whole year. I also
allowed Mom to think that he was developing as a suitable suitor
because of his intellectual and cultural qualities. After a while
she was pleased beyond measure. She was so conscious of status
and wealth that she seemed to almost be from another world.

A month or so after our first date we were completely on
our own. We'd check out the papers for any concerts, operas, or
exhibits (always something of a cultural nature), then talk it up all
week—allowing our parents to think that this was where we were.
Then we would head for a deserted lake in the warm season or an
abandoned ski shack when the weather was rainy. Our kissing and
petting soon gave way to sex, sex, sex, as long as were were together.

He used a condom each time we had intercourse, but he
would put it on only after we had been having intercourse for a while
and he thought he was coming close to an orgasm. His inquiries
about a woman's period and his fascination with the question of where
the "blood" came from were very naive for an eighteen-year-old boy
who seemed so knowledgeable about everything else. One time we
were having a very wild and thrashing around kind of intercourse,
and I remember his stopping and whispering that we had better stop

because he did not want me to start menstruating from it. I said nothing, but we did slow down a bit, just in case he was onto something I didn't know about.

Our sex acts were <u>all</u> in the normal range. I was quite happy to do it the same way time after time. I always had a very satisfying orgasm unless he was too fast, and even then it did not matter if we had a lot of time, because I would have one the second time we would have intercourse.

All of this ended just before my family moved to Los Angeles, because we were found out from things I let slip out at home, and the mothers did the rest. Neither of us minded.

DISCUSSION   *What personality variables do you recognize in Elaine that enabled her to undo much of her earlier conditioning in this relationship with a young man who was equally limited?*

When we moved to Los Angeles, I went to work in a bank. Mother thought a brand-new bank would be a great place to find an acceptable husband, and I just seemed to keep working there because I didn't have much desire to go back to school.

A bank is a very bad place to get dates. The only men interested in girls working there are much too old. Sometimes I felt so hungry for a man that I think some of the customers must have worried that I was going to pull them through the hole of my teller's window.

DISCUSSION   *American women have traditionally been reluctant to discuss their sexual frustration with others, whereas men have often been free and outspoken. What was the source of this difference? To what extent do you think this has changed? What may be some of the consequences?*

A few months before I left the job and enrolled in college the "big event" happened. My mother and father separated. Mother hated Los Angeles, and, frankly, some of her personal behavior had become quite odd and upsetting to the rest of us. She returned to live in an apartment near our old home in the East, where she could be near the children who "really loved" her.

This event caused some changes in my role. I became mother-housekeeper-cook-mender-of-socks, and all. I don't mind the arrangement at all. I can date boys and be out as long as I wish, with no one saying one damn thing.

My experience with men in college has been more than interesting. Since my twentieth birthday I have been to bed with seven boys. I have sex needs, and I have a right to get them satisfied! I still have some guilt hang-ups about sex, but they're gradually disappearing. I can work pretty well around them with the right guy, but finding the right guy is not always easy.

My religious conflicts really hurt me sometimes. While I feel my church has some very out-of-date ideas about sex and morality, I do want to marry in the church some day. I think that I can be a very faithful wife to a good husband, and my present pattern of sex behavior is just what must be until I find the right guy. This includes the need to find the right sex partner. I know they're all different in their sexual behavior. Several of these guys were very nice, but their sexual approach did not match their personalities at all. I don't think a girl—or, for that matter, a boy—should trust her intuition about the other's sexuality before marriage. I hope that God will someday be able to forgive my stupidity, but I worry about spending eternity with a dud.

DISCUSSION   *What should constitute reasonable proof that a man is not sexually a "dud," and will not become one in the future? Would Elaine easily accept the idea that she could be a factor in any sexual dysfunction that might occur in a sexual relationship?*

What have I learned from these boys? I found that some of them were only interested in their own satisfaction and cared little for what was happening to me. I discovered that I don't like the following:

guys who want sex during my menstrual period

guys who have too much hair all over their bodies

guys who have no interest in foreplay

guys who never will talk during sex

guys who try to enter my vagina too soon

guys who are not clean and showered

guys who do not like to kiss and lick my breasts

guys who cannot keep from coming too soon

guys who have bad breath

guys who want to smoke while having intercourse

guys who think only they can call the plays (positions)

guys who get a thrill from hurting if they can

guys who will not hold me after their orgasm

guys who have very large or small penises
(or strangely bent)

guys who do not like to feel my genitals

guys who do not on occasion like to kiss them
(let's face it, I love this before actual intercourse,
but it has not interested some of my bedmates,
which I think is a misfortune)

The list could go on, but so much of it is hard to put in words because it's all about feelings and very delicate to communicate with another.

Perhaps I could tell you what I liked from the best of them. First, I like to be able to go to a nice place, one with a stimulating and romantic spirit about it (no hotels, motels, or back seats of cars). I like to feel the guy really likes me, and that it's not just a one-night roll in the hay. He should have sexy eyes and a very manly body, with gentle fingers. A nice sense of humor can make going to bed seem like fun instead of a hospital operation. A willingness to talk about his sexual desires before he tries them out is important if something far-out is in his head. (I'm willing to try almost anything at least once, but I don't want it to sneak up on me, though—like rectal intercourse!) I find mutual oral copulation very nice for part of the sex act but would never want the guy to have an orgasm with me that way. I like complete privacy for sex. He should be willing to let me have some choice of position, especially after the first few times.

DISCUSSION   *Elaine has obviously given a lot of thought to what she wants and does not want in a sexual relationship. How realistic are her expectations? Does she seem to have a greater or lesser capacity to adjust to a sexual partner now than during her first sexual relationship? As female sexual expectations increase as the result of continuing experience, does this pose additional problems for the male in satisfying their needs?*

I can see I have come a long way in a short time. The main problem now is to find a young man who fits my particular combination of sex needs and personality. I will eventually find him, but it may take a little time. There is a very good possibility that I am just at the beginning of my struggle to become sexually mature. When I get married, I want a definite feeling that my husband and I are well matched in sex as in other things. I would hate to think that my sex life in marriage was some sort of problem to be solved instead of a natural joy and pleasure. The problems of marriage are difficult enough without having to discover far-out sex quirks in oneself or the other.

This sounds like the end, but I believe for me it is just the beginning.

MARGARETA   *Margareta feels that she and Elaine have had something in common concerning their sexual learning, but wonders how they can be so different. The comparison illustrates the importance of social and psychological change in adulthood. Margareta's commentary also reveals that growing up in a sexually permissive society is not in itself a guarantee of finding gratification in heterosexual relationships. Her parents hardly seem the best of models from which to cast attitudes relating to heterosexual intimacy. Margareta describes in some detail her struggle to break away from early social and sexual conditioning. For her these years of young adulthood have brought many changes in attitude and behavior.*

I am surprised that Elaine could come out so sexually free after her bad life with her family, especially her mother. Somehow I believe that she is still hiding a lot from us and herself. Maybe she has forgotten, or wants to forget. But if her childhood was much worse than she tells us, perhaps it is better for her to think of her present problems. It is to her credit that she can talk about her life with some freedom.

I am one year older than Elaine, and an only child. Both my father and my mother belonged to the working class. We always lived in a medium-sized apartment building in Stockholm, which has by now become quite old and less than beautiful. Now that my parents have more money for a better apartment it is impossible to find.

Like Elaine, I did not have much contact with my mother. When my mother was very young, she expected a child, but my grandmother forced her to have an abortion, with the result that she was never able to have children. I think that this greatly influenced her attitudes toward sex and me. I was adopted, and I do not think my mother ever really loved me. I always felt that she expected too much of me, as if she wanted some kind of reward for taking care of me as a small child.

During my childhood and teen years I had a feeling that something was wrong, and I wondered a lot about whether I was their child. I found them so different. Most children have this kind of thought, from what I have read. I was fifteen years old when I learned that I was adopted, and I was very shocked by the way I learned. My mother got very mad about something and threw it in my face. It was like, "You better learn to know it— we are not your parents." My father tried to comfort me, but it was impossible. I felt so lost and will never be free of the feelings I had then. I should have been told at the earliest time.

Perhaps it is just a normal and natural thing for many girls to love their fathers more than their mothers. Anyway, this is the way I felt. My father was engaged in educational work for the people, and he loved music and played several instruments. Much of my love for literature and music came from him. He always tried to answer my questions.

My sex education at home was zero. When I once asked my mother how children came into the world, she said that I came from a flower. I thought about it and came to the conclusion that she must be wrong. When I was about ten years old, I discovered from a class that babies came from the mother. But she told me that I should not talk about such things. I remember very clearly that I could not understand why she did not want to talk about such a fascinating matter.

What I learned at school was incomplete—that children were made by the mother and father coming together with the sperm and eggs and that many months later there would be the birth. The thing that troubled me was that the mothers had to stay for a while at the hospital to do some terrible things to themselves and the children. Doctors and nurses at the hospital were frightening to me. I pitied all persons who had babies and was even afraid about my own future. I started to think about this when I was about seven. I never played with dolls from that time on, and I never wanted to have any babies.

My mother and father were very quiet with each other. My father had his music, and my mother had her reading. I never thought about their having a sexual relationship until I was thirteen years old. For several nights when I was this age, the three of us slept in one room because my father was painting and fixing some cabinets in our bedrooms. In the middle of the night I woke up and saw my mother and father having intercourse. I did not know what they were doing. I only saw my naked father lying on my mother, behaving strangely. I watched them very quietly and could see in the darkness fairly well. My mother saw me and whispered something angrily to my father, who then got off her. I saw his large, stiff penis for the first time. Like Elaine, I did not know that men had erections. I did not say anything to them but pretended that I did not see what I had been looking at for so many minutes. My immediate impression was that what they were doing was nasty and ugly, and stories I heard from my girlfriends later that year added to my feeling. This picture has been very vivid in my mind, and only after I found out that intercourse was very nice did my feeling about it change.

I went to school until I was seventeen, the last seven years in a girls' school. Then it was to high school. I was not a very popular child. I was always too quiet with the other children. Unlike Elaine, there were no restrictions about whom I was allowed to be with. I played with both boys and girls. There was very little talk about sex among my playmates.

Exactly like Elaine, I remember my first menses very well. I was just fourteen. I discovered it in the morning, but I dared not tell my mother until evening. I waited and waited. Finally I had the courage to say, "Mother, I think I have got menses." Exactly like Elaine's mother, there was no talk about my growing up or about how I felt. She only told me that I had to buy those things that women use when they have their menses. At that age I was still disinterested in boys, but I suddenly discovered that boys

used to look at me, and I became aware that I was at least a little
pretty. But I did not think that I was pretty enough. My mother
would make fun of me when I spent too much time brushing my hair
and looking at myself in the mirror. She would say that I could not
do anything to become more beautiful and that I should not waste my
time with such foolishness. It was always better for me, she
thought, only to work hard on my schoolwork.

When I was still fourteen, I can remember becoming utterly
conscious of myself and my appearance. I worried so much that I
was not pretty enough that until I was sixteen years old, I blushed
and behaved very strangely when I was talking to boys. As I had no
sister or brother, I was a very lonely child. My friends from the
school were all that I had.

When I became sixteen, my romantic interest in boys increased. I remember my first kiss very well. I was at the cinema
with a girlfriend. Next to me sat a boy who knew my girlfriend a
little. During the performance he put his arm around me, and later
he kissed me. I dared not do anything to prevent this, and I liked it
very much. For years I thought about that beautiful kiss, but I never
met the boy again. Shortly after this, I met Lars at a school dance.
For two years we were very close friends. Lars was also lonely at
home. His father was very authoritarian, and would beat him when
he would seek his freedom. I used to see the marks of his beatings
on his face and feel very sorry for him.

After Lars and I had known each other for some months,
we could talk freely about almost anything. I learned theoretically
about sex and what sexual intercourse means to a boy, but we never
practiced the theory. We did not do anything more than kissing and
embracing each other. He did not have any experience either.
Maybe it was easier that way for both of us. Still, I have regretted
it many times. When Lars's family moved from Stockholm to the
north country, I felt lost for many months. We wrote each other
many times, but I never saw him again.

In high school I started to date. I also discovered masturbation. One day I was reading a very passionate story, which
described how the boy put his hand on the girl's genitals and caused
her to feel the orgasm. As I read this, I did the same. I practiced
it regularly, even after I had petted with a boy. The boys I had
dated were very clumsy about doing it just the way I liked, and of
course it was not yet possible for me to tell them how to do it. It
did not matter that much. I knew that I could take care of myself
after I got home. What he would think of me was more important

than my sexual satisfaction with him.

The girls knew everything there was to know about sex and love. One girl had to leave school because she was expecting a baby. We thought that she had no morals. We also envied her knowledge and the experience of sexual intercourse, but I am sure that there were many who were silent about what they also had done with boys. After a while the attitude seemed to change. I started to feel old-fashioned, so I seldom acted as if I were a virgin. But I was never really tempted to give in. While I was at high school, I did not feel as close to any boy as I had to Lars.

At home they controlled me pretty much until I went to the university. I could not stay out as long as I wanted in the evening. I suppose they were afraid that I would become pregnant. When I was nineteen my mother and father suddenly started to talk to me about contraceptives. Remember, they had never talked to me about sex before at all. It was a terrible time. I had the courage to tell them that I did not wish to hear any more. They never brought the matter up again. It was too late for <u>them</u> to talk with me about sex!

When I was almost twenty, I met a boy to whom I became engaged. I thought that the time had come at last. Few of my friends thought you had to be in love with a boy to have sex, but I was different. Dag was very handsome. In his bathing suit he looked like a Greek god, and I noticed that other girls, and even boys, would admire his looks. I wondered why I deserved such a wonderful boy. It was with Dag that I was first to have sexual intercourse.

DISCUSSION   *What would account for Margareta's feelings? In what ways might such a negative self-concept cause a person to feel anxiety that could result in failure to develop a desired relationship? Could feelings of inferiority also result in failure in sexual relationships?*

We were at his parents' home alone for the whole day. Strangely enough, I had to persuade him the first time. We went to his bed and took off all of our clothes. It was the first time we had seen each other completely naked. We kissed each other with passion. I felt his penis in my hand, and he put his fingers in my vagina. Dag stopped only to put on the condom. I do not know why this irritated and frightened me, but it did. Of course it was the

proper thing to do, but it bothered me that our passion should be
harmed by this rubber thing between us. He, on his side, was
terribly nervous, knowing that I was a virgin. There was no pain
and no blood. Perhaps he was relieved to find it all so easy. I
think, like Elaine, I had lost the sign of my virginity when I was
practicing athletics. We did not know whether to laugh or to cry
after he had his orgasm.

We had intercourse many times after this. While it all
grew better in the later months, I never felt real satisfaction with
Dag. But I felt very much like a woman. I liked the foreplay with
him much more than the intercourse. I did not learn everything
with Dag, but I did learn that one should not feel any shame and
guilt in whatever one likes to do with the sex partner, as long as it
does not hurt the other and both like it.

The end of my time with Dag is the other side of my story
with him. He was sexually experienced with other girls before we
planned to marry. He knew that I did not feel the right satisfaction
with him. I knew this as well. I started to believe that something
might be wrong with me. I even wondered if my masturbation had
done something to prevent me from having orgasm with a man. I
could not talk with anyone about this, so I only read books about
sex, including your Kinsey report about women. I even would make
Dag think that I had an orgasm, but I did not. After some time we
were growing apart. We had discovered some things about each
other we did not like. My family, especially my mother, was not a
good discovery for him. I began to think that he was without ambi-
tion and purpose in life, like a boy who could not grow up. If we had
married, it would have been a mistake, quite unrelated to our sex
problem. The sex problem was not all forgotten in my mind. I even
wondered about men and whether they recognized when a woman was
released or whether they didn't care. Now I even wonder why I had
this problem and Elaine did not. Maybe she experienced good sex
from the very first, and it was all natural. I wonder how she was
able to get so much experience with boys so suddenly?

DISCUSSION   *How do you think Elaine might answer Margareta's*
question?

Dag and I decided not to get married last year. I thought of
killing myself at first. I knew that I would find it difficult to live
without him. I even thought that our sexual intercourse would get
better soon. He worried about the practical things, while I was concerned about the sex. He did not want to marry anyone until he was

finished with the university.

The past year at the university has been good in giving me some new activities. I have now dated other boys, but I have not dared to have intercourse with them. It is not the fear of pregnancy, but the thing about orgasm, that bothers me. Only once have I had an orgasm with a boy, and it was with his hand instead of his penis.

I feel that Elaine now knows very clearly what she wants to do sexually with a man. Her catalog of sex activities seems very complete and uncensored by her church. I have not thought so much about the sexual act or had so much experience with all the sexual actions she has opinions about. Perhaps she is correct in saying that without experience with many boys you never will know whether you can be happy with one man for a lifetime of sex. The penis and how it moves in the vagina cannot be the most important thing about the love between a man and a woman.

I have been with a new boy for the past month. We like each other very much but do not want to go to bed yet. We shall have sex eventually if we continue to like each other. I can take care of myself very well, and he can surely do the same for himself. Lasting love must take some time to grow, or it will be a spindly thing that cannot head into the wind without breaking. When the time comes to go to bed together, we will know it. It is the only way for me. So many of Elaine's experiences with intercourse must not mean much to her at all. In many respects, we were the same when we were younger girls, but now I feel we have become different.

DISCUSSION   *What factors may account for the differences in attitude and behavior between Elaine and Margareta at this point in their lives? Does Margareta seem typically Swedish, on the basis of comparisons with our other students?*

GURLI

Gurli describes growing up in relatively modest socio-economic circumstances in a Danish farming community. Her family life and peer relationships seem to provide the ordinary experiences of childhood in this social environment. At fourteen Gurli and her friends become involved in a rather complete way in the discovery of sexual relationships. For Gurli peer group influence appears to have been significant in her behavior. Through Gurli's description and analysis of her childhood and adolescence it is possible to understand the development of relatively free and open sexual attitudes and behavior as they carry over into adult relationships. Gurli says she is quite happy in her present relationships and life as a university student, and there seems little reason to doubt her.

Elaine and I grew up under different circumstances. My father was a house painter, and my mother had no education. I lived in a little village all my life, except for the past two years. My only sister is three years older than I. I did not have a brother, but there were many boys in the village to play with. I am now twenty years of age.

My family has always been poor, but my mother and father have given my sister and me a great deal of love and care. My mother was always loving, and not afraid about our knowing things about sex, even though she was shy in the telling sometimes. She would tell me anything I would ask when I was young. When I became older, I would ask my sister, because it was more natural for us to talk. I liked my sister's point of view about boys much more than my mother's. That is probably the way with most teenage girls who have good older sisters who are free and open in sex talk. It is confusing for a mother, who wants to protect. I believe that the schools should give sex education from the very beginning of schooling, but especially when puberty comes. I agree with Elaine that the church should keep its nose out of this, although it was to affect me when I was fourteen years old.

When I went to school I was seven. Playing with both boys and girls was normal for me. I liked boys but had no sexual interest in them until I was eleven. I watched the animals on the farms mating and giving birth. I knew that the penis went into the vagina and left seed to make a birth possible later, and that the animals were very excited during the fucking. When I asked my mother if it hurt the female animal, she told me that it never hurt, and the animals liked to do it at the right time of the year.

I was twelve years old when my first menstruation happened. But I did not get afraid because my mother had told me something about it when I was nine and eleven. I knew that she had her menstruation every month, and my sister had begun two years earlier. I even looked forward to it, because my sister had told me that it was the sign of becoming a woman. But when it did come, I changed my mind. I got a maddening pain in my stomach, and I wished that I was a boy! My mother did her best to comfort me. She was a little hard after a while in telling me that it was just the way it had to be unless I was going to have a baby. I thought that it was a terrible choice for God to have forced on women. My mother made coffee for my pain. Today I still drink very strong coffee when I have pains through my period.

When I was twelve, I "went with boys." That is, we were in a group, but as couples. We often changed partners, and everything at this age went against the girl or boy who would not kiss the others at our birthday parties. It was all innocent fun. The girls and I began to talk a lot about boys. My sister was a wonderful source of information. At night when we were going to sleep she usually entertained me with boy stories. For her age she was very shapely, and the boys liked her, so her goodnight stories were certainly not dull. She had her first intercourse with a neighbor boy when she was fifteen. I was always begging her to tell me how it was, but it was a year before she would tell me everything about it. I liked the boys in the older classes best. All the girls liked the older boys better, because our own classmates were much less interested in us.

For some sexual fun, two girlfriends and their boyfriends would go with my boyfriend and me to a barn. All three boys were older than us—fifteen and maybe sixteen. My Jens was the oldest, but not the most experienced. But by the time we stopped going to the barn that summer, we were all very experienced. We would hope that it would rain while we were at school, so we could have an excuse for returning home late. Our joke at school was to ask each other, "Do you think it will rain this afternoon"? If it did, we were sure to be together in the barn. This went on for almost four months until school ended.

I was very curious about how the other couples were doing

it with each other in the hayloft. It may have been my idea that we should always stay very close in the barn. It was very exciting for me to see this lovemaking and hear the passionate sounds of the kissing. I was surprised at first to accept the way boys had their orgasms, with the rush of the milky sperm out of the ends of their penises. I did not like the mess of it at the start.

We girls had our fears about pregnancy, and we talked of this when the boys were not with us. I could not agree that we should take the chance of becoming pregnant. We knew that there were such things as condoms, but the boy who promised to get some could not. But it was not only the matter of pregnancy. I worried that it would hurt me very much. I thought it would be very difficult to put Jens's large penis into me for fucking. The other girls would watch it as I played with him in the hay. Perhaps even the other boys were fascinated about it, although they would only make jokes.

One night I told my sister what we had been doing and that I wanted to go fucking with Jens but was afraid. She was not surprised at what we had been doing, because she had also done these things with boys. She told me that the first time was something you had to get over. Then it would give me a great deal of pleasure other times. She also promised that she would get me some condoms from her boyfriend, but it was not soon enough.

It was a very warm and rainy day just before the end of school. All of us were naked. I did not think that it would be much different from the other times, but the other girls had changed their minds about it without telling me. They became very passionate with their boys, while Jens and I were much gentler in our caressing and kissing. The boys put their fingers into the girls cunts, while their bodies made very hot movements as if they were being fucked with fingers in them. Jens and I watched while the boys put their penises into the girls. They had no condoms.

The more experienced boy entered my friend first. It seemed very easy for her, and they fucked very well from the beginning. My other friend was having a terrible time of it. There were tears in her eyes, and she was crying that it hurt. He would push his penis into her, and she would fall deeper into the hay away from him. Jens was very excited by this, but I could not give him any attention except to let him hold me while we watched. I thought my friend had gone out of her mind, and I even wanted to push the boy off of her and save her. It looked so horrible to be in such a hurt way, but she held him tightly near the end, and then he tore through her virginity. It was then over very quickly, for the boy soon shot his sperm into her. When he took his penis from her, it was covered with the blood and his sperm, which he wiped away with his underpants.

Jens knew that I was frightened some, so he did not force me into more sex with him after the others were done. The girl who had hurt so much told me how she really enjoyed it, but I knew it was a lie. She said it only to try to convince Jens and me to do it after they had finished. She seemed angry that Jens and I had only watched them. It was just as well that Jens had told me that it was not our business to stop him, that the fucking was her own concern and she wanted it. Now after it was over, there was a changed attitude. I knew that the four of them would return to the hayloft many times during the next week without Jens and me. After a time things were better, and the three of us girls again became close friends, and once again we were all together in the barn. This was my turn. My sister had given me condoms, with advice to be very careful.

The day I was to lose my virginity was again a rainy day. I took the condoms with me to school and showed them to one of the girls. Jens and I met after school, and all of us walked to the barn. We talked openly about what was to happen. The girls told stories about how nice it was to have sex with their boys. I was convinced in my mind, but yet it was not the easiest thing for me to do. Jens was as wonderful as a "good boy" can be about the whole thing. He was also very scared with me. I do not think he had liked the sight of the blood from my girlfriend any more than I had.

Soon after we were comfortable in the hayloft, the others began fucking with each other, but they were also waiting and watching for Jens and me to begin. It did not bother me that they were with us. I even thought it was wise, should something go wrong. We were six good friends together.

I knew it would hurt, but for weeks I had been putting my fingers into my opening, trying to make it wider for Jens's penis. But it did not turn out so badly, after all. After much kissing and having Jens put his finger into me, I was ready. He put on the condom I had brought. I spread my legs wide and then guided his penis with my hand. With a quick push, it was over for me. He stayed inside me for many minutes before we moved very much in the fucking motions. I did have some pain at first, but it soon left me for the pleasure of at least being a mature girl with a wonderful boy. Jens had an orgasm in me. I felt it shuddering through him.

I did not have an orgasm this first time. When he took his penis
from me after some minutes, I could tell immediately that something was wrong. Yes, there was a little blood, but the condom
had broken and was all pushed around the back end of his penis
like a rubber ring. Not all of my feelings were worries though.
I had enjoyed what I had done. We were all feeling very grown up
and thrilled. For most of the rest of the summer just Jens and I
were together for fucking. We began to want our privacy.

DISCUSSION   *Gurli tells of her sexual experiences with her friends
without reticence or embarrassment. Her frankness here
suggests an ability to communicate about sex with
objectivity and detachment, even when her own behavior
is the center of focus. From a psychological view is such a
communication pattern a positive characteristic? What
kinds of social interpretations might one give to her
verbal behavior in some American settings where sex is
being discussed? Is her candor acceptable to American
college students, in your opinion?*

One of the girls became pregnant. Everyone in the village
knew it. Her family was shamed, and soon the boy left the village.
It was a terrible tragedy for her, especially. The baby was born
dead, and this made the shame worse, in everyone's view. When I
heard of her pregnancy, I became very frightened and felt that I
should share her guilt. My church became important for the first
time in my life, perhaps like Elaine's. I almost went crazy over
it. I suddenly wanted nothing to do with Jens or any other boy. I
prayed every day and before every meal, and a lot before sleeping.
My sister became upset with me. She even accused the father of
just scaring me about what I had confessed to him—and it was almost everything, except about my sister. My family even thought
I should see a doctor because my behavior at home had become so
strange. The father and I prayed together for several weeks until
my family objected to the time I spent with him.

It is the strangest thing in my life that, just as quickly as
I had fallen into this religious matter, I fled from it entirely. I
had not masturbated during all those months, and maybe it was the
day I did it that I regained my senses. Finally I listened to my
sister. She knew that I was only very scared by my girlfriend's
pregnancy. Soon I was better, but Jens never forgave me for the
bad things I had said to him when he tried to talk with me about my

religious yearnings. Now I must say I have no faith in such religious points of view at all. If I think about it much, it ⸗akes me angry for having made Jens run into the arms of other girls.

The next two years were different for me because all of us went to a large new school. I met many new girls and boys, which helped to give me a bigger view of life. I started going to parties with boys who were not from our village. I went with three boys from the school until I was seventeen years old. With each of them I had fucking and even more. We did oral sex with each other, which I found very nice. These years with them almost seem like Elaine's most recent year.

At high school I fell in love with a boy who was a very good student and a class leader. Until my family moved to Copenhagen, this boy was with me. Both my mother and my father liked him very much, and they were happy that I was through with the other boys. They falsely blamed the other boys for my spending time away from home at night. Kjell and I were more careful about what my parents thought. Kjell was more sophisticated. His father was an important merchant in a nearby city.

We had physical love right from the start, and he was very good in satisfying me. We did everything together. I hope that you will not think that I am a "naughty girl." But I saw nothing wrong in finding out as quickly as possible whether I would really like him. I do not think anything is wrong in sexual experiments. Kjell is a very good example of what can come from such an attitude. The move to Copenhagen was the end of everything but fondness for each other. He is now at the university with me.

My present boyfriend is Peter, and he is the oldest boy I have ever gone with. He is twenty-five years old and a student, who will soon be taking his final exam in psychology at the university. I think he is brilliant and will some day be a very distinguished scholar. He is the last person I have been to bed with, and I see no more reason to try others. Now Peter and I can do anything and everything to our satisfaction. Our sex life is the best there can be. I think it is fine with me (and him) that we are not married yet. But that is for purely practical reasons. We do intend to continue together for the rest of our lives.

chapter 12

Charles, Gustav, and Ole

CHARLES   *Charles describes his childhood and adolescence with a great deal of sensitivity. However, he sometimes perceives his problems from the standpoint of what he thinks is normal for the experiences of boys. Through this commentary it is possible to grasp the significance of some American sexual standards as part of the social development process. Charles has internalized many of the values and norms associated with popular images of the healthy, clean-cut, achieving American boy. Charles focuses upon some of the important social and psychological difficulties of bridging the gap between the world of adolescence and adulthood.*

    My early life revolved around my family and one special friend almost completely. As far as I can remember, my relations with my mother, father, and sister were very good and normal. I was very protective toward my sister, who is three years younger than me, and I spoiled her rotten. I can't remember why I felt so strongly, except she seemed so small and vulnerable. Despite this attitude, I did not pal around with her at all.

My best friend was a boy the same age, who shared all my early adventures. Both Derek and I were fairly well mannered, but of course we had our few wild times.

My mother was great to me during these early years. She was a shoulder to cry on occasionally, but she never babied me. She got me interested in sports and knew how to bring me out of moods. Despite my father's being gone on business much of the time, she never seized the opportunity to overprotect me and turn me into a mama's boy. I was spared having to hurdle the barrier of a mother who was too interested in the activities of her growing boy. My mother was one housewife who liked her work. She was always home when I needed her. She was very religious and got me to go to church regularly then.

My relations with my father were also good, but his being away often caused me moodiness. Occasionally during the summer he would take me along on a local sales trip. I think this experience helped establish in me a strong male identity that I needed to pattern myself after. Especially in my early years, many of my relatives would comment that "he has his father's smile," or "his father's walk." Of course, I wasn't aware of this as being important except that it just made me feel good. My admiration and love for my father were strong. My dad and I had the most in common on a sports basis. Sports were to become my main obsession, which perhaps diverted some of my attention away from sexual matters later.

DISCUSSION   *How important does this father-son relationship seem in contributing to sex role learning and masculinity at this point?*

After we moved to our new home and I was started in the third grade, I began to notice that our home life was rapidly falling apart. My dad had developed a drinking problem. My parents began to have many bitter fights over it, and each fight was an upsetting crisis. My mom ranted and raved over his drinking, usually with justification, but that irritated me almost as much as my dad's drinking did. Their constant fighting must have had some bad effects on me, but luckily this was balanced by the affection my parents displayed to each other and to my sister and myself. Though I tended to be down on boy-girl relationships because of the grief involved in things at home, I could also see the joy and happiness that could be achieved at times. But in general I was puzzled about what marriage was all about.

The period from the fifth through the eighth grades was somewhat difficult for me. For several years I did not understand what made me have an erection. It would usually happen while I was bathing, as a result of my handling myself. I had no real sexual knowledge of my body. I never felt like talking about "it" with my friends, or even my father. Before I was about twelve, I probably felt it was something less than clean, but this idea was in conflict with the pleasant sensations. I do not believe that I consciously sought to have an erection, and when it did occur I would be careful to avoid touching myself. That was the way I found to make it go away. Masturbation has come up only in the past year, since I graduated from high school.

The first time I experienced a wet dream was at the age of twelve. I thought there was something wrong with my glands or something else in my body. I wondered if I had some disease. During this period I did not, of course, discuss sexual matters with Mom, and unfortunately Dad was not available. My parents were separated then. I was very embarrassed about it and tried to keep my mind off of it. Fortunately, in the next year it happened only a few more times, before I heard about this type of thing happening to some of the older boys I knew at school.

By the time I was thirteen, I began to get erections when I thought of chicks or looked at issues of Playboy with my friends. In the seventh grade I was very hostile toward girls, but I began to change my view in the eighth grade. I developed a certain amount of feeling for one girl in our class. And I began to attend school dances—the first physical contact I had with girls that involved any feeling. Still I did not kiss any of them, nor did I consider going on a date. I finished the eighth grade as one of the few boys who had not gone steady with a girl. As a rule, I was still somewhat hostile around most of them. I feel this was due to a number of factors. My parents did not have any words of encouragement concerning the dating activities of my friends. But the more likely reason was my shyness. I tended to put down girls in my discussions with friends and couldn't figure out why everyone was so interested in them. A third factor may have been a late-blooming sex drive. I was still obsessed with sports, which drained away my attention from sexual matters. I could also have been influenced by my cousin's explanation of sexual intercourse. It shocked me, and made me sick to think about it.

Track seemed a much more satisfying outlet. It was clean and wholesome by any standard I had been taught in my home and school.

My peer group was typical of our society. We had the various studs. Some claimed to having experienced petting, and even sexual intercourse, with girls. I thought some of them were abnormally obsessed with sex. But for a long time, well into high school, my conception of the boy-girl relationship was that it was something phony and just a game. I had a very "super" morality at this time. My "highly moral" mother must have been of some influence, although her words on the subject of sex were very few. Because of my father's absence and his drunkenness, I did not get any direction from him. I hated him much of the time but still needed his companionship. The "jibber-jabber" between my mom and sister was of little help for my boy problems, which had to stay bottled up while I lived in this female-dominated home after my dad left.

Sports were now a nine-month training period. Sports served a number of personal needs. Not only did it give me the great joy of strenuous exercise, but it was usually a great ego boost also, because I experienced a great deal of success. Without sports draining my energy and bolstering my ego, I probably would have been much more eager to play the boy-girl games.

Naturally my physical drives were increasing all the time. I often got semi-erections at school from looking at girls. Still, masturbation did not occur to me, mostly because my need for orgasm was not yet strong and I did not know the technique. In this area I remained ignorant throughout my high school life. As I look back, I cannot see why I did not do it. I definitely was not made to feel that there was anything wrong with masturbation. I was specifically informed that it was quite normal. I knew what orgasm was. The incidence of wet dreams increased throughout high school.

Throughout my freshman year I felt that my dad would never change and that the family situation was doomed. So I became very much less involved with my family, which was the only sane thing that I could do. Yet this unnatural coldness may have had a detrimental effect on my relations with the opposite sex. I rarely kissed my mother or my sister, and this hardness may have carried over into the outside world. I was very stiff and did not often think of making it with girls. Not that I didn't want to, but I couldn't help the way I was.

My sophomore year was the turning point in my relations with girls. At the start of the year I noticed a brunette, for whom my affection was to grow throughout the year. Still, my shyness and fear that maybe she didn't like me held me back. As the year went on, I began to feel that I was getting too far behind other guys socially.

My moral attitude was incredibly romantic and straight. The peer group did not affect me at all. My attitude was that there should be no petting, because it might lead to sex, which I felt was best reserved for marriage. Of course, kissing was fine.

Finally, at the end of my sophomore year, encouraged by "inside reports" that this girl liked me, I asked her out, and a great relationship began. Those first weeks that I experienced that summer were memorable. We liked each other very much and soon were going steady. I am sure that it was not just the fun of being with a girl that caused me to like this girl. I thought she was very attractive, and enough other guys did too. She was a hippie type, outgoing, and experienced in dating. In reality she was not so radical as she pretended to be, and once I got over my shyness I was more outgoing than most people imagined. We necked a lot, but not nearly enough to suit me. Her curfew was midnight, and we always didn't have time to mess around. I was true to my belief and did not try to fondle her.

DISCUSSION   *Charles is obviously more inhibited socially and sexually with the opposite sex than most of his peers. Sports are often promoted as a desirable substitute for heterosexual activities for the adolescent male. What are the social and psychological implications of such a pattern, taking Charles into consideration as a case in point? Do athletic activities effectively serve as a compensatory mechanism for sexual frustration and anxiety in adolescence and adulthood?*

I felt some awkwardness walking around with Darlene my first week back at school in my junior year, but that soon faded. However, although I enjoyed her company at school, I just as often was bored sitting around with her. I began to notice others, and one in particular. Our relationship began to have some bad moments. Still we continued to enjoy each other more and more, so our communication and our commitment to each other deepened. I was getting a little serious. When we really hit it off it was great, and we both knew it. It was a good experience to show me how much the happiness of your life is related to your relationships with chicks.

After going with Darlene for about seven months, I finally felt her breasts. She liked it, as I did. If I had been more experienced, we would have done more. I realized that this type of petting was just a harmless pleasure. Soon after, she broke up with me. It was a profound shock to me, coming so suddenly. My opinion of girls took a nose dive. This incident affected my sexual attitudes profoundly. My morality headed downward, and my personality became more and more far out.

The next girl I took out helped restore my faith in sexuality. We necked a lot, and I played with her breasts all the time. I did not get as worked up with this girl, but I still liked her very much. At the end of my junior year we drifted apart.

That summer saw the most radical change in my sexuality. Without the friendship of a girl, I saw girls more and more as sexual objects. For the first time in my life, I was horny. However, I did not score and dated only rarely. Sex glands became more and more the matter of discussion among my friends. Guys would brag about the size of their cocks, and since mine was smallest (at least when flaccid), I began to wonder if girls would be satisfied as much as me. I talked about making it with girls much more than I ever had before. I was much more outgoing at that time than most people. When I returned to school, I was confident of my ability with girls and more content in my role of using girls for pleasure without becoming involved.

DISCUSSION   *Evaluate Charles's feelings of physical sexual inferiority from the standpoint of psychological and social outcomes. Do such anxieties ever persist beyond adolescence? How do they cope with such feelings as they relate to heterosexual situations and relationships?*

My senior year was the most exciting year of my life. Although you may get the impression that sexual matters had become an obsession with me, sports were still the most important thing. The tremendous need for achievement still outweighed my sexual drives, although by now it was a nip-and-tuck race. With each girl I attempted as much as she would let me, which wasn't much because I always seem to be attracted to "nice" girls. I began dating Kitty, the only girl I've ever been very much in love with. She was beautiful and had a good figure and a great personality. We dated for only seven weeks, but I was deeply involved. This was probably because she was unattainable for much of the year since she had been going with someone else. She broke up to go out with me, but she continued to date her old boy-friend. I was never so happy. Unfortunately she was extremely moral, and I no longer was. When she went back to her old boy-friend, it was a shock along the lines of my first girlfriend, only five times as bad.

This relationship has had the greatest influence upon my sexual attitudes. I know that love of this magnitude can be worth more than anything in the world. For this reason I fully expect to marry someday. Yet, the effect also was bitterness and disdain for most girls. It has made me a little tired with the games involved in dating. And it has made me wonder about myself. I honestly feel that I am an interesting person and an inoffensive one most of the time. Yet what could make me lose the three girls I liked most in my life so far? Whether it's coincidence or something in me that comes out when I get involved, I don't know. In addition, my moodiness seems to be out of proportion.

As I left high school, I was still a virgin. But because of peer-group pressure and an ever-increasing sex drive, now less hampered by my sports career, I felt that I had to engage in sexual intercourse. That summer I did, after being alone with a "loose" girl. I didn't like this girl at all. I hated her personality, though I was somewhat attracted by her excellent body. We had inter-course three times, and I achieved orgasm a few other times through petting. I had one great experience in which she really got excited. I felt so great it was unbelievable. Yet she and I were not greatly attracted to each other. Sex will be much finer when I find someone I can care a little bit about. A couple of times I was unable either to get or maintain an erection, due, I believe, to fatigue caused by the intense long-distance running I was doing and lack of confidence, plus her lack of stimulation and excitement. I worried that there might be something wrong with me. But since then I have conquered this fear (at least in my conscious mind) by my sex play with a couple of other girls and a knowledge that fatigue and lack of manual stimulation can cause this. I think lack of confidence can kill you!

DISCUSSION   *Has Charles correctly estimated the potentialities of fear and anxiety in causing this sexual dysfunction (impotence)? Is this problem usually resolved successfully by greater conscious control and concentration? Would Charles do well to consider the factors that may*

*contribute to his fear and anxiety? How important are
the attitudes and behavior of a sex partner in relating to
this kind of experience, in your opinion?*

Only a few days after my first intercourse I masturbated
for the first time. I found it extremely pleasurable and relaxing.
Since that time (a little less than a year ago) I have established
masturbation as a regular habit, as often as daily for a week or
two at a time. At first I wondered if masturbating so often might
be harmful. However, I am now sure that it is not.

Since high school I have dated a greater variety of girls
than before. In high school I was probably more in love with love
than with the girls. Now I am looking for some real qualities. I
am more willing to date girls who I considered less attractive before. I have learned that looks aren't important if you can communicate.

I've dated Kitty and Darlene, two of the three girls that I
"lost" in high school. While I had a great time with both, it wasn't
the same in a romantic way. Time both heals wounds and dims
passion. When I attempted to win Kitty back, it didn't work out. I
wasn't hurt by this second try, because I could see that the image
I had created of her was a false one. With Darlene I had three good
dates, but again I realized that turning back was not for me.

This past year in college has brought me into contact with
other girls. But I find living at home is not the best way to get the
full benefits. What I probably need is some kind of a beach pad,
where I can complete the picture of who I am. I feel at the age of
nineteen, I am now ready to discover the rest of life on my own.

GUSTAV   *Gustav has been eager to expose the frailties of Charles and what he understands to be American sexual patterns. Charles's case history turned out to be a kind of projective psychological test, in some respects, for bringing out many of Gustav's own social and sexual attitudes. He not only lets us know what some Swedes may think about Americans, but often gives us a view of what he thinks about himself. In a brief description of his childhood and adolescence he shows that not everything in his social and sexual development has been trouble free. Part of Gustav's approach to sexual matters is at least a verbal downgrading of the importance of sex in social relationships. At times he seems truly bored by sex, not an uncommon Swedish posture, especially when dealing with Americans.*

There is a clever story about an eight-year-old boy, Bent, who is in school for the first day, when his teacher starts to tell the class that they shall have their first sex education lesson. Bent seems a little worried about it and at last puts up his hand and asks, "Miss, couldn't we who already know how to fuck be allowed to go out and play football"? My friends and I like this story because most of us have come to the point where it is now boring and dull to give much attention to sexual matters. Sex has become something very easy and natural to most of us. The only problem is to find a good partner.

This history about Charles has left me very tired and a little discouraged about American society and its sexual ways. I read much suffering between the lines, although he tries very hard to prove his honesty. He desires very strongly to be a typical American man who wants to fuck with "loose" women to prove he is masculine, and then he also wants to fall in love with a pure and virginal princess. Isn't that the American sex dream? Of course, such an attitude is in horrible conflict and can only result in failure. He must feel that it is wrong for women to want sex with someone they like for either a short or a long time. I believe sex is normal for many different relationships we have in our lives. Perhaps Charles has a jealous rage inside about girls who have had the pleasures of knowing many men sexually.

Another idea occurs to me, which may be an important part of his confusion. Since he was twelve, he has been running away from his sexual desires. I find it hard to believe that he could have begun masturbating only when he was eighteen or nineteen, after he had had his first fucking. But even if it is not true, it is what he desires us to believe. That must be because he has much fear and guilt about his sex wishes. He still does not believe that satisfying sexual desires is a natural and healthy thing for all of us.

It is much easier for me to think about my own life and sexual matters than to go further into the life of this American student. So now let me think of what to tell you about myself, despite my boredom with this topic. I am in my second year at the university. I am soon going to be twenty-two, which may incidently explain some of the differences between Charles and myself. I have had the advantage of already living with a girl for more than a year, although I have known her since my graduation three years ago. We do not think of marriage for ourselves at this time, but when we wish it, it will probably change nothing about our situation.

We seem to have a very good relationship in all respects that really matter. We live in comfort in a small apartment near the institute at which we both study. Unfortunately we must move soon, and this is the most serious problem we have had to face together. To find a place to live in Stockholm with little money and without the help of friends and family is very difficult. It would be much less of a worry to have a sex problem between us.

Our sex experience with each other is a source of joy, relaxation, inspiration, and probably much more. There is not much to say about it, as I find such description very boring to relate to someone I do not know. It is just part of our being together, as if you were to think of us as happily married. We are fully aware of all of our sexual desires, and we do our best to satisfy each other in all the different sex actions our experiences have shown to be pleasant. My experiences with girls before were dull, compared to our time together now.

DISCUSSION   *The Swedes have an international reputation for their practical and utilitarian approaches to most every social situation and problem. Does Gustav suggest that this may also be true for Swedish sexual behavior? How might such an attitudinal set influence the expression of affection and sexual emotion in their relationships?*

I spent my first nineteen years in a smaller city about eighty kilometers from Stockholm. Both of my parents were academicians in the lower schools, so there was always much concern about my education and those of my younger sister and brother. My family was quite bound by the social schedules and standards of their profession and friends. My mother and father were not very different from the parents of other children I have known. There were occasional quarrels between them, but seldom did they let such matters concern their children. Both of them were very strong in their opinions on problems in the home. Sometimes my mother would have her way, and other times my father would be the strong one. When it was a question of following the wishes of our parents, there was little doubt in our minds that it was wise to do as we were told. My father was especially forceful with us. As a matter of fact, he was much too stern for my liking until I was in the late teenage years. He was quite free in punishing my brother and me with his belt. If warmth and intimacy have been lacking between us, I think it is because of this very old fashioned way of controlling us. When this happened, my mother would usually defend his action, even though I knew in my heart that she thought he was too severe. Sometimes I wished for the completely uncontrolled freedom that many of my best friends had.

My relationship with my younger brother, who was two years younger, was quite close and good. We were together a lot during the summers and even shared many of the same friends. My sister is five years younger, and all the family treats her like a little baby, with much attention and love.

My sex education began fairly early. I was probably about five or six when I began to ask about babies and sex. I always was given natural answers. When I was about seven or eight my parents gave me a very good book, which showed in pictures and very simple words how children are created from the sperm and egg and are later born. I never felt there was anything unnatural about it. Unlike the attitudes I have heard about in America, in our family we all had a healthy view of our bodies and never had reason to hide our nakedness when dressing and bathing.

My father was very free about explaining sexual matters to my brother and me. I remember asking him at about the age of eight why my penis would get hard when I pulled it in the bath. His answers were very straight and honest, but perhaps more complicated than they needed to be. I probably did a better job of explaining it to my brother, who was also curious. I do not recall masturbating very much until I became twelve and was beginning to have the advantage of growing bigger there, with the start of puberty. Before I was to have my first ejaculation, my knowledge about it was well in hand, from what I had heard from older boys and from my sex education at school.

As for my experience in school, it was not as good as the children now get. Our teacher was very formal and blushed while talking with us. But I do remember that the pictures and plastic models were very good for our age. The movies that were shown in the following grades gave more complete knowledge of sex. Now that I look more critically at this education, I see that more should have been done to show how sex is connected to psychology and sociology, in being part of the meaning of people's living together in love. There was never any time for students to talk about such things. The instruction was only about the physical facts of sex and the dangers of becoming pregnant if you were not married.

The teachers fortunately did not turn the lessons into moral lectures in the American fashion. Sex was never presented as a sin or something dirty. It was only taught that to cause a young girl to become pregnant was irresponsible. But I think there should have been much more. And the same could be said even for my father. He and I often talked about this problem after one of my good friends made a girl pregnant when he was only fifteen. But I think my father's main interest was that I should be careful with the girls. He was not one who could talk about love and what I was feeling toward girls. I thought his talk was a little too rough and concerned only the sex side of being with them.

When I was sixteen, my father gave me a package of condoms after I had been going with a girl for several months. I was sure that he thought I was having a sex relationship with her, and I was not. So that made me angry, and I told him that it was not his business. I believe this was the only time in my family life that sex topics caused an argument.

DISCUSSION   *Gustav has expressed rather rancorous views about American sexual attitudes that supposedly define sexual behavior as sinful or dirty, and at the same time has implied that Swedes, and especially he, are free of such negative feelings or conceptualizations. How can you account for Gustav's very emotional protest to his father's practical behavior if he is as free as he has been suggesting?*

My activities with girls were not very sexual until I was sixteen. Between thirteen and sixteen I only went to school dances and parties and only kissed and petted with girls in my class. I knew that some of my friends were doing more, especially with girls who were not in our school, but I was a little more shy. It was quite enough for me to be with them romantically so that we could have fun and be good friends. I have always thought that it was important for a girl to respect you for seeing something in her beyond sex. And then, equally important was my idea that a girl should really want to do it with me.

After I had gone with a girl for four months, that time came for me. I had my first fucking with Annika, who had invited me to her home while her parents were on a short holiday. It was the first time for both of us, and it was the beginning of a steady sexual relationship for a whole year. We enjoyed this part of our relationship more than any other part. After a while we grew apart because I felt she was much too demanding in some social respects. I learned one very important thing from Annika—and perhaps she did, too—that sex is only one part of being in love. We ended the connection with a very bad fight over another girl's wanting to talk with me at school. It was a very insignificant issue, but enough to make clear our immaturity.

Until graduation I went with several other girls for longer times. With each of these I also had sexual relations when it was possible. Birgitta and Karin were quite alike, but their parents were quite different. Birgitta's parents were quite traditional and fearful about sex. She also was quite fearful about becoming pregnant, although we always used a condom. Birgitta and I are still like childhood friends when I visit home, but our romance ended when we drifted apart during the summer holiday that had separated us. The last summer before my graduation brought Karin into my life. For this year I was to have the pleasure of a very beautiful and wonderful girl. She had had sexual experience with other boys before me, unlike both Annika and Birgitta, but without much satisfaction, according to her. I am not sure how I should dare to describe her sexually. She was by far the most gentle and pleasant to be with in all of our nonsexual activities but seemed to enjoy fucking much less. So, many of our times together she did not have orgasm. Gradually we stopped spending so much time together, and then I met the girl with whom I live now.

As I stated earlier, I do not particularly care to describe or analyze my present personal life in detail. I am happy to let this relationship remain within my own knowledge for the time. I will only say in a general way that it is better in almost all respects than any I have had before. I believe that to have real love between people they must live together, and this was not possible with the girls who came before.

OLE

Ole does not hold out much hope that Charles will find personal happiness in the "frightening" American system, but he seems more gentle in his observations than Gustav. Possibly part of Ole's attitude is because he acknowledges the uncertainty of his own future. Ole has been living for the past several months in a recently organized commune with other Danish students near the university. Ole makes many positive comments about the quality of this experience and its validity as a substitute for more traditional life style, but he is also aware of some of the problems intrinsic to such group life, such as how to adapt sex roles learned during childhood and adolescence to communal relationships.

Charles seems to be disadvantaged in his sexual upbringing, but that is not so very unusual for children growing up in America. The girls seem to be taught to be pure and clever about sex matters, and the boys must learn to be forceful and push to get what is wanted sexually from these pure and clever girls. The whole system is frightening, and it is no surprise that some boys like Charles come out of it all with confusion and ideas that work against happiness.

The idea that something is wrong with girls who like to have sex—all that about loose girls—is terribly childish and typically American. To treat girls like mud in the secrecy of one's mind because they trust you to go fucking with them is crazy. I would really like to meet Charles now, and then in a few years to see how he has turned out from this American influence. Because he has some gentleness in his spirit, which he has had to fight in order to become like his friends, I want to wish him good luck in finding himself.

My own life has been much different from Charles'. My
mother and father have been very good parents. I think they are
still very much in love with each other, and both have given my
younger sister and me all the love and attention children need.
My relation to my sister has always been good. We teased each
other, but we never fought. We have not had very much money
because of the illness of our father. But our little family has managed very well by careful saving and avoiding waste. My family
has always lived in the same flat in Copenhagen, so we have known
all our friends a long time.

When I was about eight, I became interested in another
girl in my class. I remember giving her ten ore (two cents),
which at that time was a huge financial sacrifice. There was no
special reason, except that I liked her very much. I prayed to
God every night that I could be married to her. Of course, I
never told her such nonsense—or anyone else, for that matter.
I often turned warm to a girl who was very good-looking and nice
to me. But at this time there was no sexual contact with them.

Between ten and fourteen, my interest in sports was also
large. I spent my whole time playing association football with my
friends. I made some very close relations. And in one boy I
came to have 100 percent confidence. When I was about twelve,
my attention turned to sexual matters, and Erik and I spent some
of our time together talking about girls. We both began to develop
in our sex organs at this time.

Some sex play occurred between us. One day, when we
were at his home alone, we were looking at some pictures of
naked girls. Our penises became quite hard, and we started to
wrestle with each other. The game turned out to be pulling down
each other's pants to see how big we had become. For about a
year we played this way with each other. We discovered masturbation together during one of these episodes, although we had heard
older boys at school speaking of it. Trying it out together made
both of us have "little" orgasms, in which only clear fluid came out
in some drops that we thought were the seeds for making babies
with a girl. I think that was only our imaginations.

Because of these experiences with Erik, I began to masturbate regularly at home. It would usually be at night when I could
lie under my covers in bed and think of the pictures of girls and how
nice it would be to cuddle with them and perhaps to feel between
their legs. At first I did not have much desire to think of fucking
with them. It took me a little while longer to think of putting my

penis inside their vaginas. I was not immediately aware that the
vagina could become large enough for me to put my penis in. I
thought it would hurt me as much as give me pleasure. Such a
fantasy was quickly abandoned when Erik and I got hold of some
good porno books, which showed some excited and swelled penises
fucking with no difficulty. By the time Erik and I were fourteen,
we stopped the homosexual play, although we were the closest of
friends until we graduated.

When we were thirteen, sex education began in school.
It was not very good. The teacher was red with embarrassment
over the subject and did not care to answer the questions. Of
course the boys made it into a joke when she became so frightened
by it. While I didn't learn much, what was said was enough to encourage me to find some interesting and informative books about
pregnancy at the library. Some good changes have come to the
schools in Denmark in recent years, and now it is not necessary
to hunt for such materials. Also, I think the porno shops make
such private searches unnecessary. The older boys can get the
younger ones all they need for understanding. The freeing of
porno has been a wonderful lifting of repression for everyone.

By the time I was fifteen, my knowledge about sex was
almost as complete as it is today. What was lacking was experience, but I was content in my relationships with girls only to kiss
and pet. Erik and my other friends and I often talked about what
we should allow ourselves to do with a girl at this age. I did not
want to go to bed with a girl until I could love her very much and
know her for some time very intimately. I had a steady girlfriend
when I was fourteen, but we agreed not to do more than pet.

I got to know Jytte when I was sixteen and a half. She
was one class below me. From the beginning we kissed and petted.
In a few months we moved ahead to full orgasms using our hands.
We talked about ourselves and how we felt with each other with
full honesty. After about four months we discussed going to bed
with each other.

Unfortunately, we did not decide to begin fucking. I was
quite ready, but Jytte was still thinking much as her parents
wanted her to think. That view was that fucking was something
you did only when you were married, so we stayed as virgins for
another three months. During this time, we were in bed with one
another once without fucking, with orgasms only from the hand
and rubbing my penis between her legs, but not inside her vagina.
It was very clear to us both that we were just doing some harmful

teasing of our true love, and we needed to express it more fully.

A few weeks later when the opportunity came again to be alone for loving, we did our first fucking with each other. It was beautiful for both of us. The hurt in pushing through the maidenhead was the only bad part for Jytte, but that was over very quickly and was smothered by the passion of our connection. The cuddling and kissing was like never before, and we talked about how good it was to be rid of our virginity at last. I thought our love could never end after those beautiful hours together. And that was so for the next two years.

A few weeks after our first fucking, Jytte told her mother what we had done. They had very good communication. At first her mother was somewhat unhappy, but then she and Jytte went to the doctor to have a contraceptive device fitted. It was agreeable to her father, as well. During the next two years I became almost like a son with this family, and I think my mother and father understood my love for Jytte, too.

During our last summer together I lived with her in her parents' summer cottage like husband and wife. I learned that you could not find love just in bed with a girl. You must be able to inspire each other and have interests together. If you cannot do this, the strong spiritual impulse to love leaves the relationship. It was at this point that some trouble began to show between us. When I graduated, Jytte still had a year of schooling. It may have been a mistake for me to tease her that her interest in music was childish. I also made fun of her friends in school, who would take her time with schoolgirl matters that I thought were immature.

Within a month we had learned how to make each other very unhappy with our words. Soon our regular sex life was over. It ended when her parents became tired of our quarreling in their home. Early in the summer they took Jytte to the summer cottage without me for what was supposed to be a short holiday, but Jytte did not return with them and instead invited her girlfriends to be with her for most of the summer. It was a very sad end to what had been a good relationship.

My first year at the university was a success, at least with the examinations and in finding some good friends. Gradually I was invited to some parties, and then I began to notice some girls who had an eye on me, which I reciprocated. These girls were all very experienced in sexual relationships. Going to bed with them was never a problem if it was convenient. I went fucking with four of them.

Of course, I learned a great deal about these girls, and I liked each one for reasons other than sex, or I would not have bothered. But there was always something missing. I found that three of them could not give themselves fully and completely to a fellow they went to bed with only a few times.

In these three relationships I quickly missed the trust and confidence I had had with Jytte. All I learned from these three girls was that sex was best with true feelings of love. Only one of the four girls of this year came to have a meaningful emotional connection with me.

Yrsa and I went to bed the very first night we met each other at a party. We stayed the whole night in a guest room with another couple. That night was anything but a private matter between us, but I think we enjoyed the variation, not suspecting that we liked each other for something beyond sex. She was a very serious and good student of Danish literature at the university. I was also impressed by her beautiful body. Yrsa was quite experienced and did not mind the other boy and girl in our bed at all. For me it was an embarrassment, happily dulled by spirits and the four of us laughing so much. To go fucking under such circumstances with a girl I thought I might like very much was filled with inner conflict. I felt like an actor in a porno movie—excited, but not feeling the love I wanted to give. It was just sex for its own sake, or as if we were still dancing in the parlor and the song ended with orgasms for us.

From this strange beginning a good friendship developed between us. Yrsa was quite different from the other girls I have liked very much. She was much more open in sexual matters than in telling about her feelings and thoughts. For example, I could never discover what her past relationships had been with other men. I told her everything but learned little from her. This I took to mean that the confidence between us was not complete. At the end of the year I moved from home to live with her in her apartment near the university for the last month of the term. We worked together on my papers, but we became aware that we did not truly share too many interests out of bed.

At first we ignored the little irritations between us, but we soon felt that it was not the best relationship between a man and woman. Her style of unhappiness was silence, and I must admit that mine was to talk too much. By the end of the term we had come to the conclusion that living together was a mistake, despite the enjoyable sex together. Fortunately, we broke with each other as very good friends, but knowing that our relationship could not be anything deeper. Yrsa is now living with another man, and I am happy to know she is in love with someone who can understand her strange moods.

DISCUSSION   *This experience illustrates the importance of personality and social role compatibility in finding success in intimate relationships. Communication is often cited as a critical variable in such relationships. Is this usually an over-simplification?*

I went fucking with a number of girls, but our attraction was only a thing of the bodies. Certainly, nothing is wrong with good fucking, even as simple exercise, if that is all there can be for the persons. But that is not much to describe.

DISCUSSION   *Ole distinguishes between sexual behavior that is relevant and that which is of no importance to the individual. Can evaluations of sexual experience always be so simple? Is sexual feeling and experience better conceptualized on a gradient or continuum?*

For the past two months I have been living in what I believe is the solution to my needs for giving and receiving love. I am now living with Anni in a kollektive. Perhaps you know this institution as the German komune. We are five couples who have been living together as one. One of the couples has brought two children, two and four years old. For the children it is like a Tivoli of affection. No need to worry about them. To describe the girl and the others who are part of this beautiful experience in living would be wrong for me. The individual is nothing, now that consciousness of the group has been given form in our personal lives. My interest in the collective is not because of a need of sex. Our fucking is not group sex. We are private in our sexual relationships. We are still trying to grow up to reach our ideals of a better form of loving together.

The problems we must face in growing out of old ways of feeling and thinking are not easy for all of us to solve, and this includes me. We have many new practical problems to solve in trying to change our lives this way. But we hope to find some solution to the troubles that have beset all of us in what we are trying to do.

Because our experience is only two months old, I cannot say how
it will end for us. But now that I look at my old dreams of marriage,
I see how limited such a structure is for some of us. The questions
I have about our way of living are many. I wonder whether we are
strong enough to give ourselves to so many others for a long time
of living together. Some of us have already shown the weaknesses
of our individuality and revealed the scars of bad homes and the
pressure of society to make us selfish and mindless about the wel-
fare of others. We are painfully aware that the collective idea has
failed in the past, although we have heard that there are more than
a hundred still working in Denmark. We have tried to learn as much
as we can from others.

DISCUSSION   *Does Ole appear to have a social background and
personality that would fit a communal pattern of social
living as he has described it? How might Charles and
Gustav fit into such a life style? How do you feel about
such a living style for yourself? How adaptable is your
personality and sex role behavior to such a social
environment? What social and psychological needs would
it meet, and what would be your likely frustrations and
anxieties?*

We first came together as a social experiment. For several of us it was purely for intellectual and scientific interest at the
beginning. We wanted to see what would happen to us and each other.
We were even looking for answers before we knew what questions to
ask. Now I think we are at the point of asking ourselves the question
that is really important to our new sense of being—can man really
learn to love outside of himself?

BIBLIOGRAPHY

Bell, Robert R. Premarital Sex in a Changing Society. Englewood
  Cliffs, N.J.: Prentice-Hall, 1966.

Berne, Eric. Sex in Human Loving. New York: Simon & Schuster,
  1970.

Boëthius, C. G. Facts and Life: Toward New Guidelines in Sex
  Education. Monograph. Stockholm: Public Commission on Sex
  Education, 1971.

Breasted, Mary. Oh! Sex Education! New York: Praeger, 1970;
  New American Library, Signet Books, 1971.

Brecher, Ruth, and Brecher, Edward. An Analysis of Human Sexual
  Response. New York: New American Library, Signet Books,
  1966.

Brown, Fred, and Kempton, Rudolf T. Sex Questions and Answers.
  2d ed. New York: McGraw-Hill, 1970.

Cannon, Kenneth L., and Long, Richard. "Premarital Sexual Behavior in the Sixties." Journal of Marriage and the Family,
  February 1971.

Christensen, Harold T., and Gregg, Christina F. "Changing Sex
  Norms in America and Scandinavia." Journal of Marriage and
  the Family, November 1970.

Claësson, Bent H. Det där med blommor och bin... Stockholm:
  Swedish Association for Sex Education (RFSU), 1969.

Connery, Donald S. The Scandinavians. New York: Simon &
  Schuster, 1966.

Crosby, John F. Illusion and Disillusion: The Self in Love and
  Marriage. Belmont, Calif.: Wadsworth, 1973.

Crowley, L. A.; Malfetti, J. L.; Stewart, E. I.; and Dias, N. V.
  Reproduction, Sex, and Preparation for Marriage. 2d ed.
  Englewood Cliffs, N.J.: Prentice-Hall, 1973.

DeLora, Joanne S., and DeLora, Jack R. Intimate Life Styles.
  Pacific Palisades, Calif.: Goodyear, 1972.

Dodson, Fitzhugh. How to Parent. New York: New American
Library, Signet Books, 1970.

Engström, Lars. Socio-economic and Medical Aspects of Planned
Parenthood. Monograph. Stockholm: Swedish Association for
Sex Education, 1971.

Fullerton, Gail Putney. Survival in Marriage. New York: Holt,
Rinehart and Winston, 1972.

Gagnon, John H., and Simon, William, eds. The Sexual Scene.
Chicago: Aldine, 1970.

Hegeler, Inge. An ABZ of Love. New York: Medical Press, 1963.

Hutt, Corinne. Males and Females. Baltimore: Penguin Books,
1972.

Israel, Joachim. The Onset of Heterosexual Activity and Its Sociological Context. Monograph. Uppsala, Sweden: University of
Uppsala, 1969.

——————————."The Liberation from Sex Taboos." Papers of the
International Symposium on Sexology, 1969. Stockholm: Swedish
Association for Sex Education (RFSU), 1970.

Jones, Kenneth L., Shainberg, Louis W., and Byer, Curtis O. Sex.
New York: Harper & Row, 1969.

Karlen, Arno. Sexuality and Homosexuality. New York: W. W.
Norton, 1971.

Katchadourian, Herant A., and Lunde, Donald T. Fundamentals
of Human Sexuality. New York: Holt, Rinehart and Winston,
1972.

Kennedy, Eugene C. The New Sexuality. Garden City, N.Y.:
Doubleday, 1972.

Kogan, Benjamin A. Human Sexual Expression. New York: Har-
court Brace Jovanovich, 1973.

Larsen, Knud S. "An Investigation of Sexual Behavior among Norwegian College Students: A Motivational Study." Journal of
Marriage and the Family, February 1971.

Liljeström, Rita. Is the Nuclear Family the Answer for a Changing Society? Monograph. Stockholm: Swedish Association for Sex Education (RFSU), 1971.

Linnér, Birgitta. Sex and Society in Sweden. New York: Random House, Pantheon Books, 1967; Harper & Row, 1971.

——————. "Sexual Morality and Sexual Reality—the Scandinavian Approach," American Journal of Orthopsychiatry, July 1966.

——————. "The Sexual Revolution in Sweden." Impact of Science on Society, October-December, 1968.

McCary, James L. Human Sexuality. 2d ed. New York: Van Nostrand Reinhold, 1973.

Mannila, Elina Haavio. "Some Consequences of Women's Emancipation." Publication No. 64 of the Institute of Sociology, University of Helsinki; Journal of Marriage and the Family, February 1969.

——————. "The Position of Finnish Women: Regional and Cross-National Comparisons." Publication No. 68 of the Institute of Sociology, University of Helsinki; Journal of Marriage and the Family, May 1969.

Masters, William H., and Johnson, Virginia E. Human Sexual Response. Boston: Little, Brown, 1966.

——————. Human Sexual Inadequacy. Boston: Little, Brown, 1970.

Miller, Howard L., and Siegel, Paul S. Loving: A Psychological Approach. New York: John Wiley & Sons, 1972.

Millet, Kate. Sexual Politics. Garden City, N. Y.: Doubleday, 1970.

Putney, Snell, and Putney, Gail J. The Adjusted American. New York: Harper & Row, 1964.

Reiss, Ira L. The Social Context of Premarital Sexual Permissiveness. New York: Holt, Rinehart and Winston, 1967.

Saxton, Lloyd. The Individual, Marriage, and the Family. 2d ed. Belmont, Calif.: Wadsworth, 1972.

Schulz, David A. The Changing Family. Englewood Cliffs, N. J.:
    Prentice-Hall, 1972.

Sjöberg, E.; Hansson, K.; Sjövall, T.; and Engström, L.
    What the Swedes Teach about Sex. Stockholm: Swedish Asso-
    ciation for Sex Education, 1970; New York: Grosset and Dunlap.

Somerville, Rose M. Introduction to Family Life and Sex Education.
    Englewood Cliffs, N. J.: Prentice-Hall, 1972.

Udry, J. Richard. The Social Context of Marriage. 2d ed. Philadel-
    phia: Lippincott, 1971.

Wiseman, Jacqueline P., ed. People as Partners. San Francisco:
    Canfield Press, 1971.